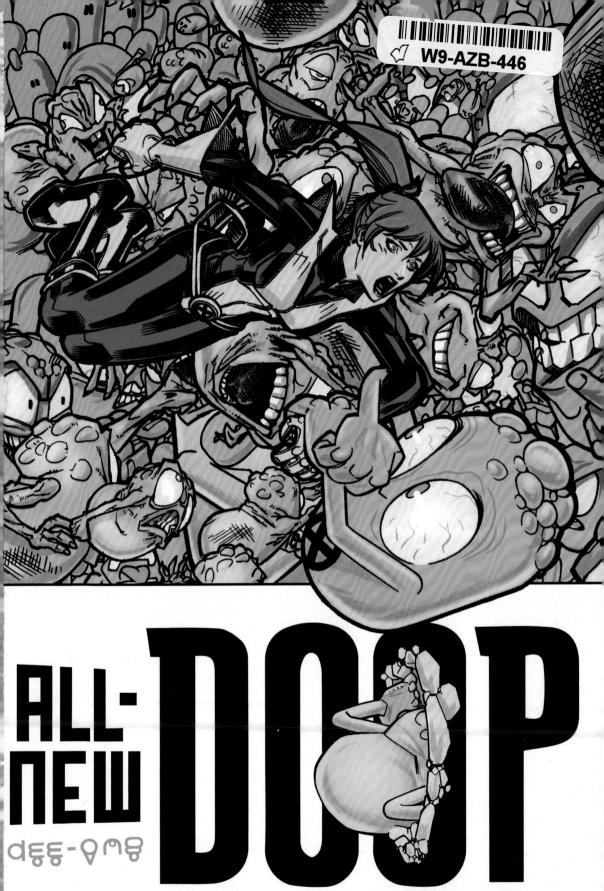

ALL-NEW DOOP

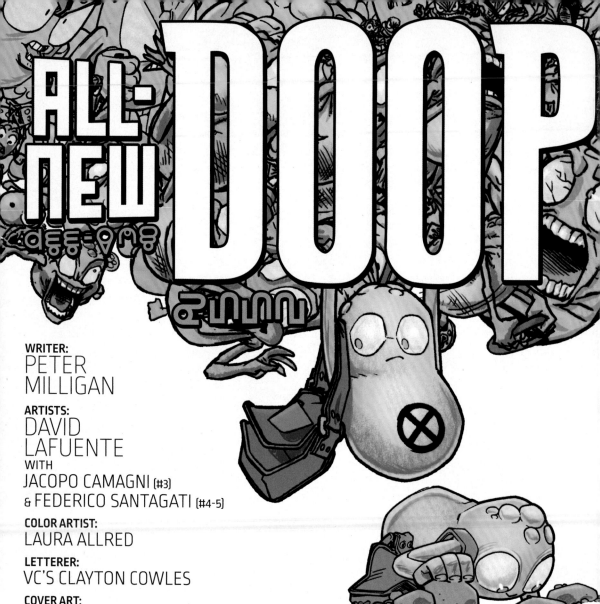

ALL-NEW DOOP

WRITER:
PETER MILLIGAN

ARTISTS:
DAVID LAFUENTE
WITH
JACOPO CAMAGNI [#3]
& FEDERICO SANTAGATI [#4-5]

COLOR ARTIST:
LAURA ALLRED

LETTERER:
VC'S CLAYTON COWLES

COVER ART:
MICHAEL ALLRED & LAURA ALLRED

ASSISTANT EDITOR:
DEVIN LEWIS

EDITOR:
NICK LOWE

COLLECTION EDITOR: JENNIFER GRÜNWALD
ASSISTANT EDITOR: SARAH BRUNSTAD
ASSOCIATE MANAGING EDITOR: ALEX STARBUCK
EDITOR, SPECIAL PROJECTS: MARK D. BEAZLEY
SENIOR EDITOR, SPECIAL PROJECTS: JEFF YOUNGQUIST
SVP PRINT, SALES & MARKETING: DAVID GABRIEL
BOOK DESIGNER: RODOLFO MURAGUCHI

EDITOR IN CHIEF: AXEL ALONSO
CHIEF CREATIVE OFFICER: JOE QUESADA
PUBLISHER: DAN BUCKLEY
EXECUTIVE PRODUCER: ALAN FINE

ALL-NEW DOOP. Contains material originally published in magazine form as ALL-NEW DOOP #1-5. First printing 2014. ISBN# 978-0-7851-9042-4. Published by MARVEL WORLDWIDE, INC., a subsidiary of MARVEL ENTERTAINMENT, LLC. OFFICE OF PUBLICATION: 135 West 50th Street, New York, NY 10020. Copyright © 2014 Marvel Characters, Inc. All rights reserved. All characters featured in this issue and the distinctive names and likenesses thereof, and all related indicia are trademarks of Marvel Characters, Inc. No similarity between any of the names, characters, persons, and/or institutions in this magazine with those of any living or dead person or institution is intended, and any such similarity which may exist is purely coincidental. **Printed in Canada.** ALAN FINE, EVP - Office of the President, Marvel Worldwide, Inc. and EVP & CMO Marvel Characters B.V.; DAN BUCKLEY, Publisher & President - Print, Animation & Digital Divisions; JOE QUESADA, Chief Creative Officer; TOM BREVOORT, SVP of Publishing; DAVID BOGART, SVP of Operations & Procurement, Publishing; C.B. CEBULSKI, SVP of Creator & Content Development; DAVID GABRIEL, SVP Print, Sales & Marketing; JIM O'KEEFE, VP of Operations & Logistics; DAN CARR, Executive Director of Publishing Technology; SUSAN CRESPI, Editorial Operations Manager; ALEX MORALES, Publishing Operations Manager; STAN LEE, Chairman Emeritus. For information regarding advertising in Marvel Comics or on Marvel.com, please contact Niza Disla, Director of Marvel Partnerships, at ndisla@marvel.com. For Marvel subscription inquiries, please call 800-217-9158. **Manufactured between 8/15/2014 and 9/22/2014 by SOLISCO PRINTERS, SCOTT, QC, CANADA.**

10 9 8 7 6 5 4 3 2 1

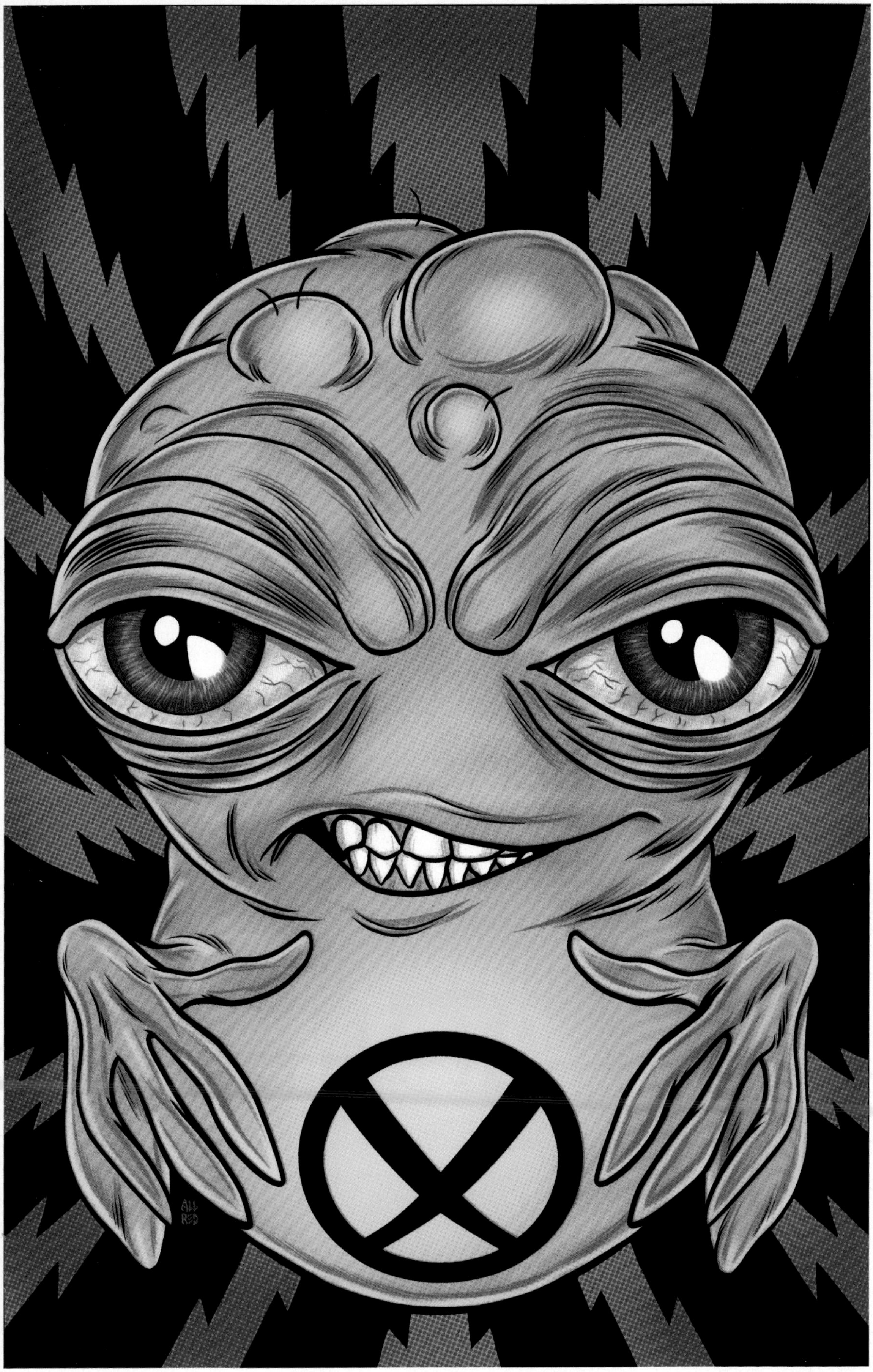

MARVEL COMICS PRESENTS

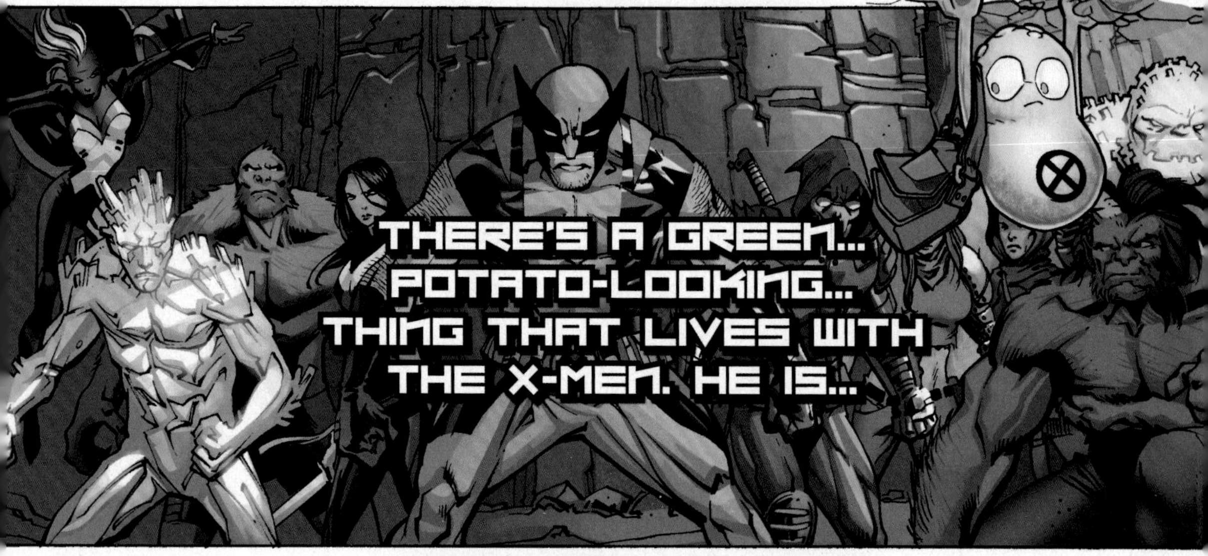

THERE'S A GREEN...
POTATO-LOOKING...
THING THAT LIVES WITH
THE X-MEN. HE IS...

DOOP

IN

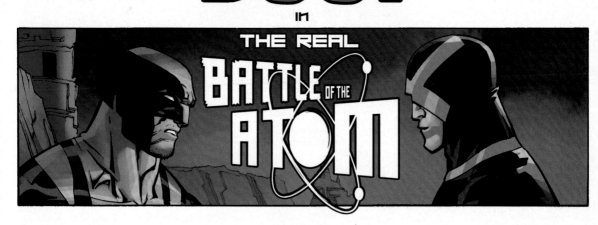

THE REAL

BATTLE OF THE **ATOM**

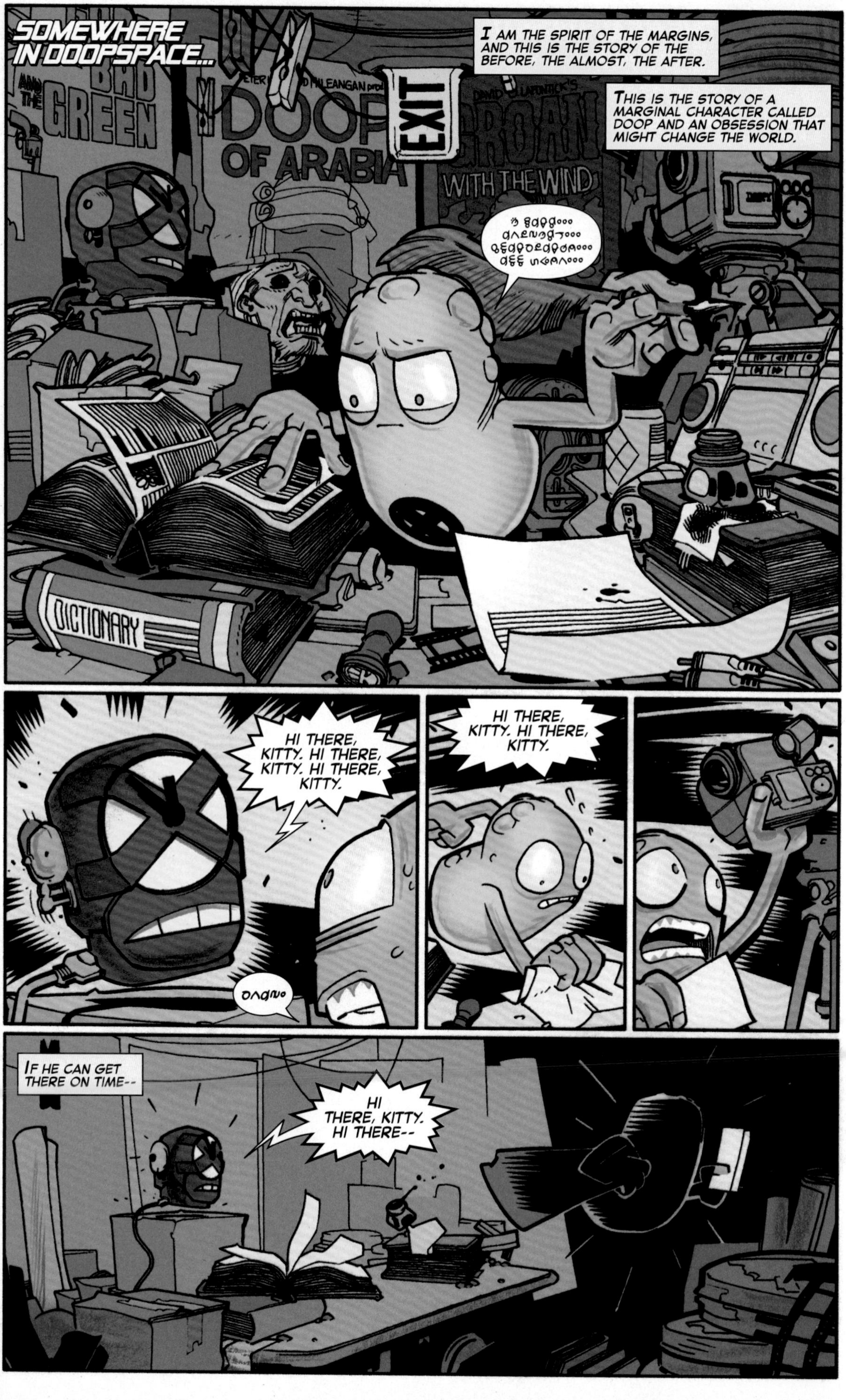
SOMEWHERE IN DOOPSPACE...
I AM THE SPIRIT OF THE MARGINS, AND THIS IS THE STORY OF THE BEFORE, THE ALMOST, THE AFTER.
THIS IS THE STORY OF A MARGINAL CHARACTER CALLED DOOP AND AN OBSESSION THAT MIGHT CHANGE THE WORLD.
BAD AND THE GREEN
DOOP OF ARABIA
EXIT
GROAN WITH THE WIND
DICTIONARY
HI THERE, KITTY. HI THERE, KITTY. HI THERE, KITTY.
HI THERE, KITTY. HI THERE, KITTY.
IF HE CAN GET THERE ON TIME--
HI THERE, KITTY. HI THERE--

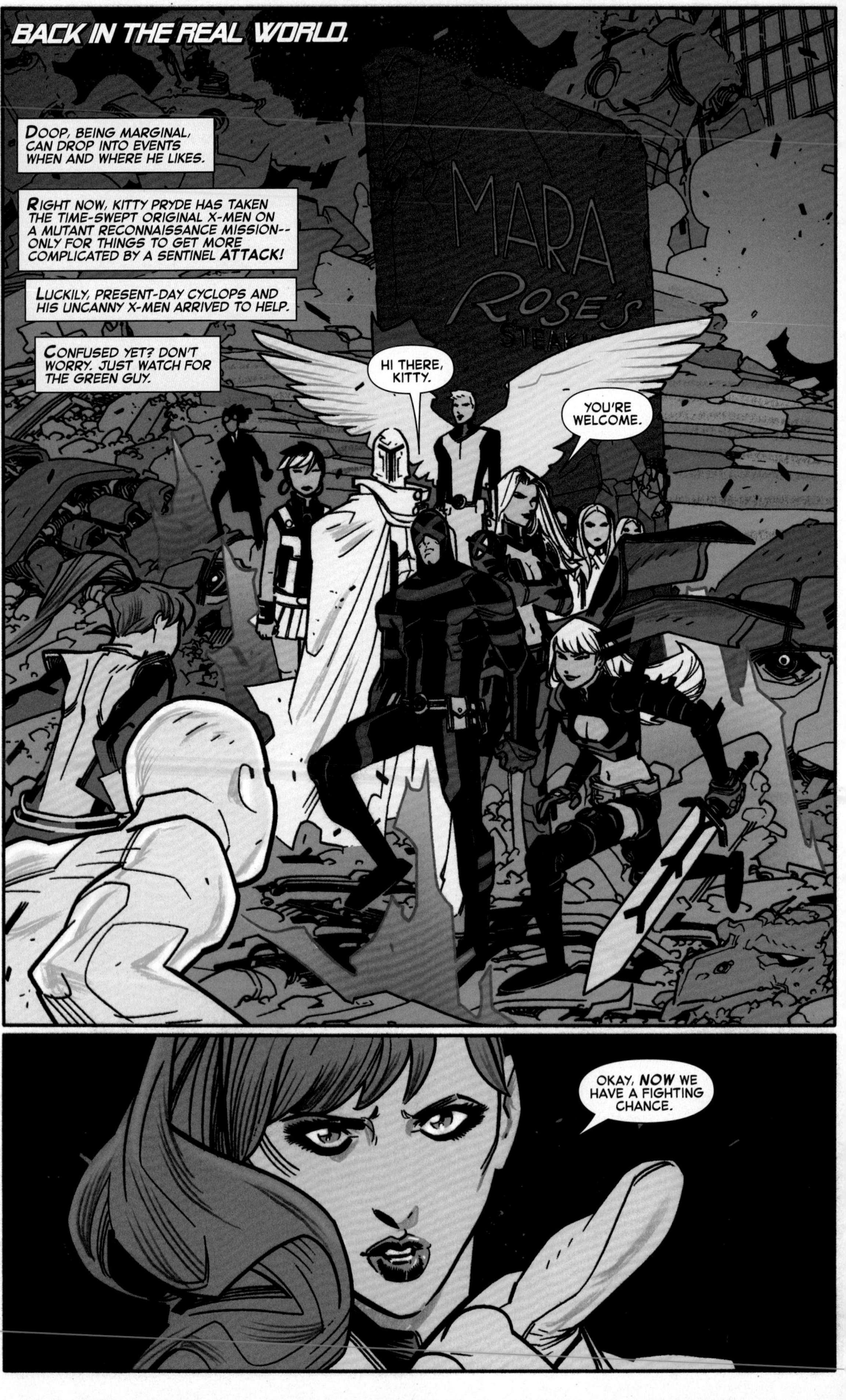
BACK IN THE REAL WORLD.
DOOP, BEING MARGINAL, CAN DROP INTO EVENTS WHEN AND WHERE HE LIKES.
RIGHT NOW, KITTY PRYDE HAS TAKEN THE TIME-SWEPT ORIGINAL X-MEN ON A MUTANT RECONNAISSANCE MISSION--ONLY FOR THINGS TO GET MORE COMPLICATED BY A SENTINEL ATTACK!
LUCKILY, PRESENT-DAY CYCLOPS AND HIS UNCANNY X-MEN ARRIVED TO HELP.
CONFUSED YET? DON'T WORRY. JUST WATCH FOR THE GREEN GUY.
MARA
ROSE'S
HI THERE, KITTY.
YOU'RE WELCOME.
OKAY, NOW WE HAVE A FIGHTING CHANCE.

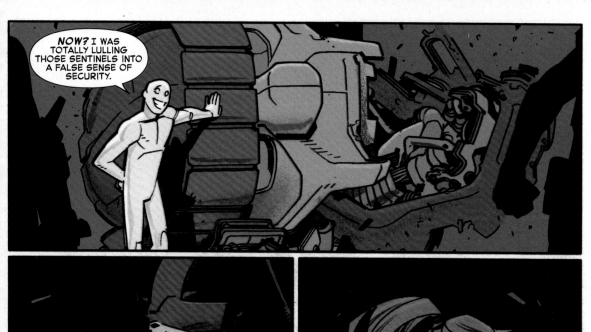

NOW? I WAS TOTALLY LULLING THOSE SENTINELS INTO A FALSE SENSE OF SECURITY.

SINCE WHEN DO YOU TAKE TIME-DISPLACED STUDENTS INTO THE FIELD WHEN THEY HAVEN'T BEEN FULLY TRAINED FOR COMBAT MISSIONS?

WE WERE OUT FOR A RECONNAISSANCE MISSION, THANK YOU.

LET'S SHUT THIS DOWN FAST.

LET'S.

FUNNY.

WHAT IS?

KEEP GETTING THE FEELING... THAT SOMEONE'S *WATCHING* ME.

GEEZ. PARANOID MUCH, PROFESSOR KITTY?

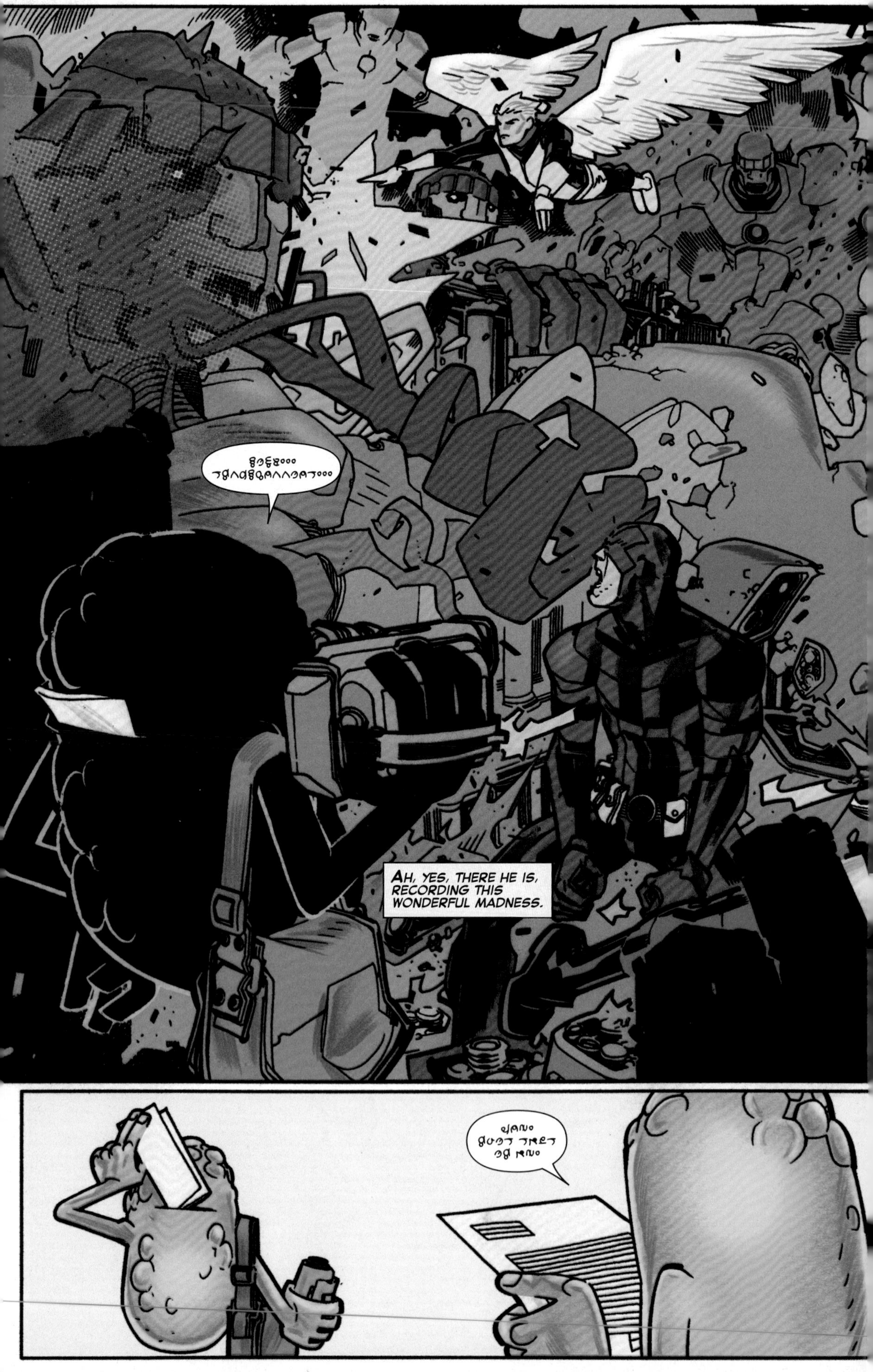
AH, YES, THERE HE IS, RECORDING THIS WONDERFUL MADNESS.

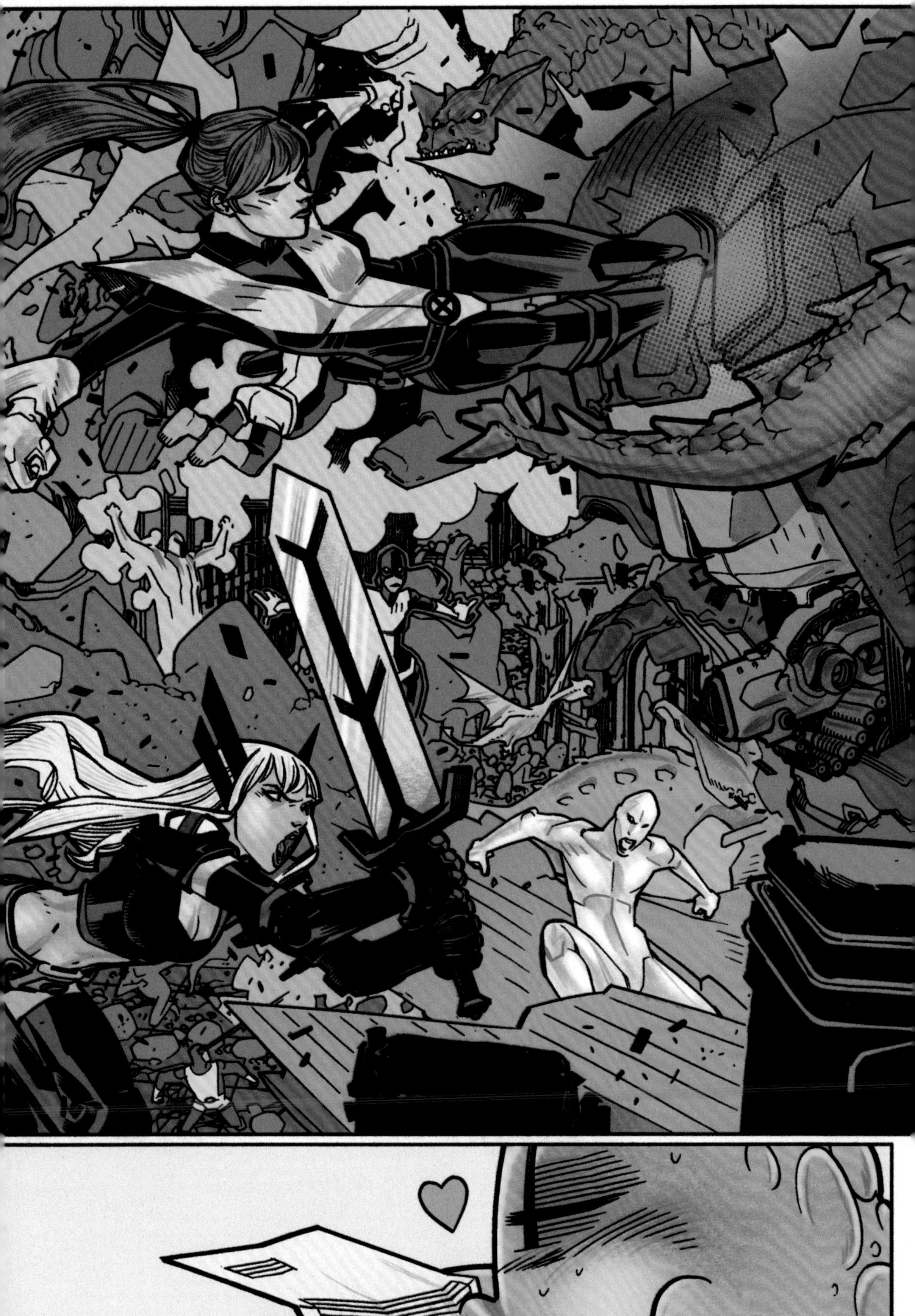

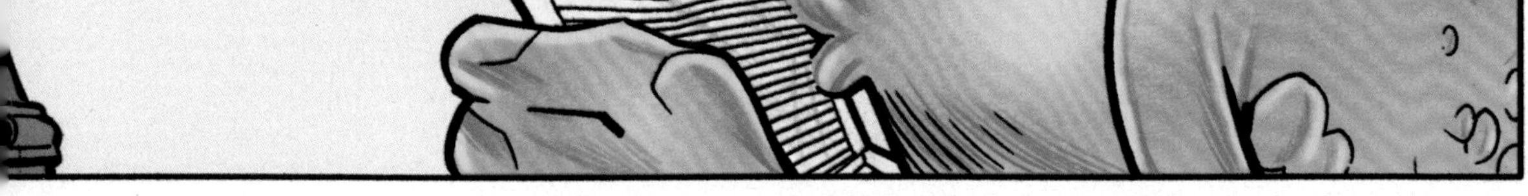

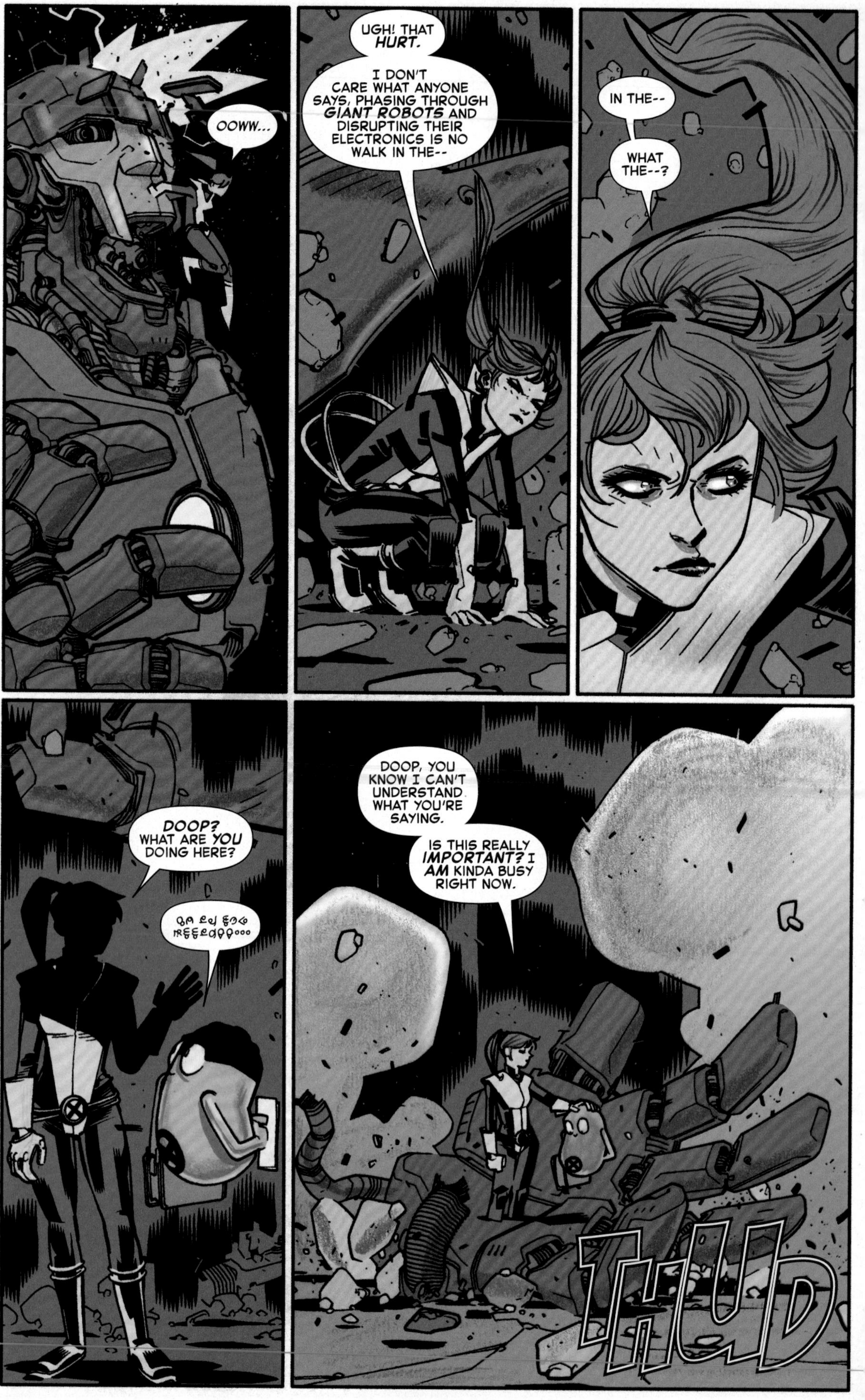

OOWW...
UGH! THAT HURT.
I DON'T CARE WHAT ANYONE SAYS, PHASING THROUGH GIANT ROBOTS AND DISRUPTING THEIR ELECTRONICS IS NO WALK IN THE--
IN THE--
WHAT THE--?
DOOP? WHAT ARE YOU DOING HERE?
DOOP, YOU KNOW I CAN'T UNDERSTAND WHAT YOU'RE SAYING.
IS THIS REALLY IMPORTANT? I AM KINDA BUSY RIGHT NOW.
THUD

WHAT'S THIS? A LETTER?

 goa natttoudooo np &unnm

FOR ME? DOOP, WHY ARE YOU--

PROFESSOR K?

I SAW YOU FALL. ARE YOU OKAY?

I DIDN'T FALL. I JUMPED. THERE'S A SUBTLE DIFFERENCE, BOBBY.

WHAT'S WITH THE *LETTER*?

OH, NOTHING. LET'S GET BACK TO THE TASK AT HAND. DID YOU DO ANYTHING AFTER FREEZING THAT SENTINEL'S EYES CLOSED?

DO ANYTHING? YOU MEAN, *BESIDES* FEELING ALL PLEASED WITH MYSELF?

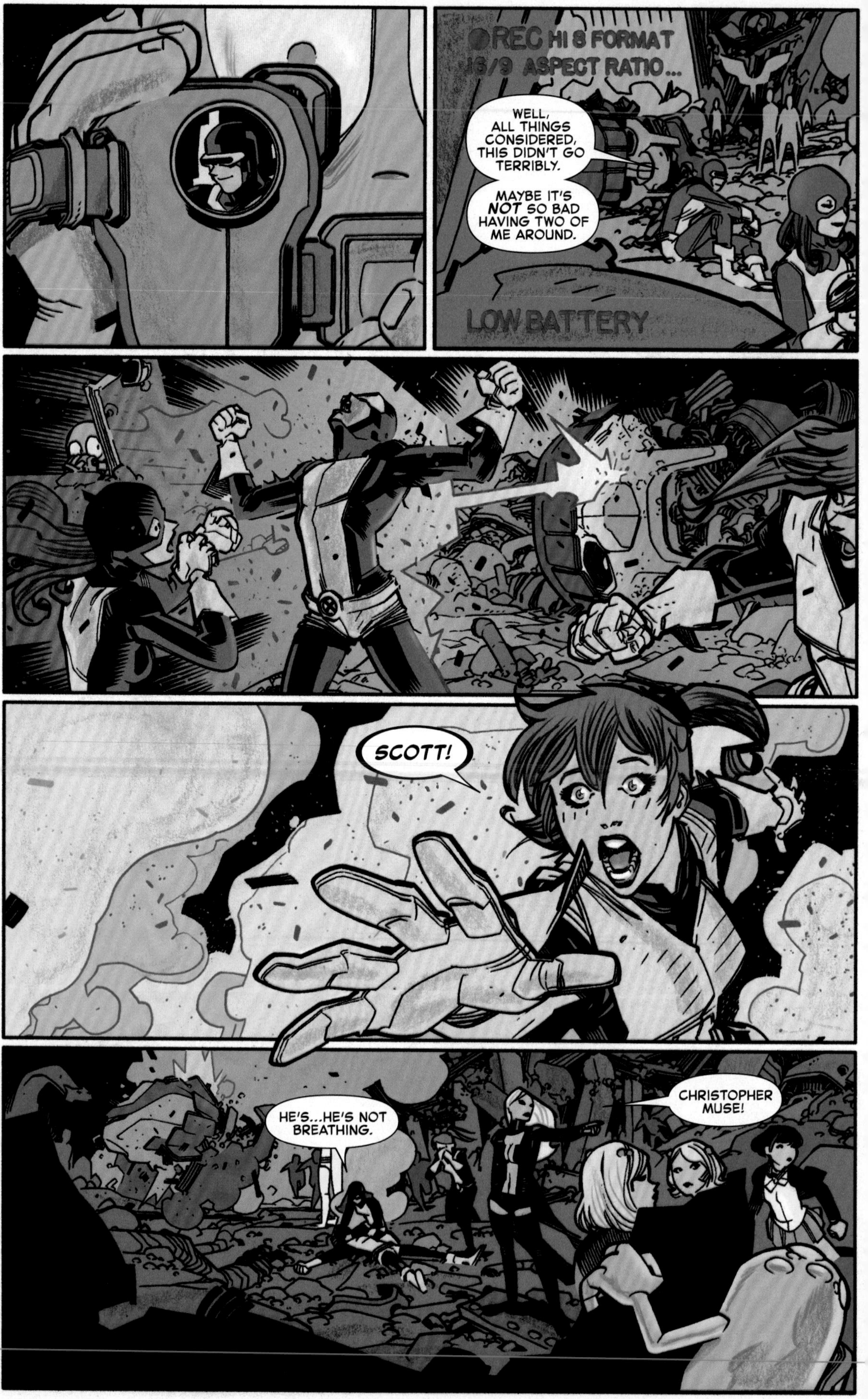
REC HI 8 FORMAT
16/9 ASPECT RATIO...
WELL, ALL THINGS CONSIDERED, THIS DIDN'T GO TERRIBLY.
MAYBE IT'S NOT SO BAD HAVING TWO OF ME AROUND.
LOW BATTERY
SCOTT!
HE'S...HE'S NOT BREATHING.
CHRISTOPHER MUSE!

THOUGH MARGINAL, DOOP REALIZES HE HAS A ROLE TO PLAY IN THIS STORY.

GREATER THAN ANYONE MIGHT HAVE GUESSED.

N-NO... NO...NO...

HUHH?

ᏖᎤᎾ ᎣᏓᏬᏬᎠᏆᏗᎠ ᎣᎪᎾ ᏗᎤᏘᎬᏓᏅᏕᎡᎠ ᏕᎤᏓᏅᏗ ᎫᎤᎾᎡᎪ ᎣᎡᎪᎡᎤ

I...I DON'T KNOW WHAT YOU'RE SAYING B-BUT I CAN'T DO THIS. THAT'S SCOTT SUMMERS. HE'S A LEGEND.

ᎣᎤᎪᏒᎧᏘᎤᏂᎤᎡᎪ ᎬᎡᏒᎤᎤ

WH-WHAT IF I SCREW UP? WHAT IF I--

SLPPP

UGHH?!

UHH...

CHRISTOPHER MUSE, GET OVER HERE!

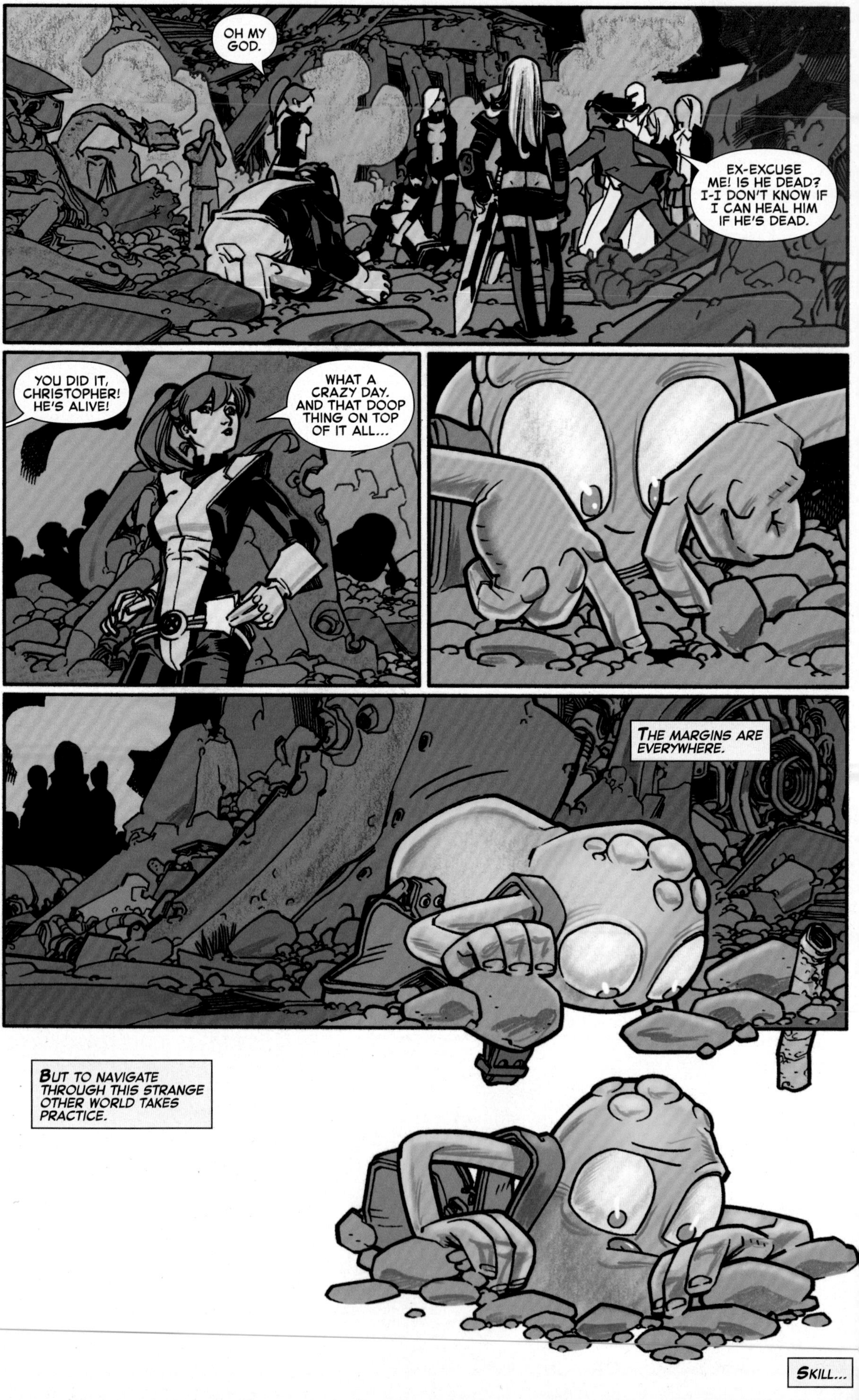
OH MY GOD.
EX-EXCUSE ME! IS HE DEAD? I-I DON'T KNOW IF I CAN HEAL HIM IF HE'S DEAD.
YOU DID IT, CHRISTOPHER! HE'S ALIVE!
WHAT A CRAZY DAY. AND THAT DOOP THING ON TOP OF IT ALL...
THE MARGINS ARE EVERYWHERE.
BUT TO NAVIGATE THROUGH THIS STRANGE OTHER WORLD TAKES PRACTICE.
SKILL...

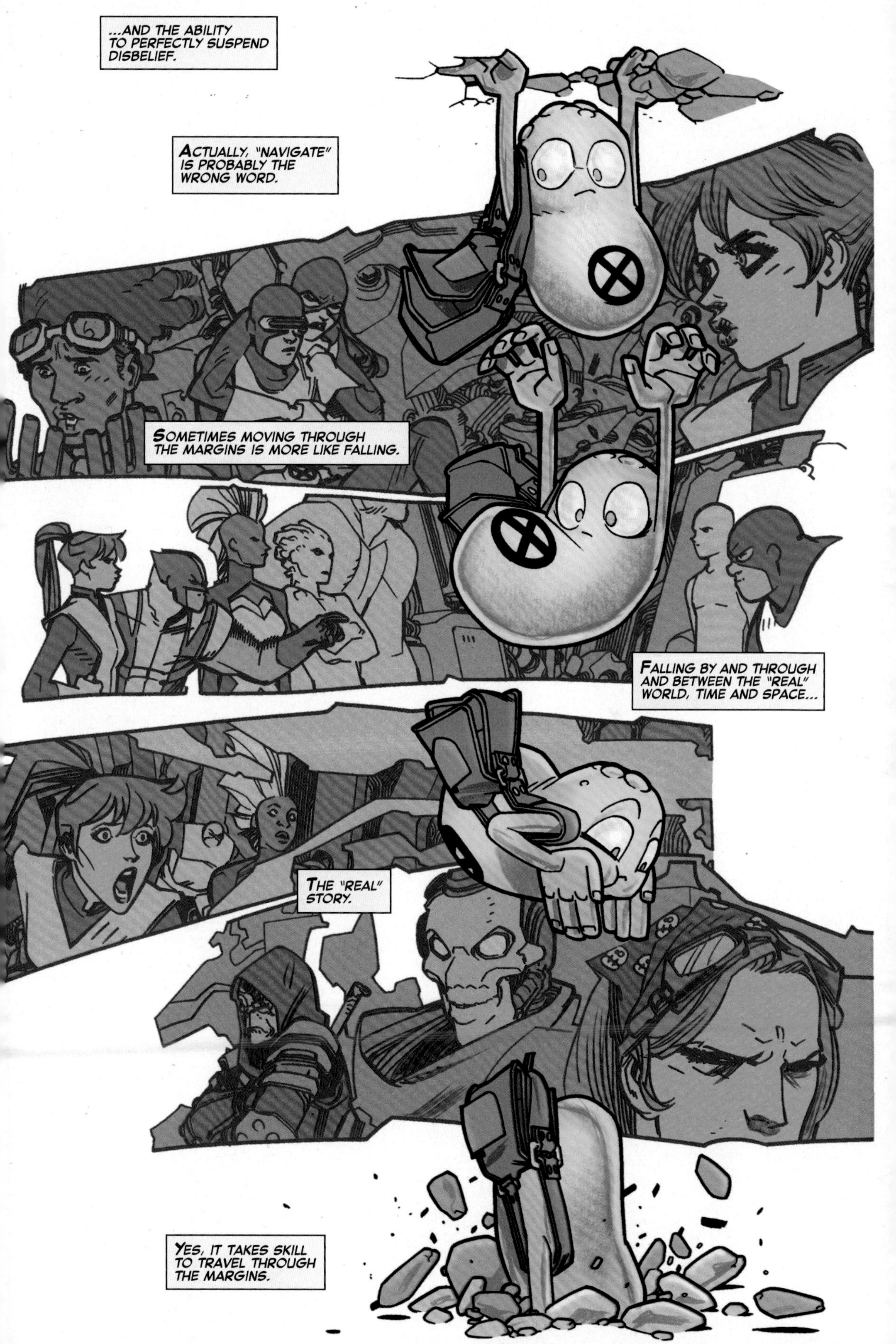
...AND THE ABILITY TO PERFECTLY SUSPEND DISBELIEF.
ACTUALLY, "NAVIGATE" IS PROBABLY THE WRONG WORD.
SOMETIMES MOVING THROUGH THE MARGINS IS MORE LIKE FALLING.
FALLING BY AND THROUGH AND BETWEEN THE "REAL" WORLD, TIME AND SPACE...
THE "REAL" STORY.
YES, IT TAKES SKILL TO TRAVEL THROUGH THE MARGINS.

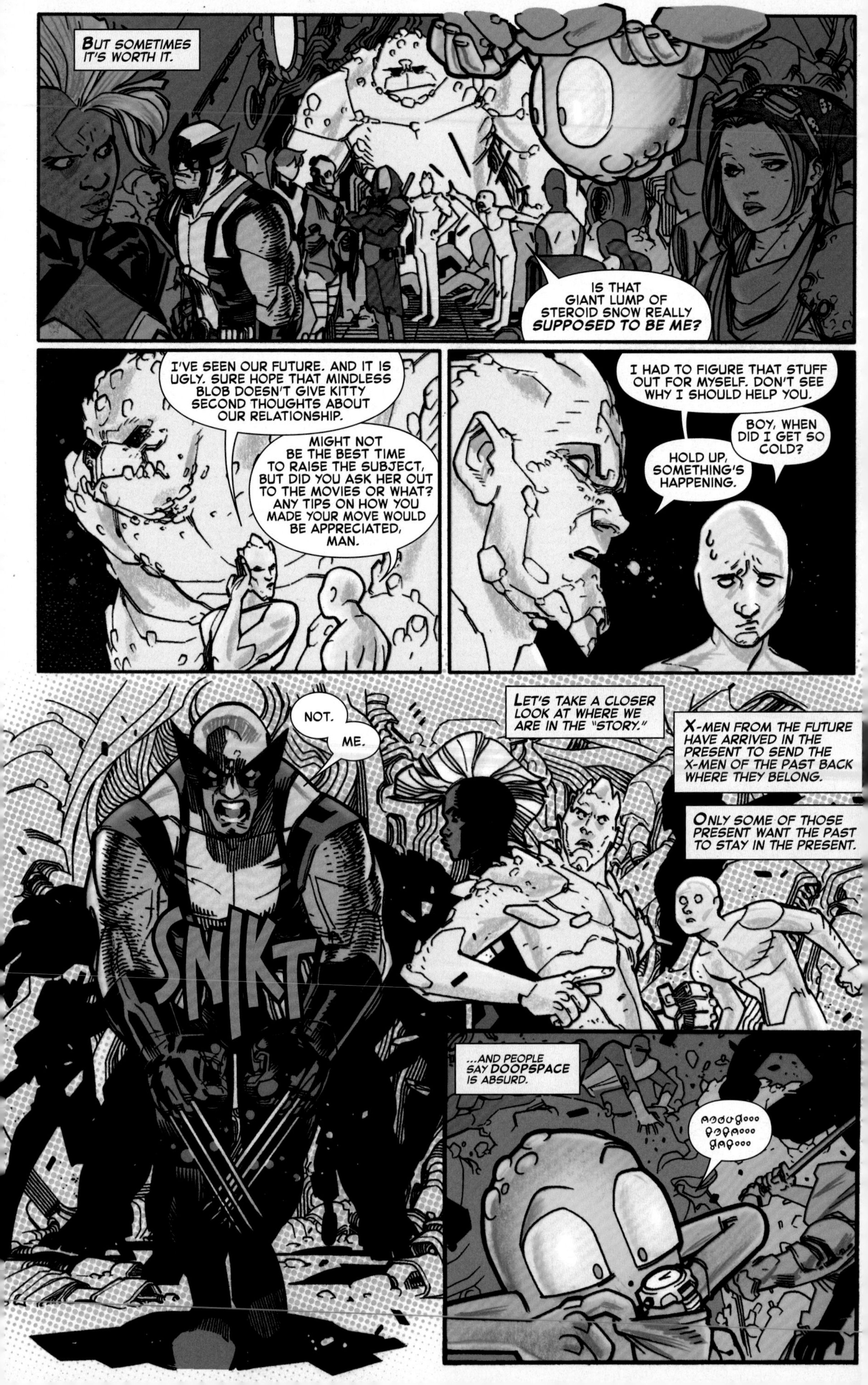
BUT SOMETIMES IT'S WORTH IT.
IS THAT GIANT LUMP OF STEROID SNOW REALLY SUPPOSED TO BE ME?
I'VE SEEN OUR FUTURE. AND IT IS UGLY. SURE HOPE THAT MINDLESS BLOB DOESN'T GIVE KITTY SECOND THOUGHTS ABOUT OUR RELATIONSHIP.
MIGHT NOT BE THE BEST TIME TO RAISE THE SUBJECT, BUT DID YOU ASK HER OUT TO THE MOVIES OR WHAT? ANY TIPS ON HOW YOU MADE YOUR MOVE WOULD BE APPRECIATED, MAN.
I HAD TO FIGURE THAT STUFF OUT FOR MYSELF. DON'T SEE WHY I SHOULD HELP YOU.
BOY, WHEN DID I GET SO COLD?
HOLD UP, SOMETHING'S HAPPENING.
NOT.
ME.
SNIKT
LET'S TAKE A CLOSER LOOK AT WHERE WE ARE IN THE "STORY."
X-MEN FROM THE FUTURE HAVE ARRIVED IN THE PRESENT TO SEND THE X-MEN OF THE PAST BACK WHERE THEY BELONG.
ONLY SOME OF THOSE PRESENT WANT THE PAST TO STAY IN THE PRESENT.
...AND PEOPLE SAY DOOPSPACE IS ABSURD.

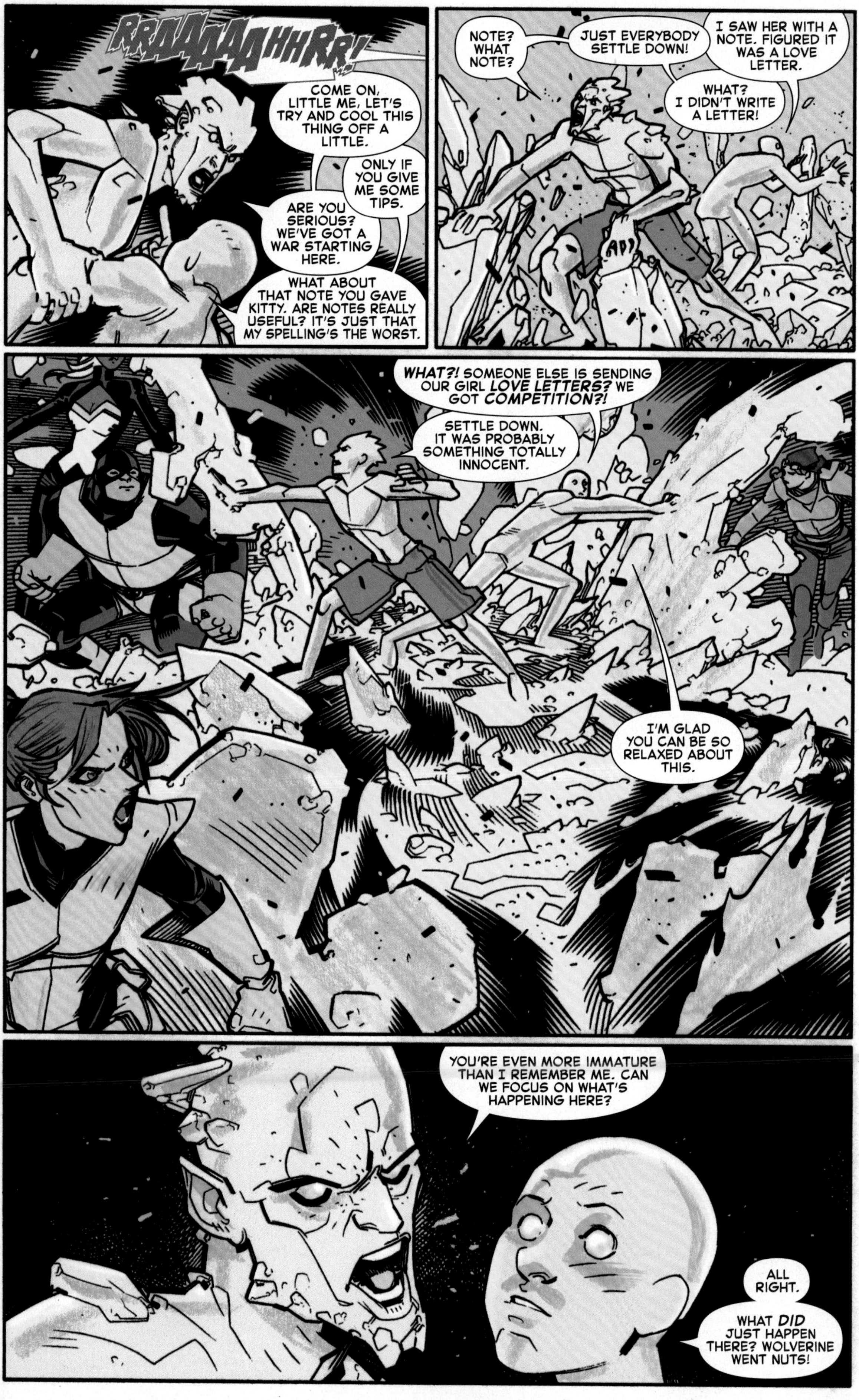
RRAAAAAAHHRR!
COME ON, LITTLE ME, LET'S TRY AND COOL THIS THING OFF A LITTLE.
ONLY IF YOU GIVE ME SOME TIPS.
ARE YOU SERIOUS? WE'VE GOT A WAR STARTING HERE.
WHAT ABOUT THAT NOTE YOU GAVE KITTY. ARE NOTES REALLY USEFUL? IT'S JUST THAT MY SPELLING'S THE WORST.
NOTE? WHAT NOTE?
JUST EVERYBODY SETTLE DOWN!
I SAW HER WITH A NOTE. FIGURED IT WAS A LOVE LETTER.
WHAT? I DIDN'T WRITE A LETTER!
WHAT?! SOMEONE ELSE IS SENDING OUR GIRL LOVE LETTERS? WE GOT COMPETITION?!
SETTLE DOWN. IT WAS PROBABLY SOMETHING TOTALLY INNOCENT.
I'M GLAD YOU CAN BE SO RELAXED ABOUT THIS.
YOU'RE EVEN MORE IMMATURE THAN I REMEMBER ME. CAN WE FOCUS ON WHAT'S HAPPENING HERE?
ALL RIGHT.
WHAT DID JUST HAPPEN THERE? WOLVERINE WENT NUTS!

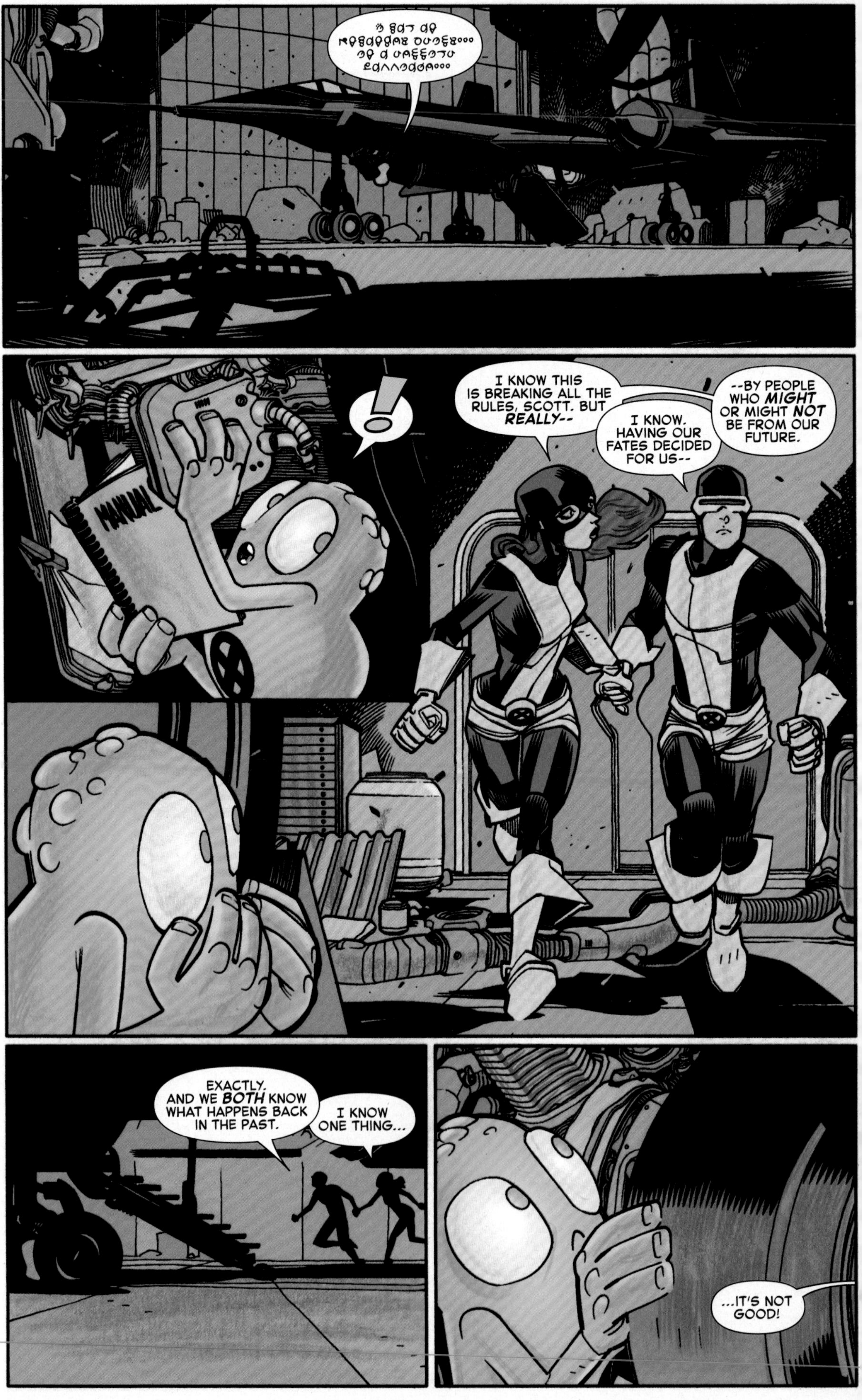
!
I KNOW THIS IS BREAKING ALL THE RULES, SCOTT. BUT REALLY--
I KNOW. HAVING OUR FATES DECIDED FOR US--
--BY PEOPLE WHO MIGHT OR MIGHT NOT BE FROM OUR FUTURE.
EXACTLY. AND WE BOTH KNOW WHAT HAPPENS BACK IN THE PAST.
I KNOW ONE THING...
...IT'S NOT GOOD!

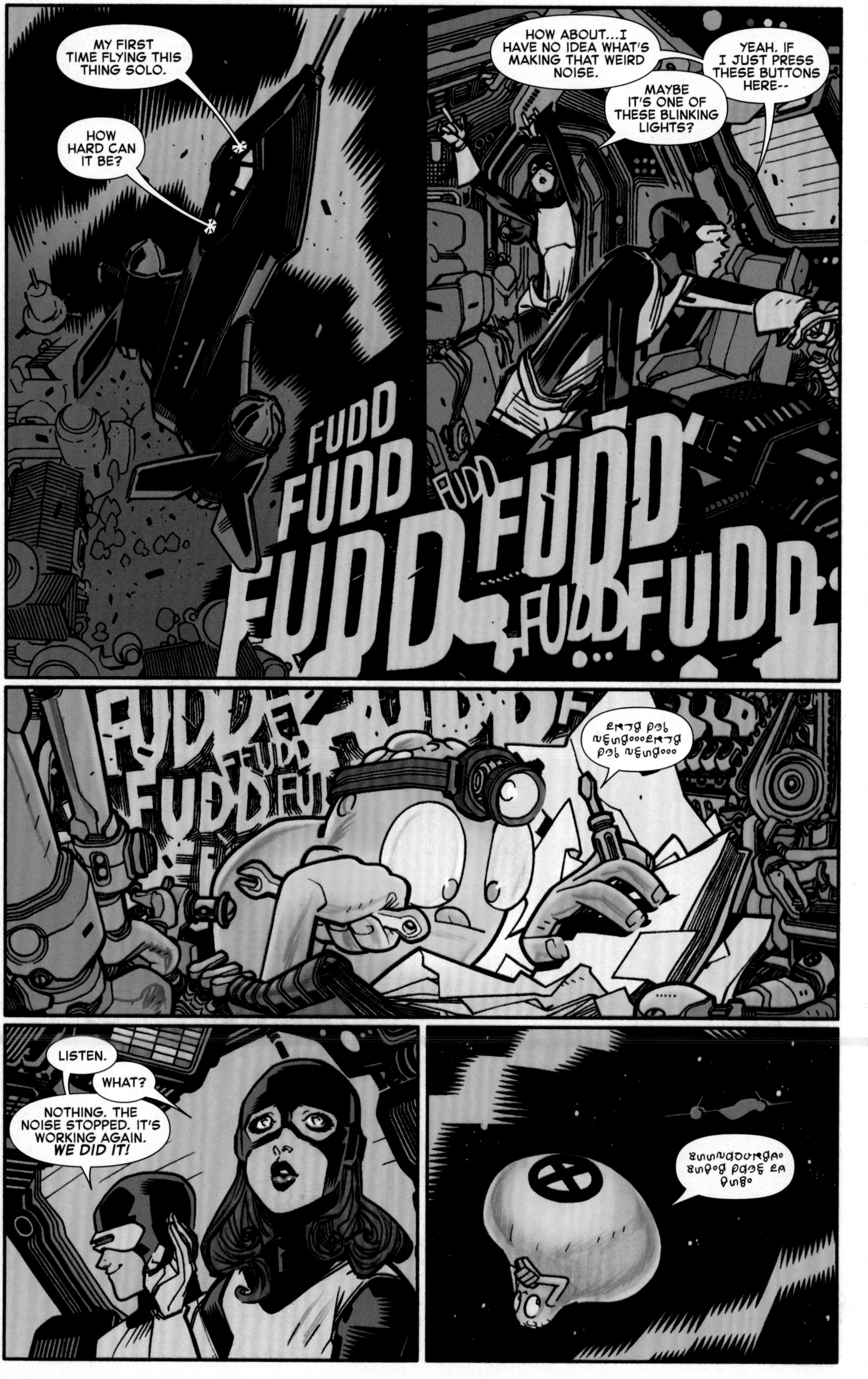
MY FIRST TIME FLYING THIS THING SOLO.
HOW HARD CAN IT BE?
HOW ABOUT...I HAVE NO IDEA WHAT'S MAKING THAT WEIRD NOISE.
MAYBE IT'S ONE OF THESE BLINKING LIGHTS?
YEAH. IF I JUST PRESS THESE BUTTONS HERE--
FUDD
FUDD
FUDD
FUDD
FUDD
FUDD
FUDD
FUDD
LISTEN.
WHAT?
NOTHING. THE NOISE STOPPED. IT'S WORKING AGAIN. *WE DID IT!*

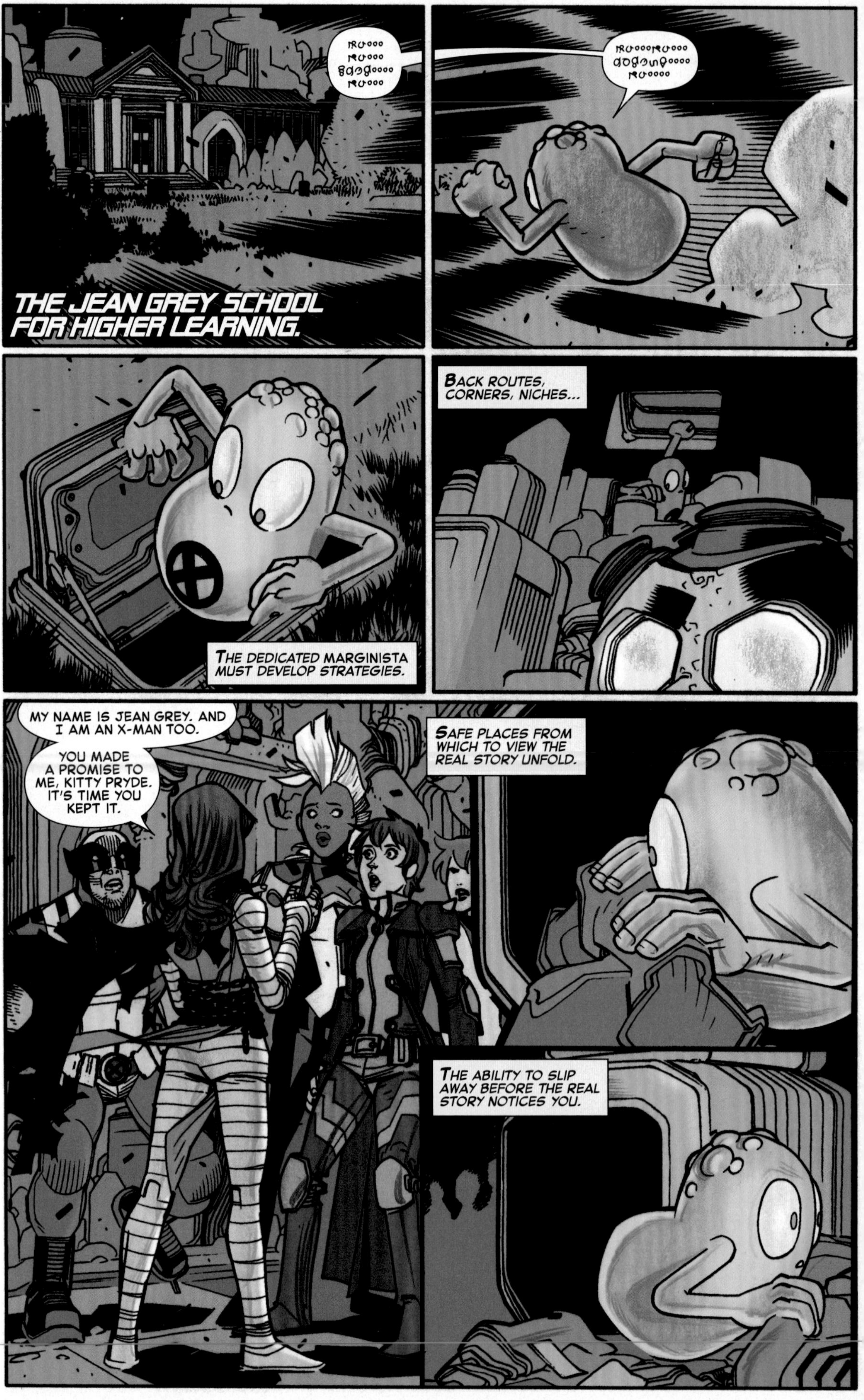
THE JEAN GREY SCHOOL FOR HIGHER LEARNING.
BACK ROUTES, CORNERS, NICHES...
THE DEDICATED MARGINISTA MUST DEVELOP STRATEGIES.
MY NAME IS JEAN GREY. AND I AM AN X-MAN TOO.
YOU MADE A PROMISE TO ME, KITTY PRYDE. IT'S TIME YOU KEPT IT.
SAFE PLACES FROM WHICH TO VIEW THE REAL STORY UNFOLD.
THE ABILITY TO SLIP AWAY BEFORE THE REAL STORY NOTICES YOU.

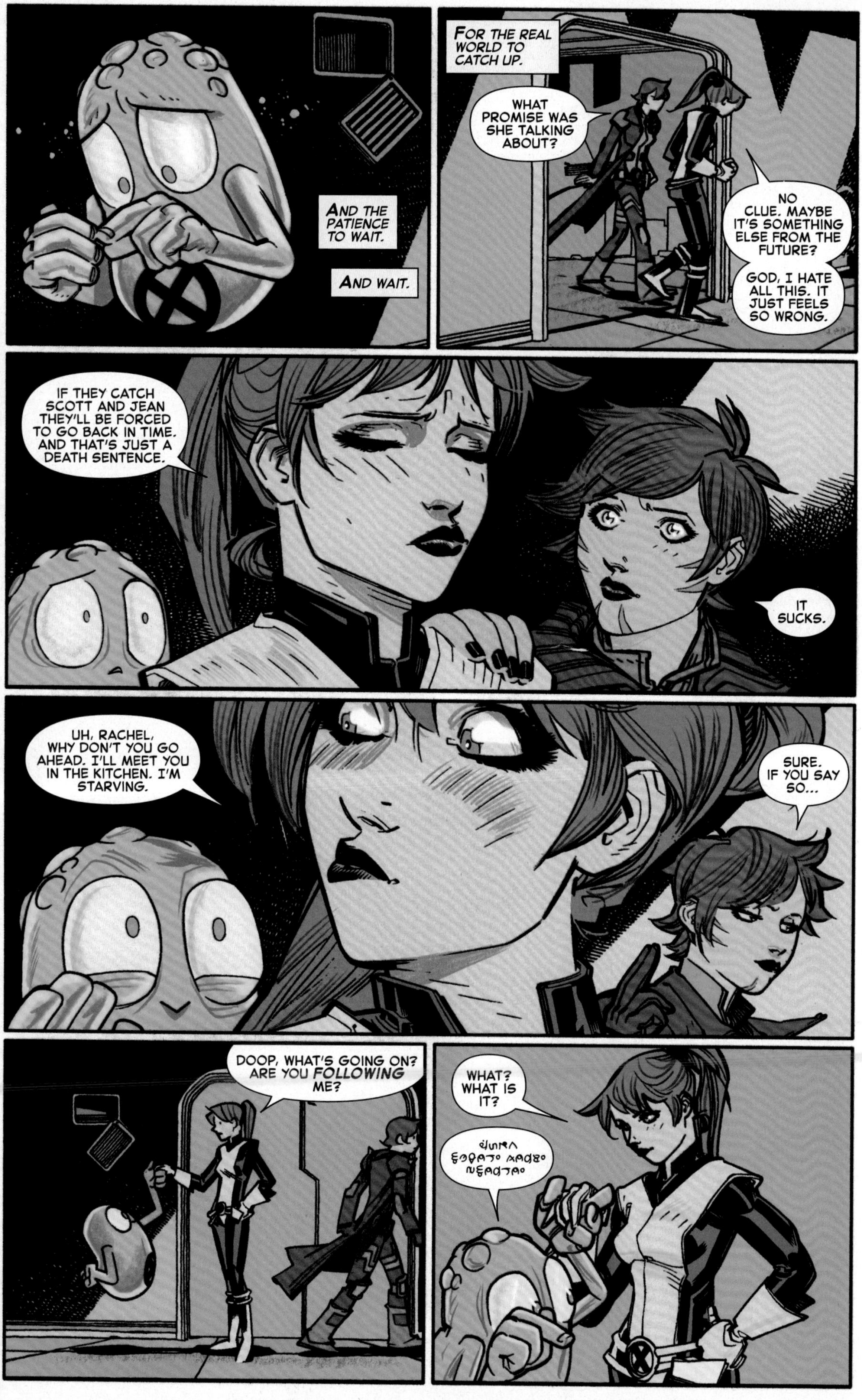
AND THE PATIENCE TO WAIT.
AND WAIT.
FOR THE REAL WORLD TO CATCH UP.
WHAT PROMISE WAS SHE TALKING ABOUT?
NO CLUE. MAYBE IT'S SOMETHING ELSE FROM THE FUTURE?
GOD, I HATE ALL THIS. IT JUST FEELS SO WRONG.
IF THEY CATCH SCOTT AND JEAN THEY'LL BE FORCED TO GO BACK IN TIME. AND THAT'S JUST A DEATH SENTENCE.
IT SUCKS.
UH, RACHEL, WHY DON'T YOU GO AHEAD. I'LL MEET YOU IN THE KITCHEN. I'M STARVING.
SURE. IF YOU SAY SO...
DOOP, WHAT'S GOING ON? ARE YOU *FOLLOWING* ME?
WHAT? WHAT IS IT?

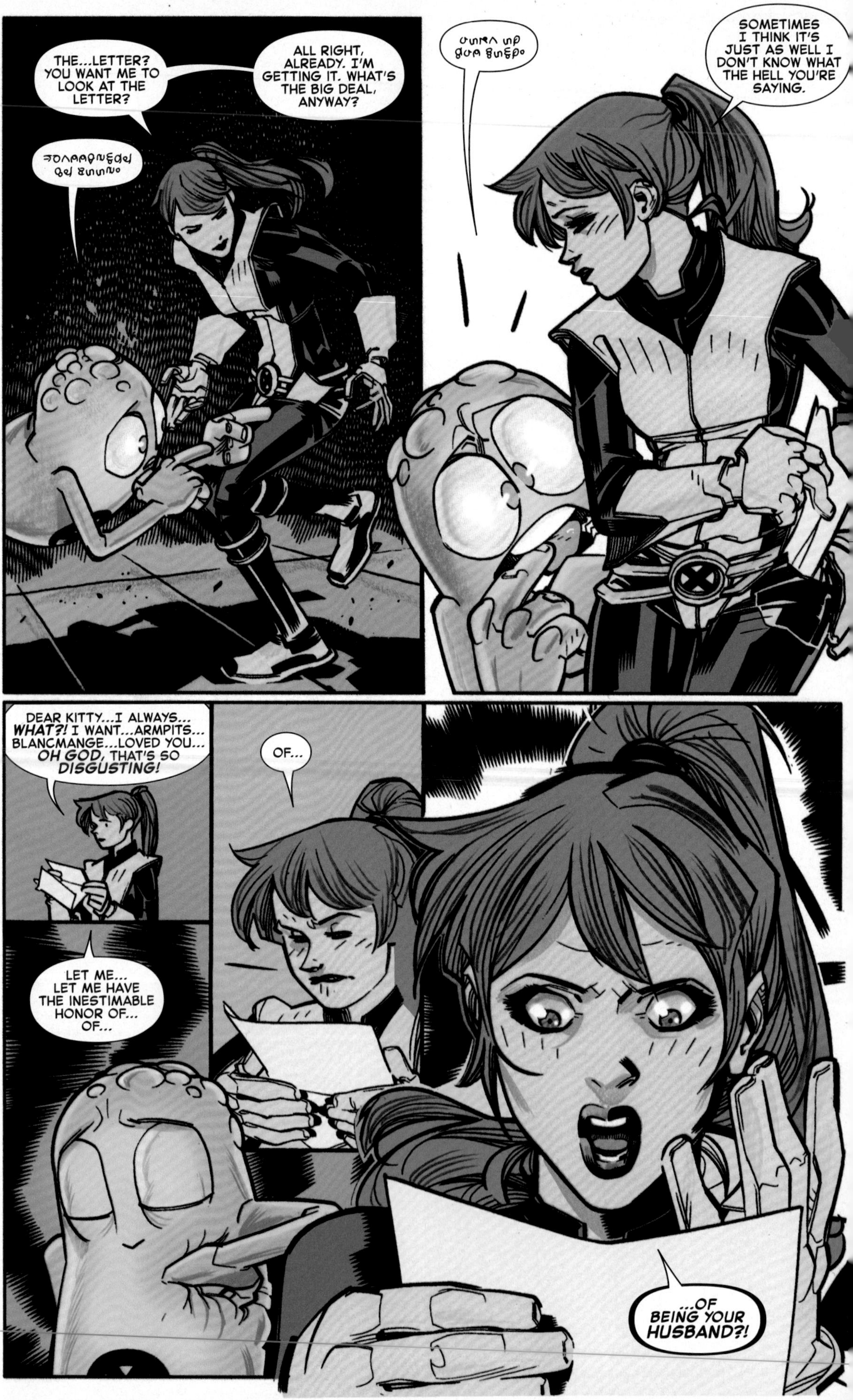
THE...LETTER? YOU WANT ME TO LOOK AT THE LETTER?
ALL RIGHT, ALREADY. I'M GETTING IT. WHAT'S THE BIG DEAL, ANYWAY?
SOMETIMES I THINK IT'S JUST AS WELL I DON'T KNOW WHAT THE HELL YOU'RE SAYING.
DEAR KITTY...I ALWAYS... WHAT?! I WANT...ARMPITS... BLANCMANGE...LOVED YOU... OH GOD, THAT'S SO DISGUSTING!
OF...
LET ME... LET ME HAVE THE INESTIMABLE HONOR OF... OF...
...OF BEING YOUR HUSBAND?!

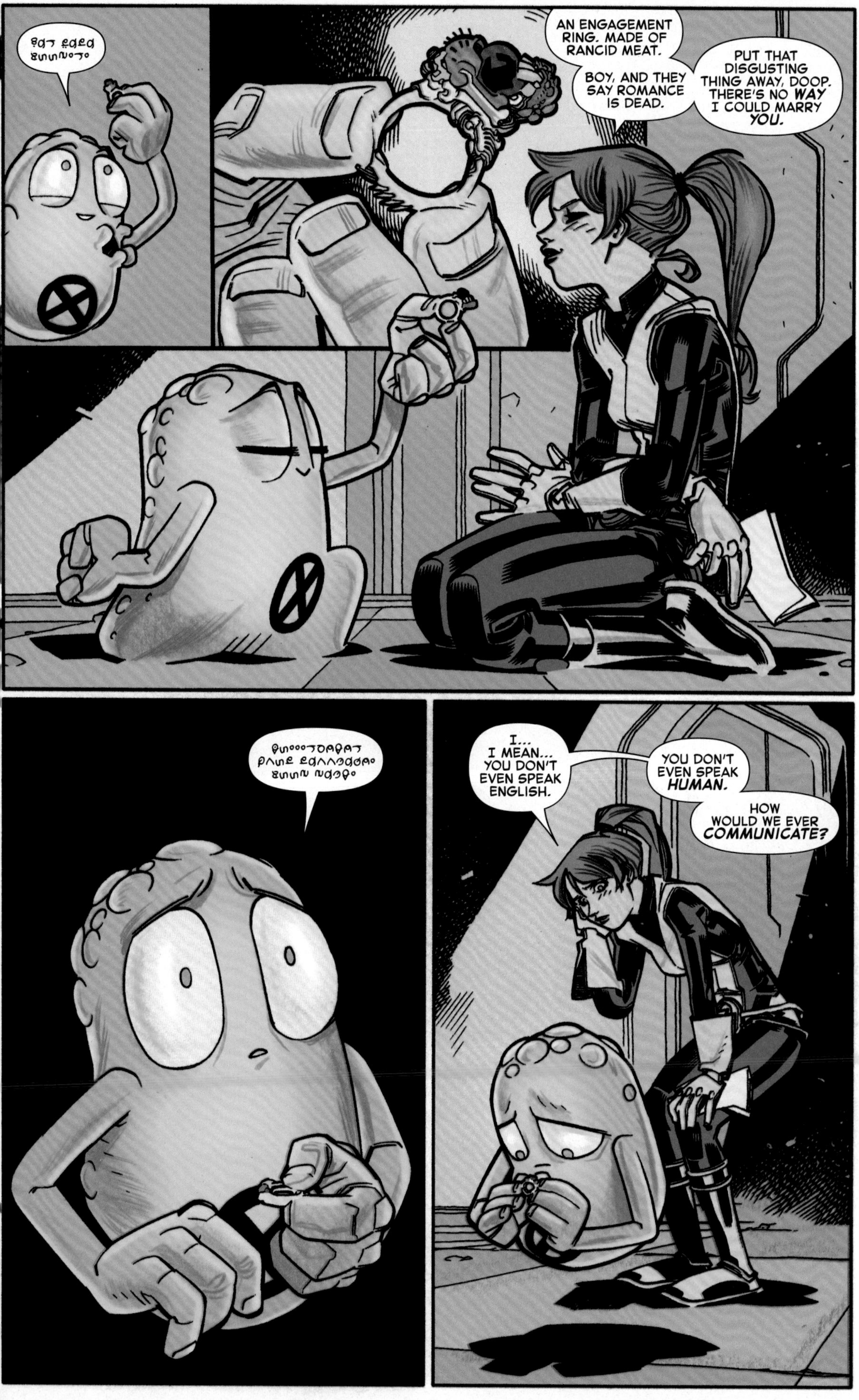
AN ENGAGEMENT RING. MADE OF RANCID MEAT.
BOY, AND THEY SAY ROMANCE IS DEAD.
PUT THAT DISGUSTING THING AWAY, DOOP. THERE'S NO WAY I COULD MARRY YOU.
I... I MEAN... YOU DON'T EVEN SPEAK ENGLISH.
YOU DON'T EVEN SPEAK HUMAN.
HOW WOULD WE EVER COMMUNICATE?

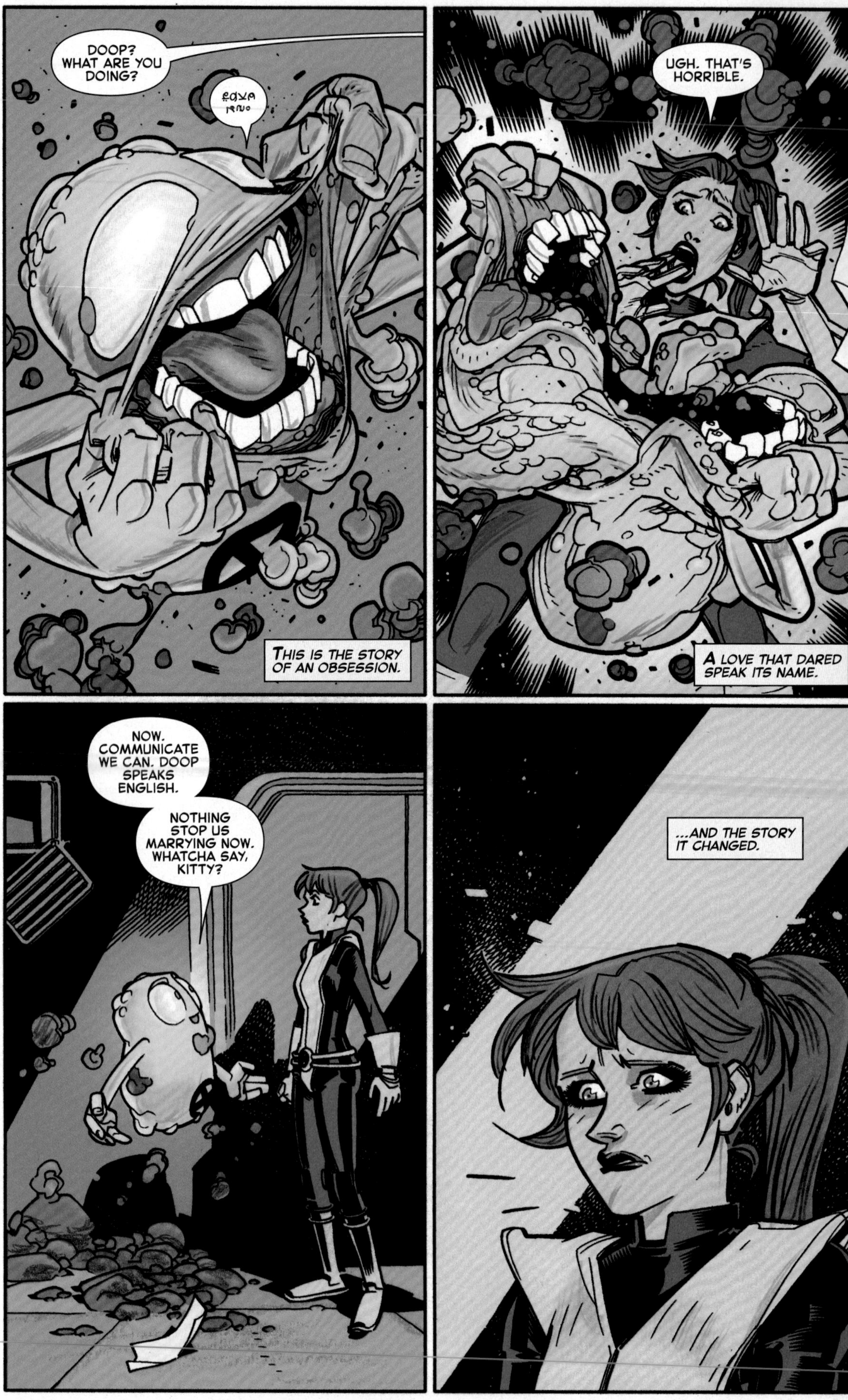
DOOP? WHAT ARE YOU DOING?
THIS IS THE STORY OF AN OBSESSION.
UGH. THAT'S HORRIBLE.
A LOVE THAT DARED SPEAK ITS NAME.
NOW. COMMUNICATE WE CAN. DOOP SPEAKS ENGLISH.
NOTHING STOP US MARRYING NOW. WHATCHA SAY, KITTY?
...AND THE STORY IT CHANGED.

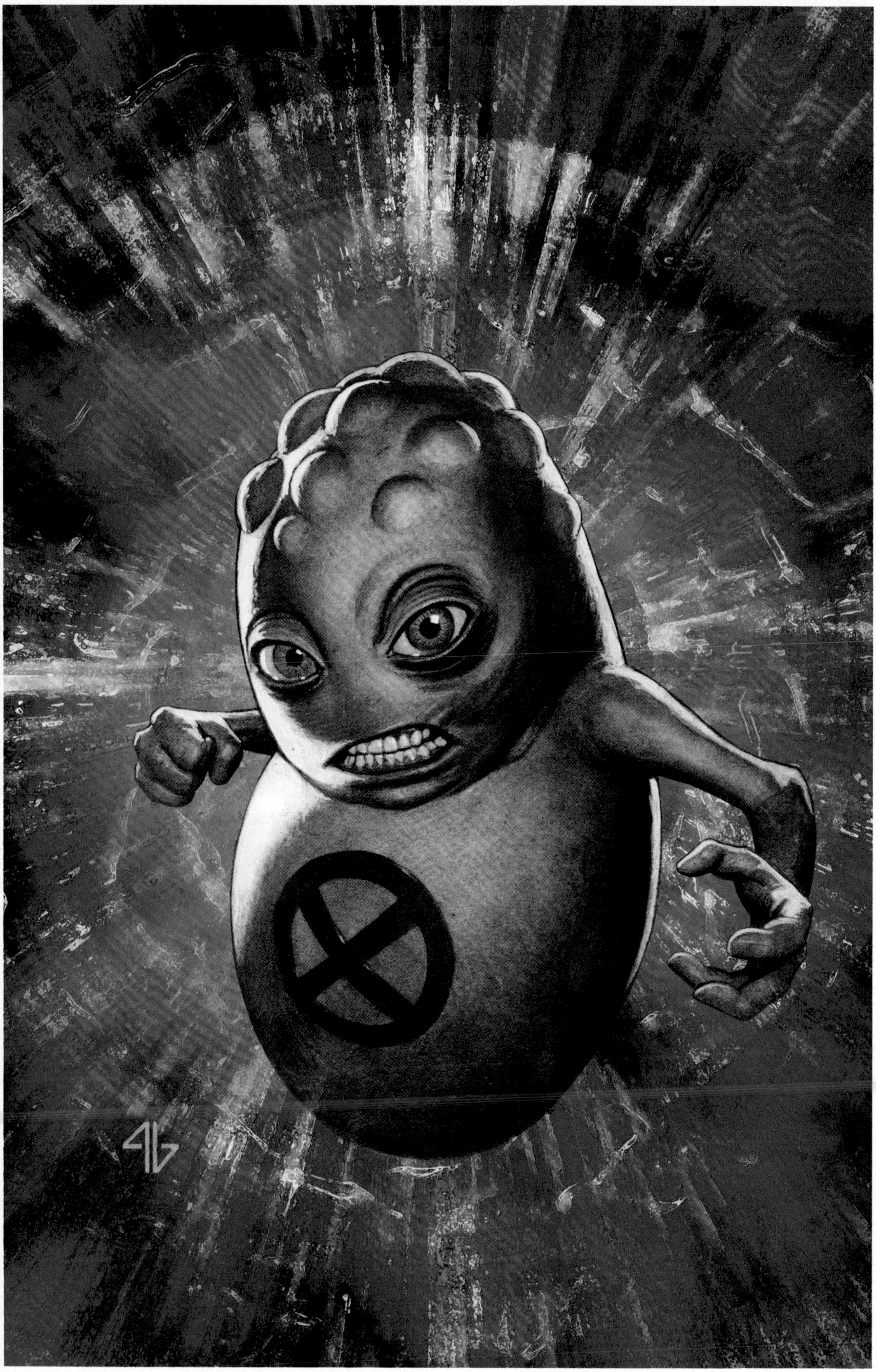

ALL NEW DOOP #1 VARIANT BY ADI GRANOV

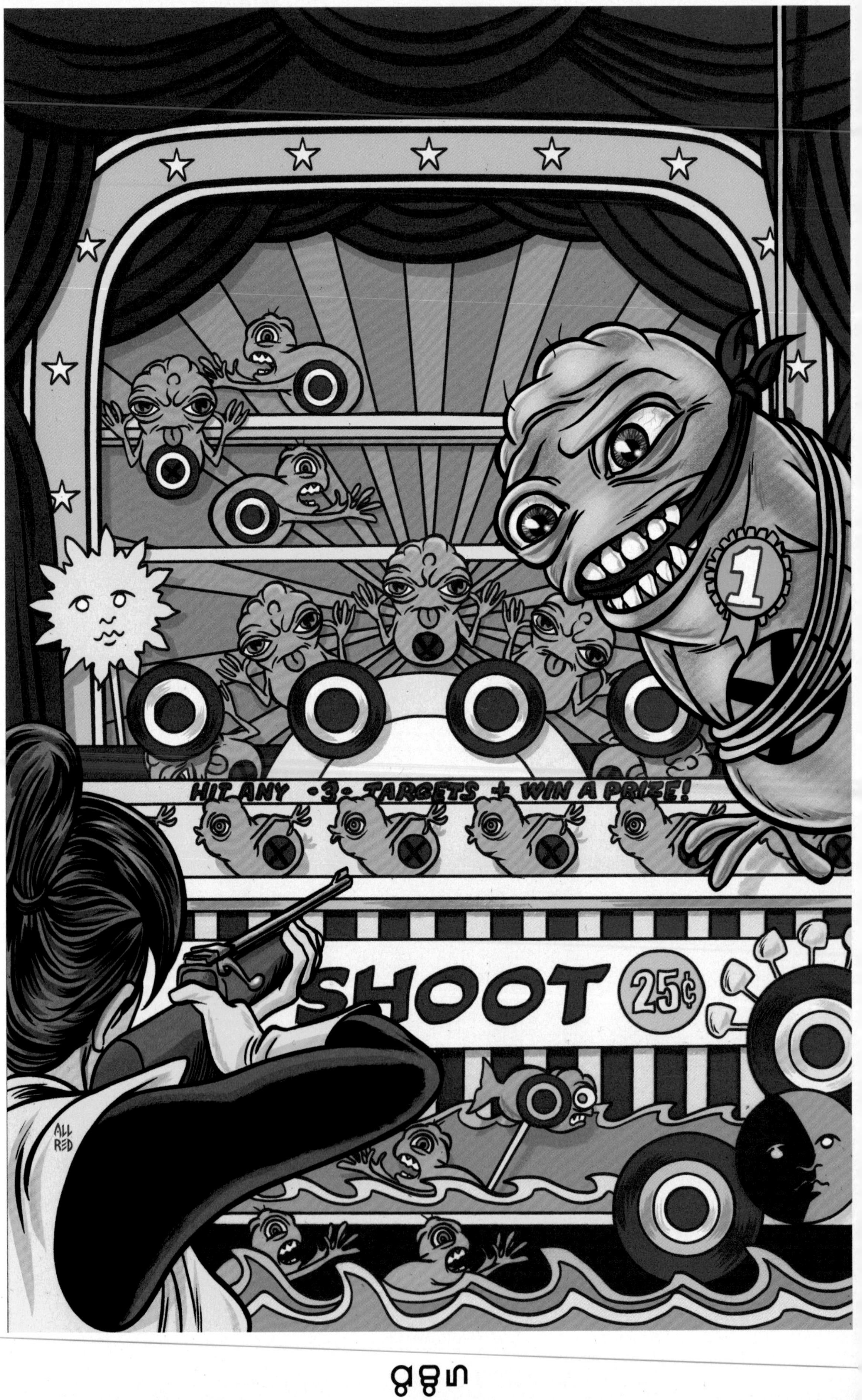
HIT ANY -3- TARGETS + WIN A PRIZE!
1
SHOOT
25¢
ALL RED

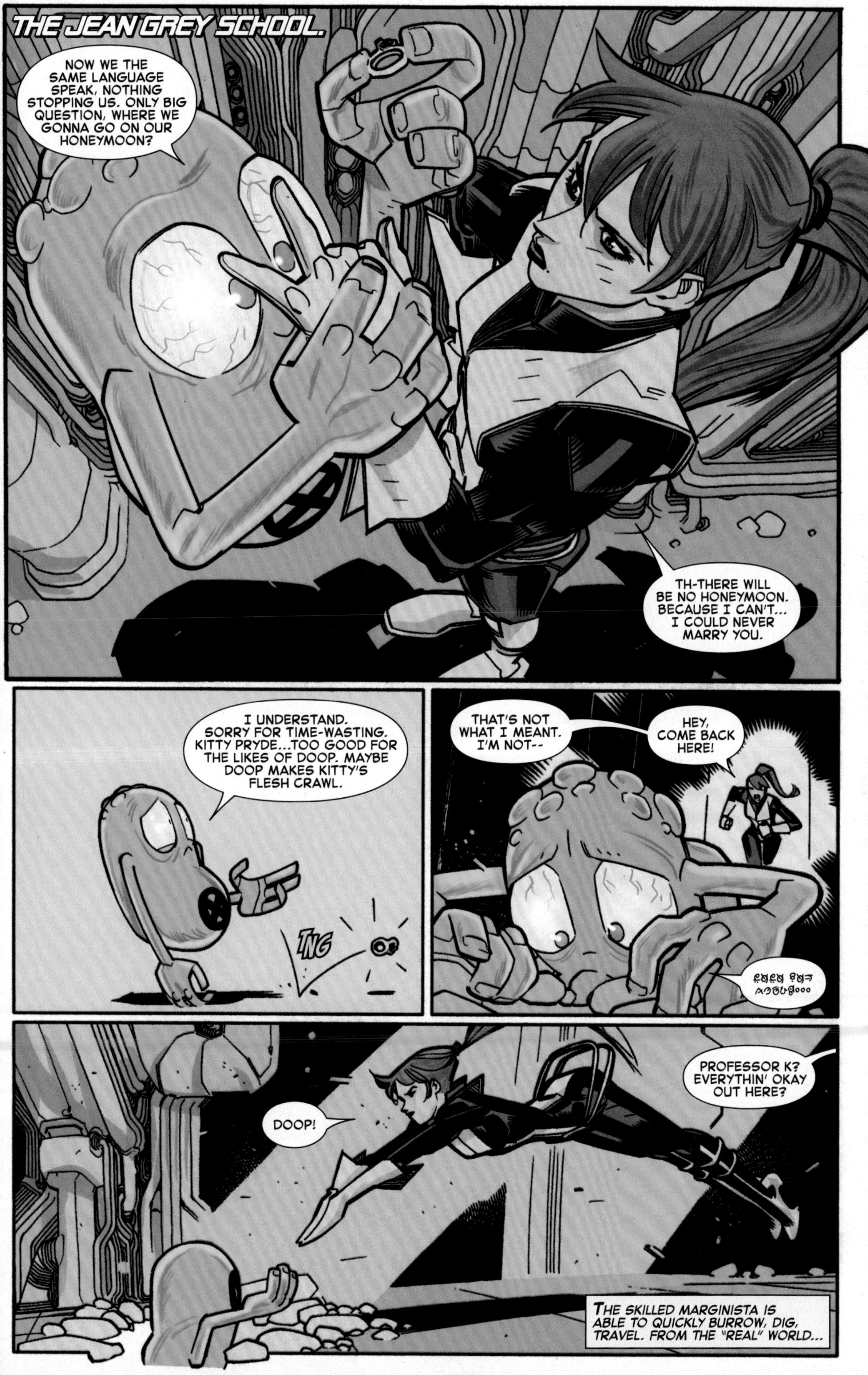
THE JEAN GREY SCHOOL.
NOW WE THE SAME LANGUAGE SPEAK, NOTHING STOPPING US. ONLY BIG QUESTION, WHERE WE GONNA GO ON OUR HONEYMOON?
TH-THERE WILL BE NO HONEYMOON. BECAUSE I CAN'T... I COULD NEVER MARRY YOU.
I UNDERSTAND. SORRY FOR TIME-WASTING. KITTY PRYDE...TOO GOOD FOR THE LIKES OF DOOP. MAYBE DOOP MAKES KITTY'S FLESH CRAWL.
TNG
THAT'S NOT WHAT I MEANT. I'M NOT--
HEY, COME BACK HERE!
DOOP!
PROFESSOR K? EVERYTHIN' OKAY OUT HERE?
THE SKILLED MARGINISTA IS ABLE TO QUICKLY BURROW, DIG, TRAVEL. FROM THE "REAL" WORLD...

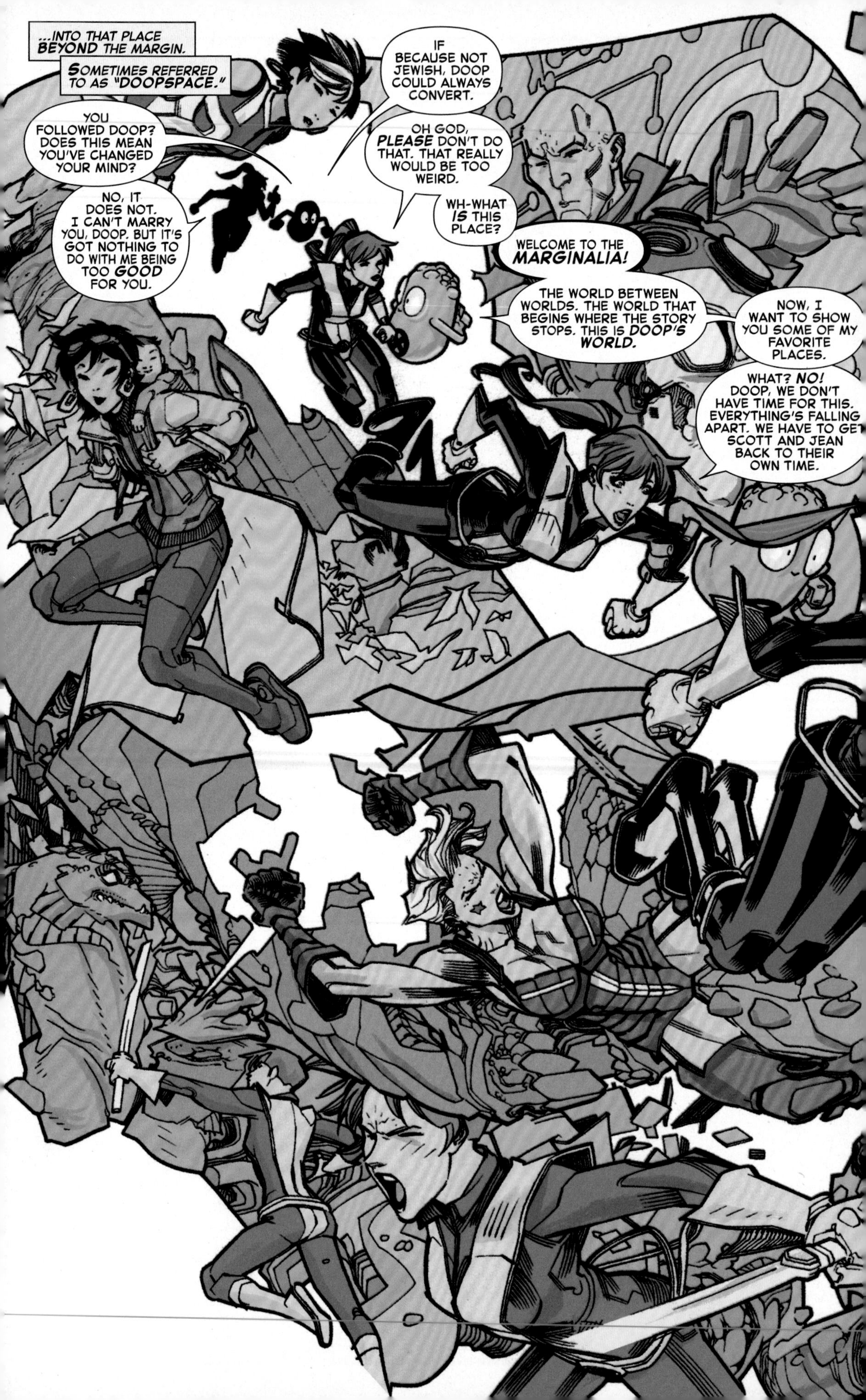
...INTO THAT PLACE BEYOND THE MARGIN.
SOMETIMES REFERRED TO AS "DOOPSPACE."
YOU FOLLOWED DOOP? DOES THIS MEAN YOU'VE CHANGED YOUR MIND?
NO, IT DOES NOT. I CAN'T MARRY YOU, DOOP. BUT IT'S GOT NOTHING TO DO WITH ME BEING TOO GOOD FOR YOU.
IF BECAUSE NOT JEWISH, DOOP COULD ALWAYS CONVERT.
OH GOD, PLEASE DON'T DO THAT. THAT REALLY WOULD BE TOO WEIRD.
WH-WHAT IS THIS PLACE?
WELCOME TO THE MARGINALIA!
THE WORLD BETWEEN WORLDS. THE WORLD THAT BEGINS WHERE THE STORY STOPS. THIS IS DOOP'S WORLD.
NOW, I WANT TO SHOW YOU SOME OF MY FAVORITE PLACES.
WHAT? NO! DOOP, WE DON'T HAVE TIME FOR THIS. EVERYTHING'S FALLING APART. WE HAVE TO GET SCOTT AND JEAN BACK TO THEIR OWN TIME.

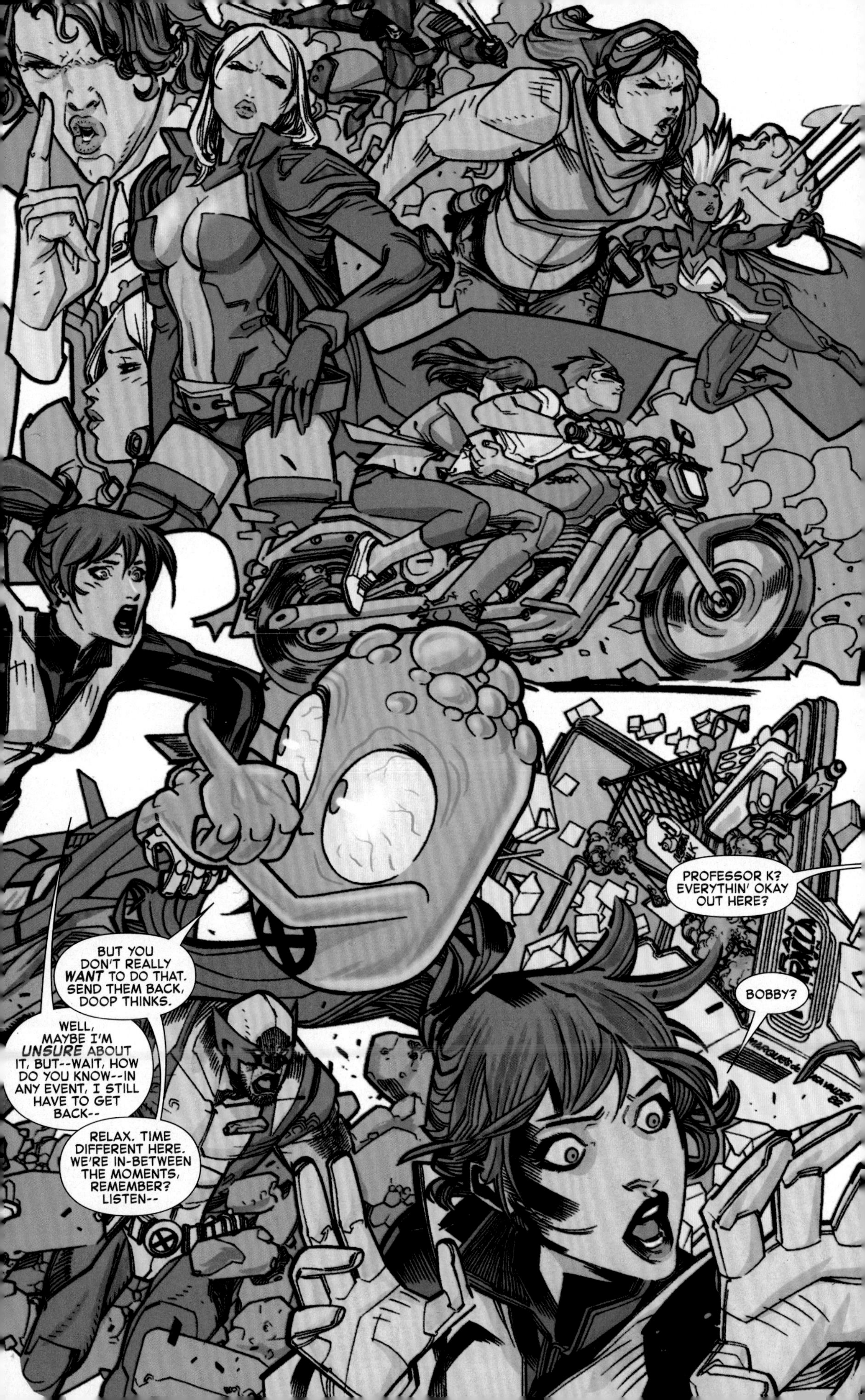
BUT YOU DON'T REALLY WANT TO DO THAT. SEND THEM BACK, DOOP THINKS.
WELL, MAYBE I'M UNSURE ABOUT IT, BUT--WAIT, HOW DO YOU KNOW--IN ANY EVENT, I STILL HAVE TO GET BACK--
RELAX. TIME DIFFERENT HERE. WE'RE IN-BETWEEN THE MOMENTS, REMEMBER? LISTEN--
PROFESSOR K? EVERYTHIN' OKAY OUT HERE?
BOBBY?

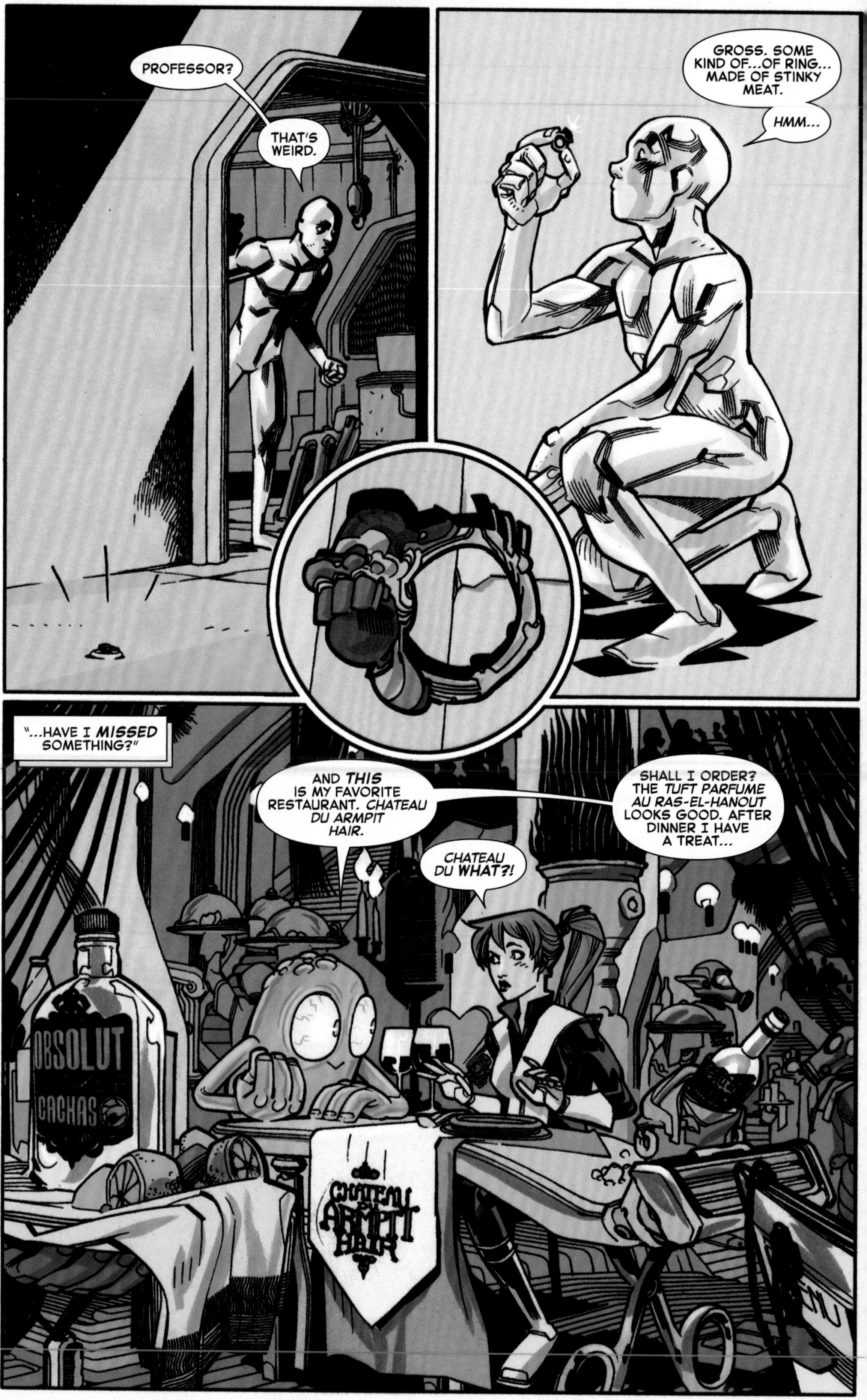
PROFESSOR?
THAT'S WEIRD.
GROSS. SOME KIND OF...OF RING... MADE OF STINKY MEAT.
HMM...
"...HAVE I *MISSED* SOMETHING?"
AND *THIS* IS MY FAVORITE RESTAURANT. *CHATEAU DU ARMPIT HAIR.*
CHATEAU DU **WHAT?!**
SHALL I ORDER? THE *TUFT PARFUME AU RAS-EL-HANOUT* LOOKS GOOD. AFTER DINNER I HAVE A TREAT...
OBSOLUT
CACHAS
CHATEAU DU ARMPIT HAIR

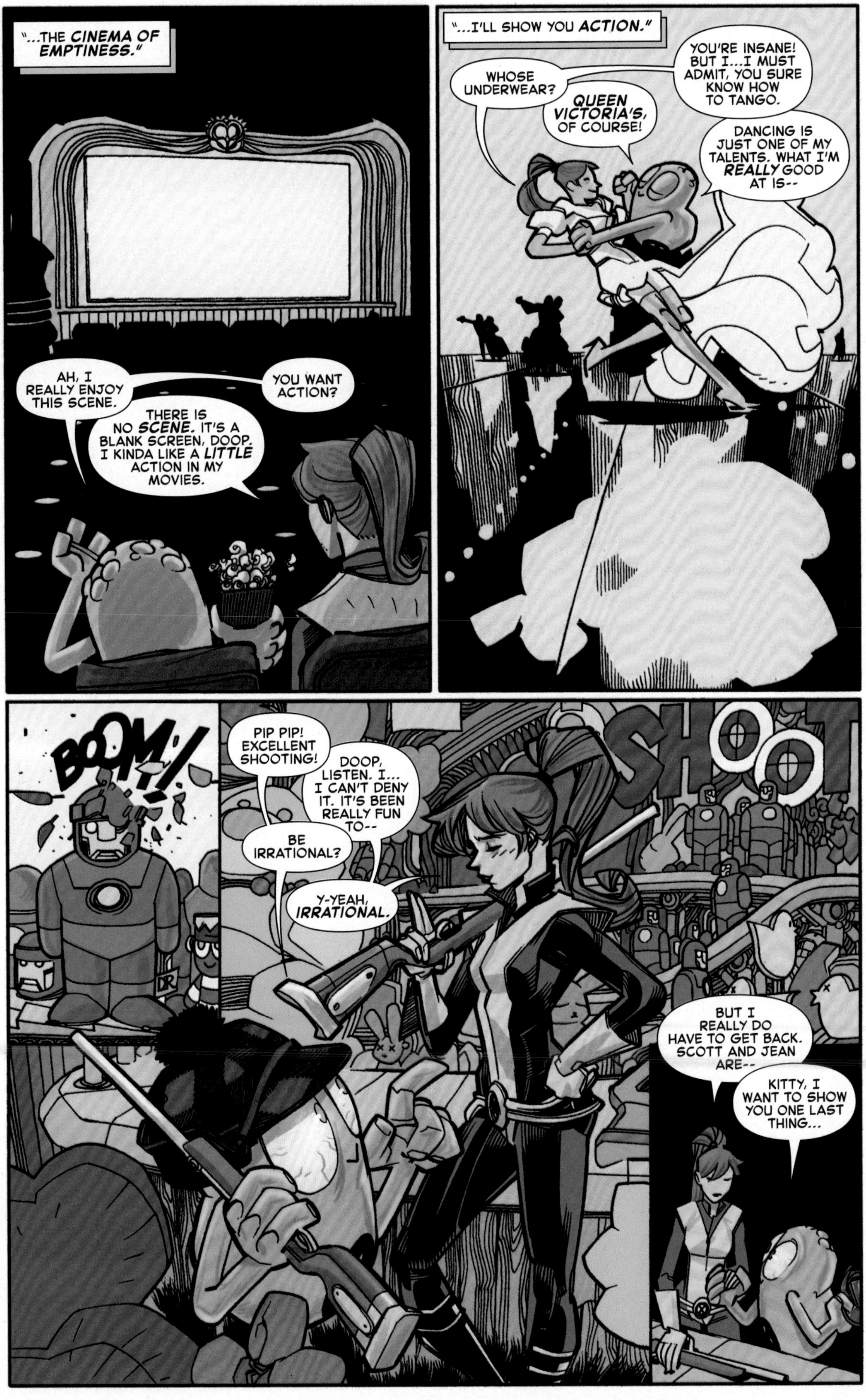
"...THE CINEMA OF EMPTINESS."
AH, I REALLY ENJOY THIS SCENE.
YOU WANT ACTION?
THERE IS NO SCENE. IT'S A BLANK SCREEN, DOOP. I KINDA LIKE A LITTLE ACTION IN MY MOVIES.
"...I'LL SHOW YOU ACTION."
WHOSE UNDERWEAR?
QUEEN VICTORIA'S, OF COURSE!
YOU'RE INSANE! BUT I...I MUST ADMIT, YOU SURE KNOW HOW TO TANGO.
DANCING IS JUST ONE OF MY TALENTS. WHAT I'M REALLY GOOD AT IS--
BOOM!!
PIP PIP! EXCELLENT SHOOTING!
DOOP, LISTEN. I... I CAN'T DENY IT. IT'S BEEN REALLY FUN TO--
BE IRRATIONAL?
Y-YEAH, IRRATIONAL.
SHOOT
BUT I REALLY DO HAVE TO GET BACK. SCOTT AND JEAN ARE--
KITTY, I WANT TO SHOW YOU ONE LAST THING...

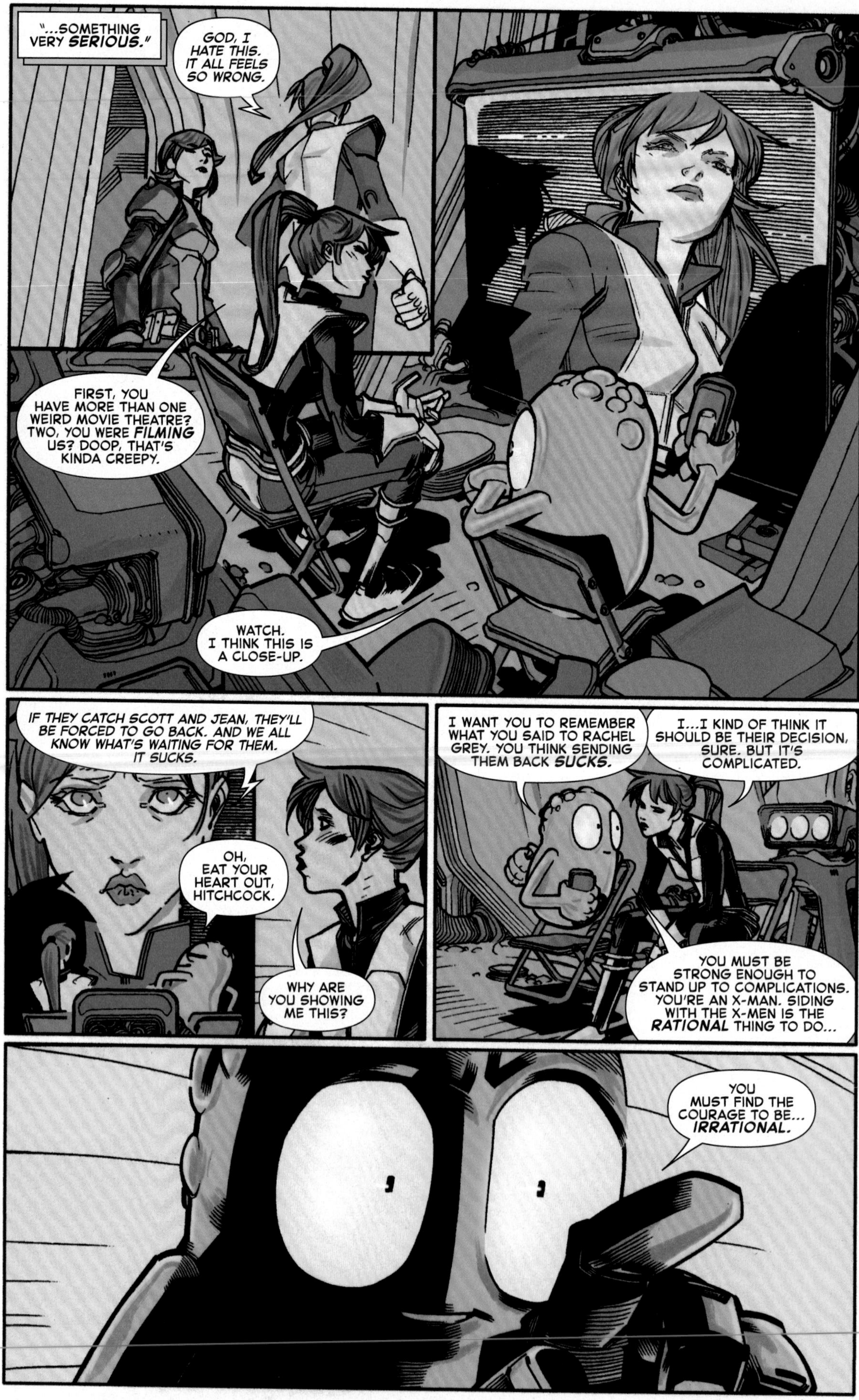

"...SOMETHING VERY SERIOUS."
GOD, I HATE THIS. IT ALL FEELS SO WRONG.
FIRST, YOU HAVE MORE THAN ONE WEIRD MOVIE THEATRE? TWO, YOU WERE FILMING US? DOOP, THAT'S KINDA CREEPY.
WATCH. I THINK THIS IS A CLOSE-UP.
IF THEY CATCH SCOTT AND JEAN, THEY'LL BE FORCED TO GO BACK. AND WE ALL KNOW WHAT'S WAITING FOR THEM. IT SUCKS.
OH, EAT YOUR HEART OUT, HITCHCOCK.
WHY ARE YOU SHOWING ME THIS?
I WANT YOU TO REMEMBER WHAT YOU SAID TO RACHEL GREY. YOU THINK SENDING THEM BACK SUCKS.
I...I KIND OF THINK IT SHOULD BE THEIR DECISION, SURE. BUT IT'S COMPLICATED.
YOU MUST BE STRONG ENOUGH TO STAND UP TO COMPLICATIONS. YOU'RE AN X-MAN. SIDING WITH THE X-MEN IS THE RATIONAL THING TO DO...
YOU MUST FIND THE COURAGE TO BE... IRRATIONAL.

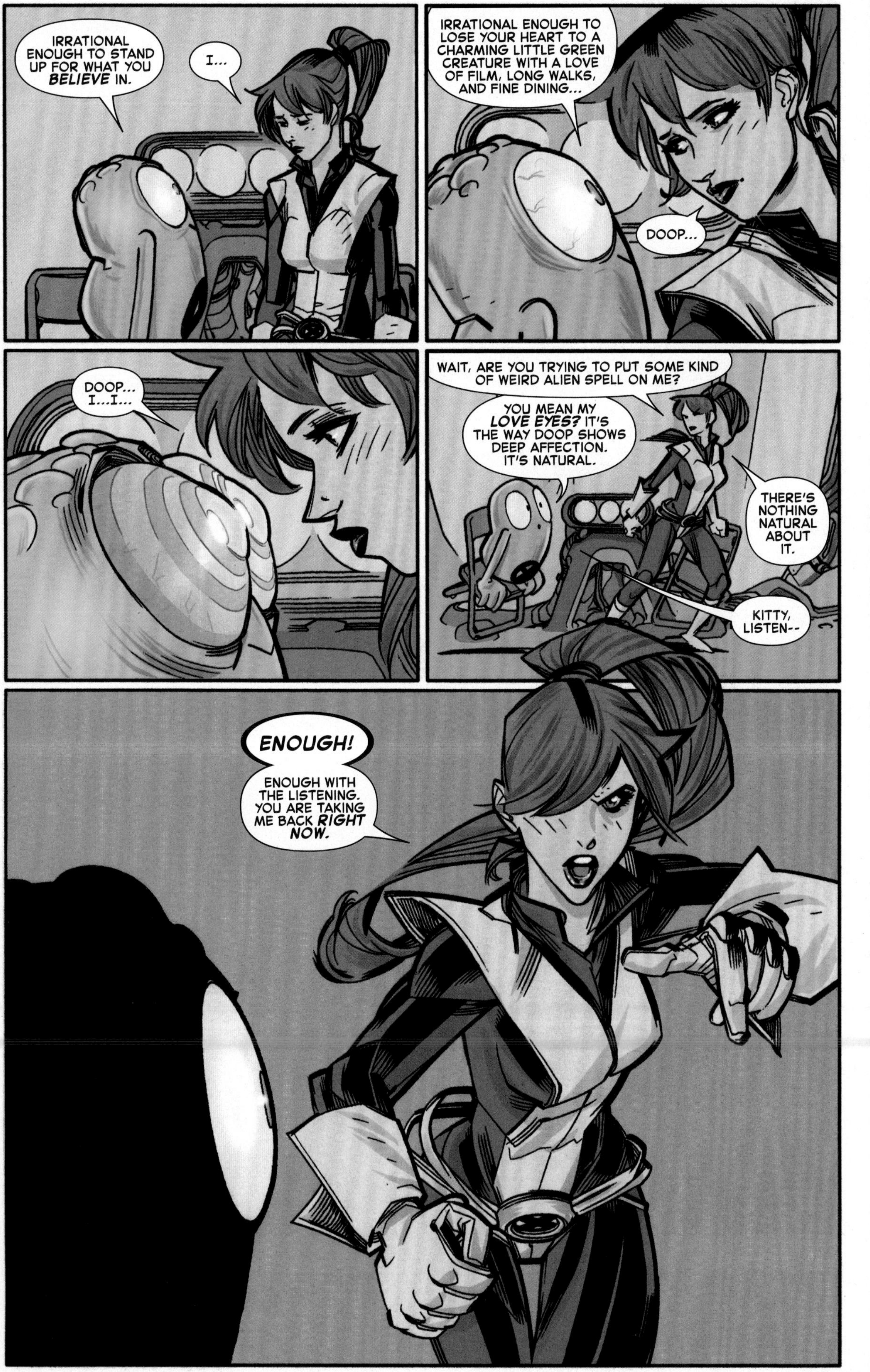
IRRATIONAL ENOUGH TO STAND UP FOR WHAT YOU *BELIEVE* IN.
I...
IRRATIONAL ENOUGH TO LOSE YOUR HEART TO A CHARMING LITTLE GREEN CREATURE WITH A LOVE OF FILM, LONG WALKS, AND FINE DINING...
DOOP...
DOOP... I...I...
WAIT, ARE YOU TRYING TO PUT SOME KIND OF WEIRD ALIEN SPELL ON ME?
YOU MEAN MY *LOVE EYES?* IT'S THE WAY DOOP SHOWS DEEP AFFECTION. IT'S NATURAL.
THERE'S NOTHING NATURAL ABOUT IT.
KITTY, LISTEN--
ENOUGH!
ENOUGH WITH THE LISTENING. YOU ARE TAKING ME BACK *RIGHT NOW.*

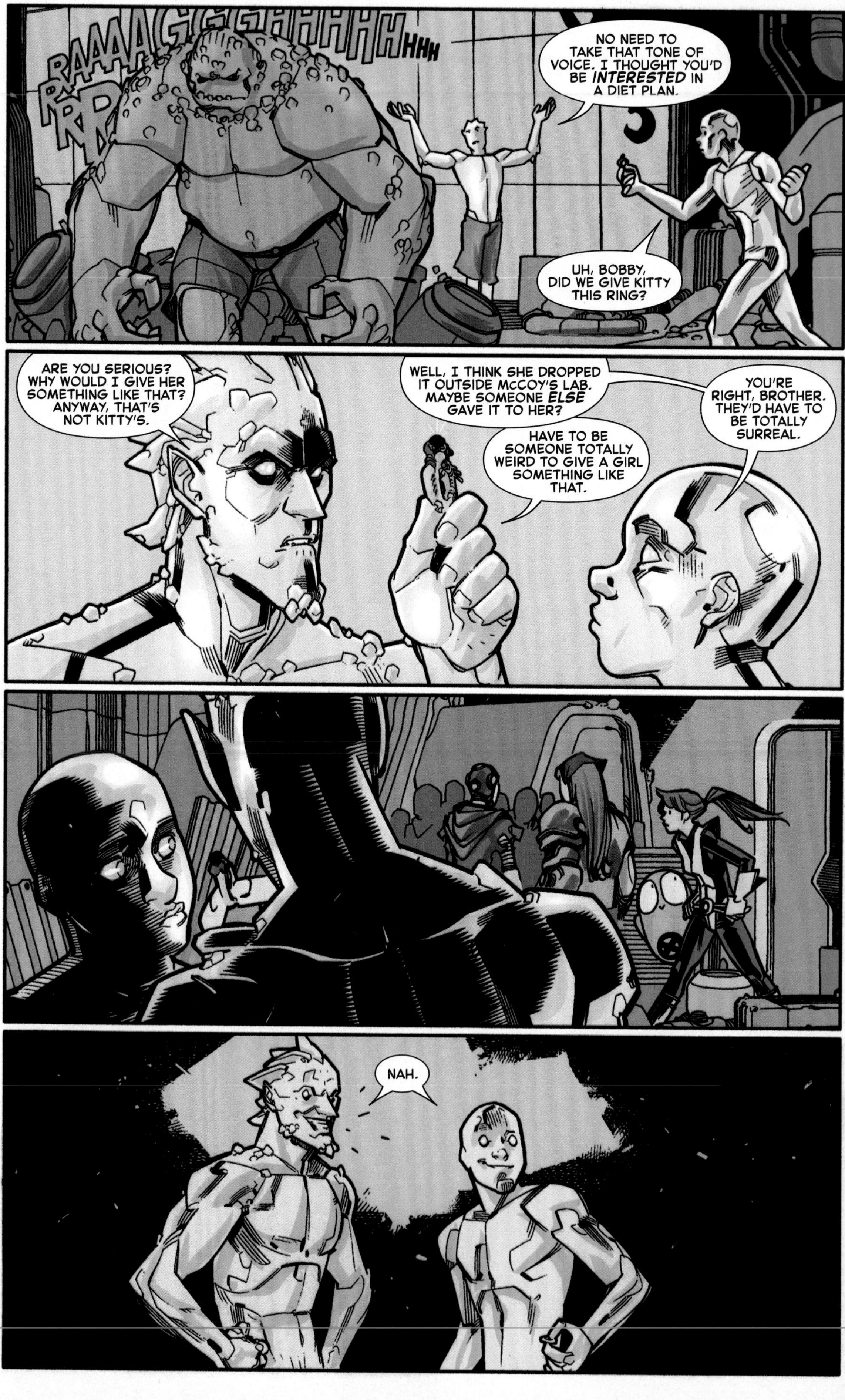
RAAAAGGGHHHHHHHHH
NO NEED TO TAKE THAT TONE OF VOICE. I THOUGHT YOU'D BE *INTERESTED* IN A DIET PLAN.
UH, BOBBY, DID WE GIVE KITTY THIS RING?
ARE YOU SERIOUS? WHY WOULD I GIVE HER SOMETHING LIKE THAT? ANYWAY, THAT'S NOT KITTY'S.
WELL, I THINK SHE DROPPED IT OUTSIDE McCOY'S LAB. MAYBE SOMEONE *ELSE* GAVE IT TO HER?
HAVE TO BE SOMEONE TOTALLY WEIRD TO GIVE A GIRL SOMETHING LIKE THAT.
YOU'RE RIGHT, BROTHER. THEY'D HAVE TO BE TOTALLY SURREAL.
NAH.

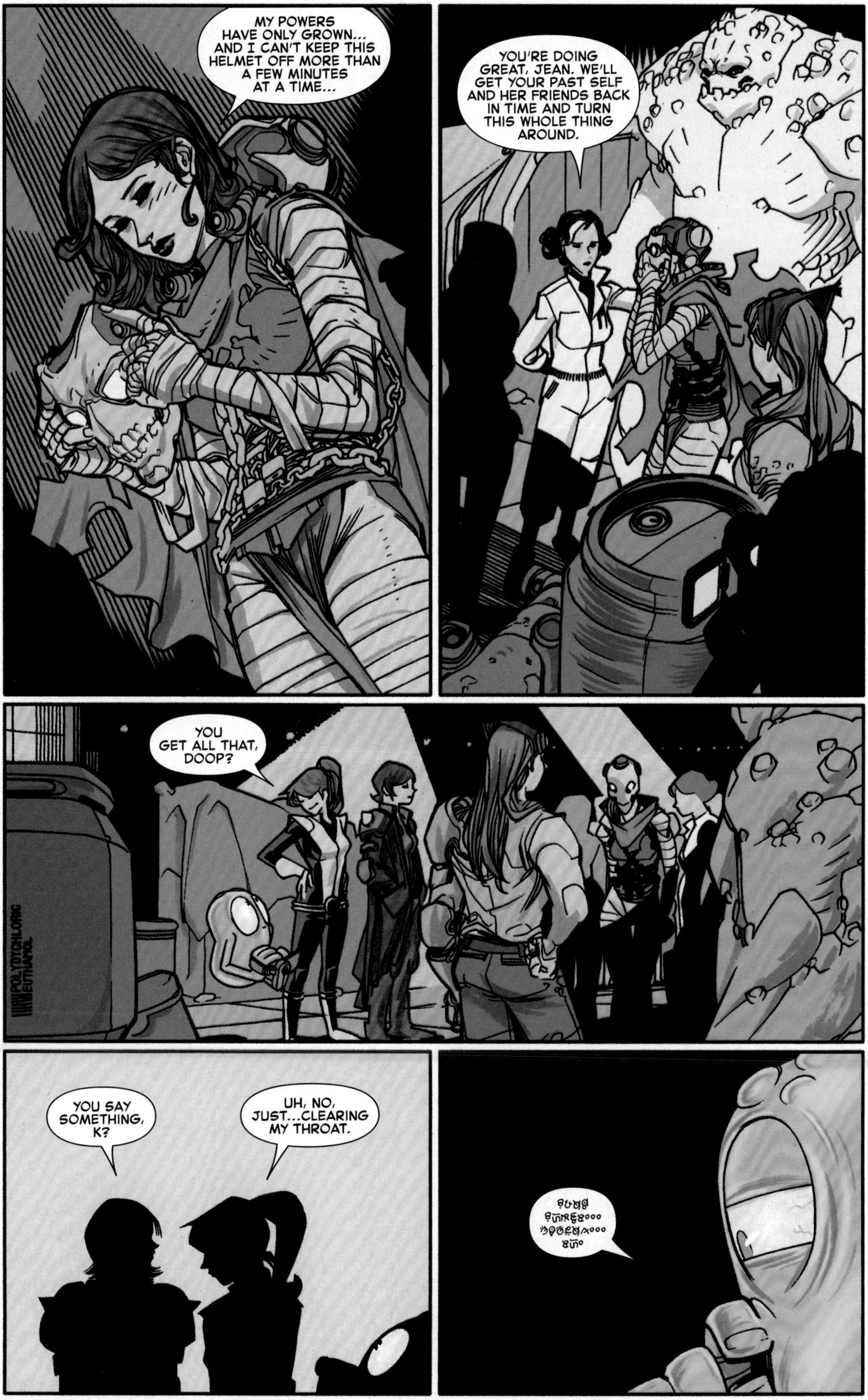
MY POWERS HAVE ONLY GROWN... AND I CAN'T KEEP THIS HELMET OFF MORE THAN A FEW MINUTES AT A TIME...
YOU'RE DOING GREAT, JEAN. WE'LL GET YOUR PAST SELF AND HER FRIENDS BACK IN TIME AND TURN THIS WHOLE THING AROUND.
YOU GET ALL THAT, DOOP?
YOU SAY SOMETHING, K?
UH, NO, JUST...CLEARING MY THROAT.

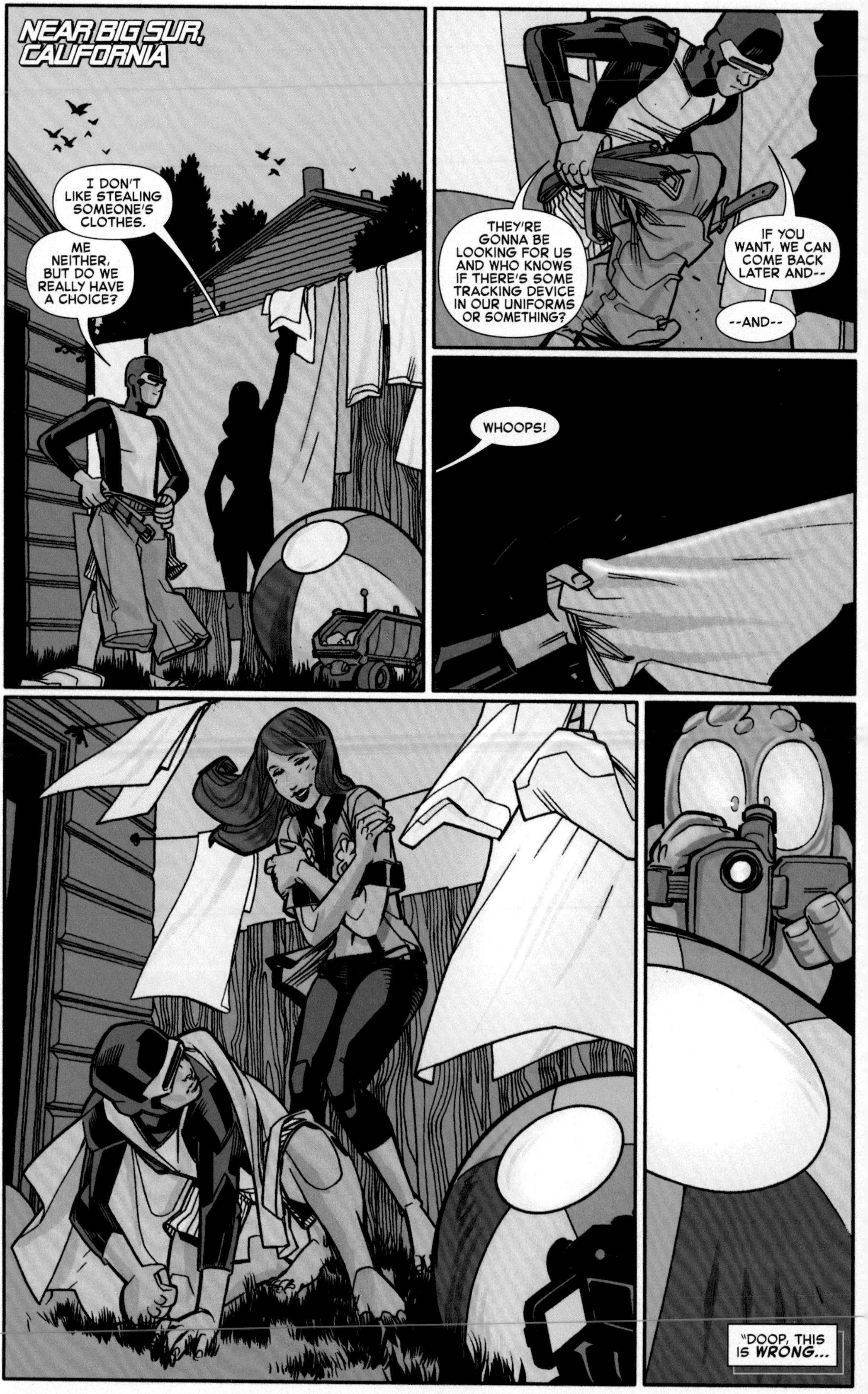
NEAR BIG SUR, CALIFORNIA
I DON'T LIKE STEALING SOMEONE'S CLOTHES.
ME NEITHER, BUT DO WE REALLY HAVE A CHOICE?
THEY'RE GONNA BE LOOKING FOR US AND WHO KNOWS IF THERE'S SOME TRACKING DEVICE IN OUR UNIFORMS OR SOMETHING?
IF YOU WANT, WE CAN COME BACK LATER AND--
--AND--
WHOOPS!
"DOOP, THIS IS WRONG...

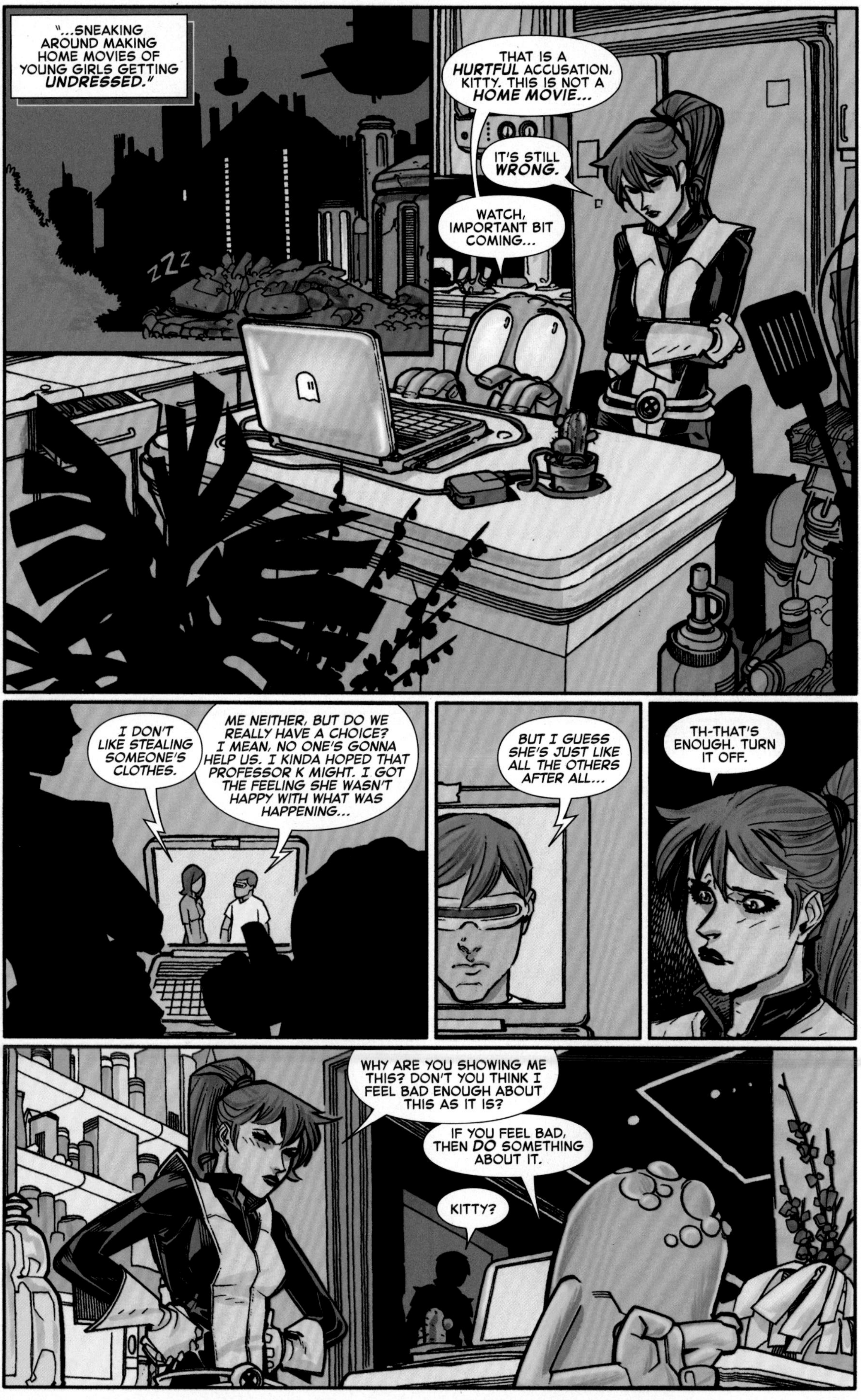
"...SNEAKING AROUND MAKING HOME MOVIES OF YOUNG GIRLS GETTING UNDRESSED."
THAT IS A HURTFUL ACCUSATION, KITTY. THIS IS NOT A HOME MOVIE...
IT'S STILL WRONG.
WATCH, IMPORTANT BIT COMING...
ZZZ
I DON'T LIKE STEALING SOMEONE'S CLOTHES.
ME NEITHER, BUT DO WE REALLY HAVE A CHOICE? I MEAN, NO ONE'S GONNA HELP US. I KINDA HOPED THAT PROFESSOR K MIGHT. I GOT THE FEELING SHE WASN'T HAPPY WITH WHAT WAS HAPPENING...
BUT I GUESS SHE'S JUST LIKE ALL THE OTHERS AFTER ALL...
TH-THAT'S ENOUGH. TURN IT OFF.
WHY ARE YOU SHOWING ME THIS? DON'T YOU THINK I FEEL BAD ENOUGH ABOUT THIS AS IT IS?
IF YOU FEEL BAD, THEN DO SOMETHING ABOUT IT.
KITTY?

I'M STARVING. I WAS THINKING... A TRIPLE DATE. YOU, ME, THE FRIDGE.

HMM. YOU'RE TALKING MY LANGUAGE.

WHAT'S UP?

THIS PLACE... IT SMELLS...

THIS *PLACE* IS HOME TO DOZENS OF PUBESCENT KIDS. OF *COURSE* IT SMELLS.

THIS IS DIFFERENT. THIS IS KINDA...

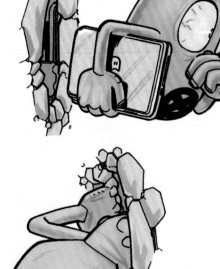

"...GREEN."

&7¢!*&

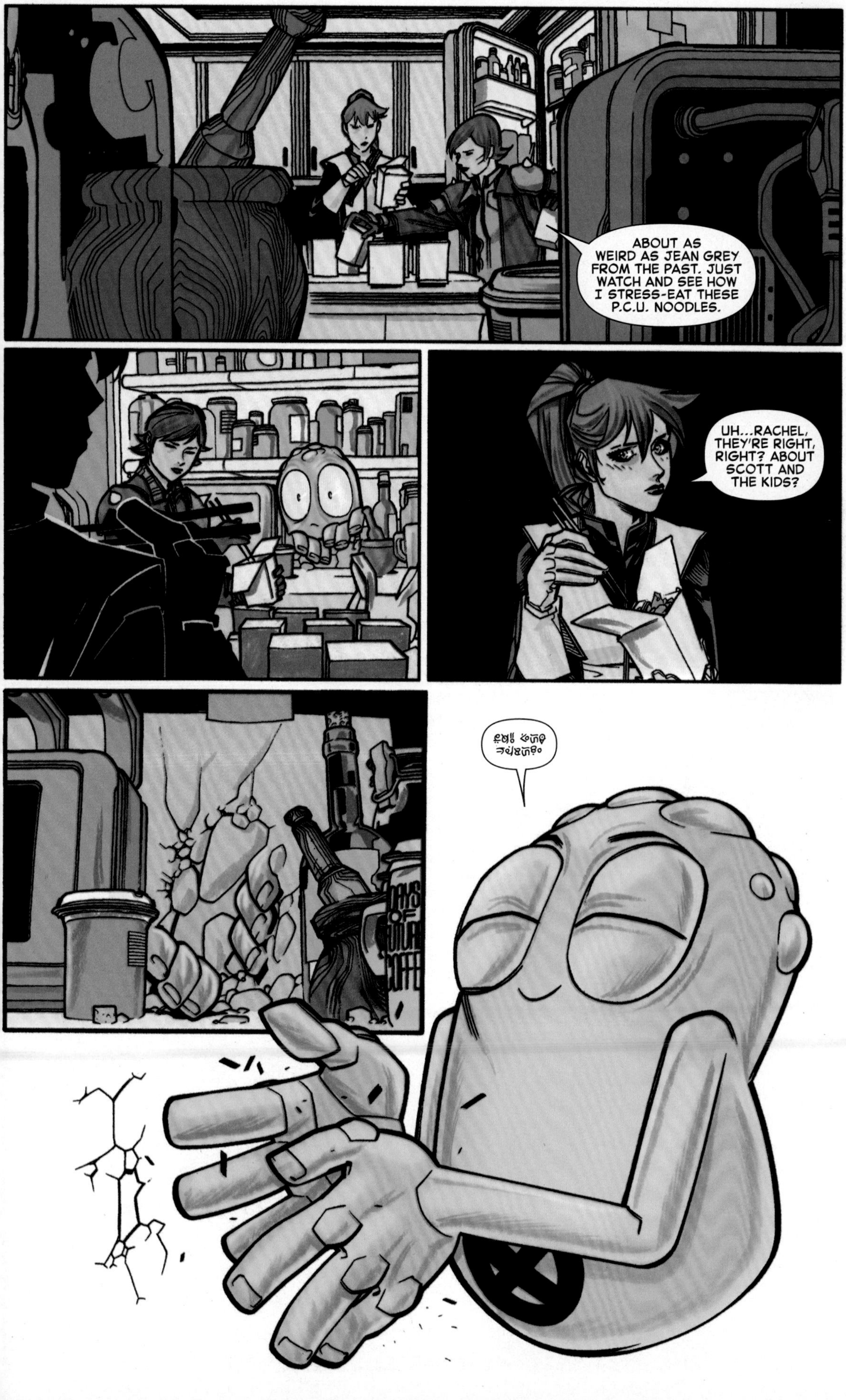
ABOUT AS WEIRD AS JEAN GREY FROM THE PAST. JUST WATCH AND SEE HOW I STRESS-EAT THESE P.C.U. NOODLES.
UH...RACHEL, THEY'RE RIGHT, RIGHT? ABOUT SCOTT AND THE KIDS?

DOOP, YOU'VE HELPED ME COME TO THE RIGHT DECISION WITH THE X-MEN. AND NOW I'VE COME TO THE RIGHT DECISION WITH YOU.

I LOVE YOU, DOOP. I AM YOURS. LET'S NUZZLE EACH OTHER UNTIL OUR NOSES DEVELOP BLISTERS.

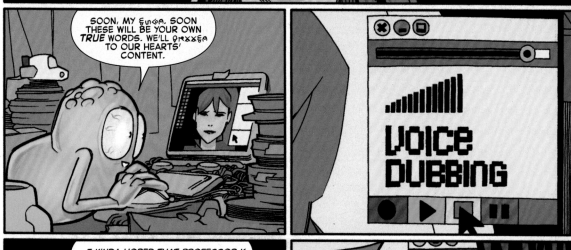

SOON, MY ꖜ⚬ꞡⴰ. SOON THESE WILL BE YOUR OWN *TRUE* WORDS. WE'LL ⴲꞄⵝⵝꞡⴰ TO OUR HEARTS' CONTENT.

VOICE DUBBING

...I KINDA HOPED THAT PROFESSOR K MIGHT. I GOT THE FEELING SHE WASN'T HAPPY WITH WHAT WAS...

Erase

WHAA
WHA

WHAVAMMMMM
WHAAAMMMM

ꞡⴲꞡ ⵝꞡⴰⵝꞡꞥⴰⴲⴰⵝⴰꞡⴰ

BOBBY PROBABLY ISN'T GOING TO LIKE THIS! BOBBY PROBABLY ISN'T GOING TO LIKE THIS!

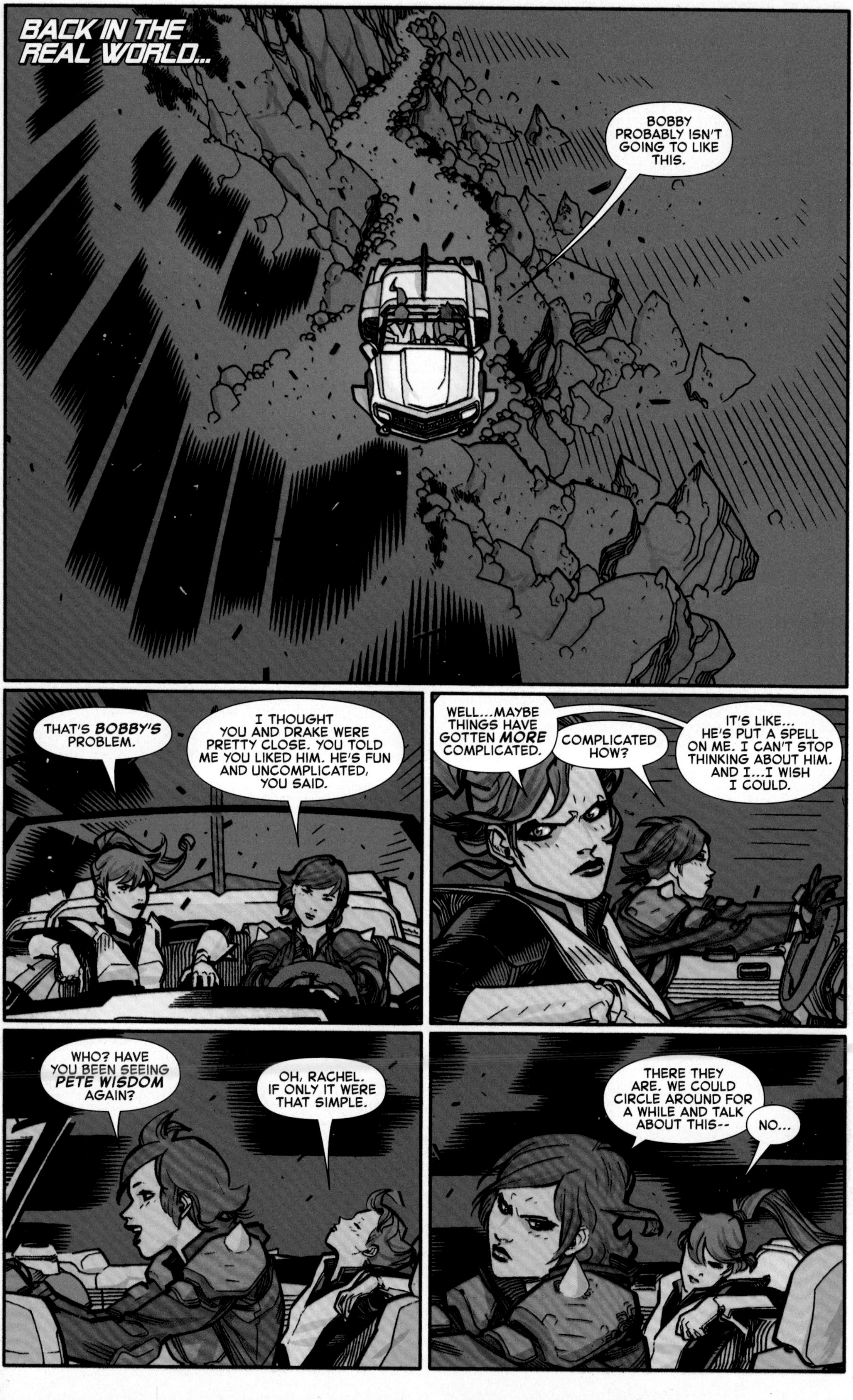
BACK IN THE REAL WORLD...
BOBBY PROBABLY ISN'T GOING TO LIKE THIS.
THAT'S BOBBY'S PROBLEM.
I THOUGHT YOU AND DRAKE WERE PRETTY CLOSE. YOU TOLD ME YOU LIKED HIM. HE'S FUN AND UNCOMPLICATED, YOU SAID.
WELL...MAYBE THINGS HAVE GOTTEN MORE COMPLICATED.
COMPLICATED HOW?
IT'S LIKE... HE'S PUT A SPELL ON ME. I CAN'T STOP THINKING ABOUT HIM. AND I...I WISH I COULD.
WHO? HAVE YOU BEEN SEEING PETE WISDOM AGAIN?
OH, RACHEL. IF ONLY IT WERE THAT SIMPLE.
THERE THEY ARE. WE COULD CIRCLE AROUND FOR A WHILE AND TALK ABOUT THIS--
NO...

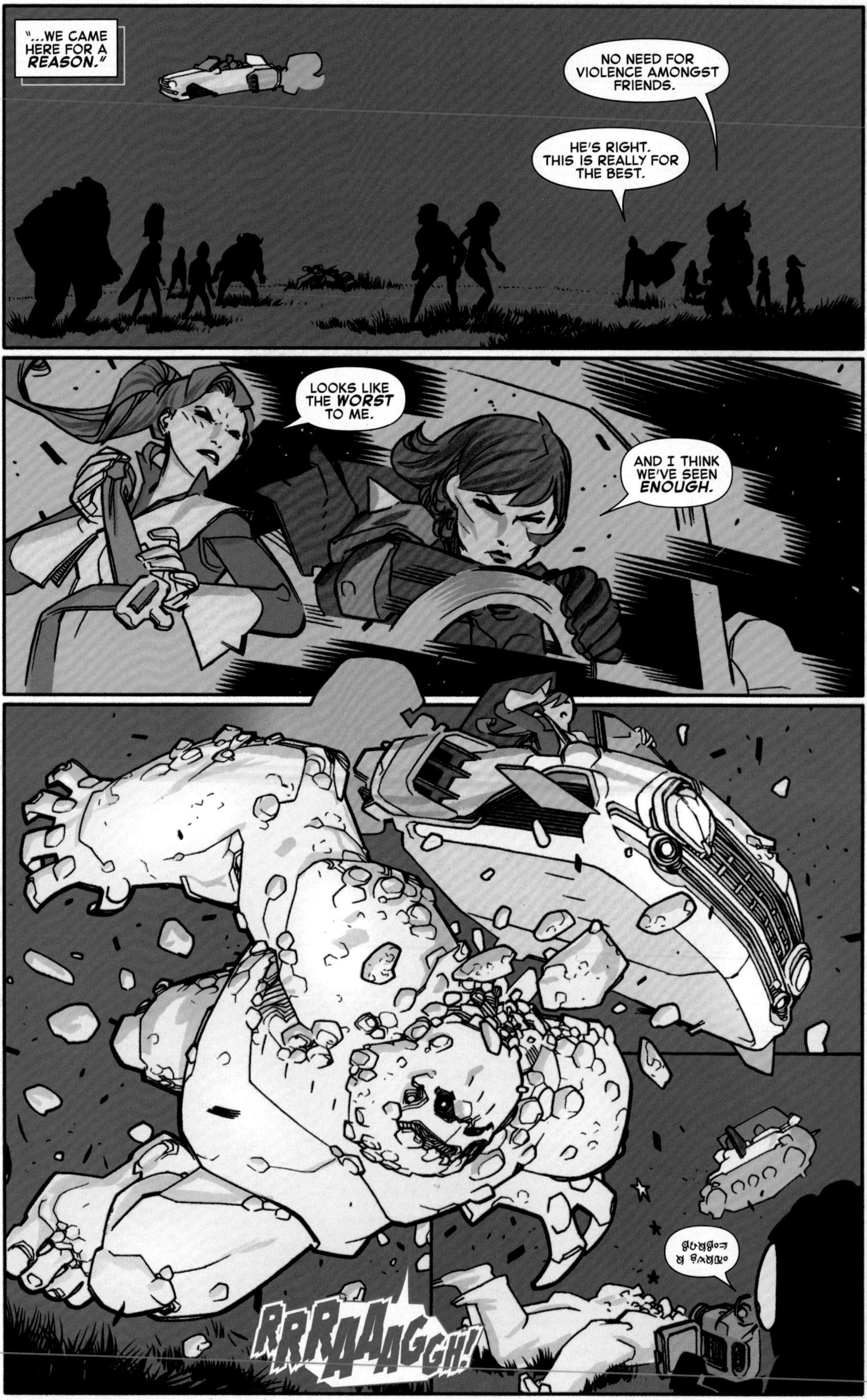
"...WE CAME HERE FOR A *REASON.*"
NO NEED FOR VIOLENCE AMONGST FRIENDS.
HE'S RIGHT. THIS IS REALLY FOR THE BEST.
LOOKS LIKE THE *WORST* TO ME.
AND I THINK WE'VE SEEN *ENOUGH.*
RRRAAAAGGH!

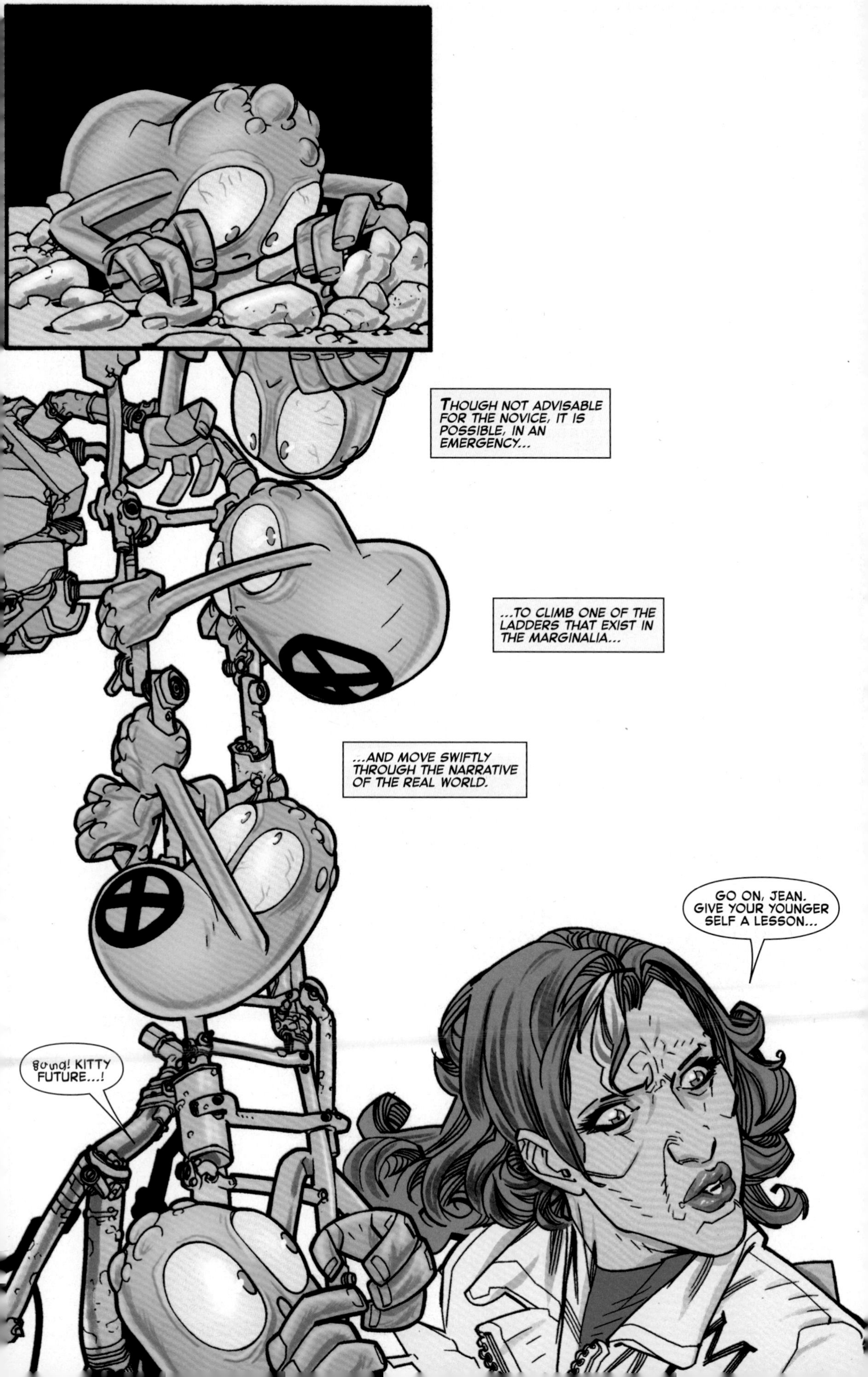
THOUGH NOT ADVISABLE FOR THE NOVICE, IT IS POSSIBLE, IN AN EMERGENCY...
...TO CLIMB ONE OF THE LADDERS THAT EXIST IN THE MARGINALIA...
...AND MOVE SWIFTLY THROUGH THE NARRATIVE OF THE REAL WORLD.
GO ON, JEAN. GIVE YOUR YOUNGER SELF A LESSON...
KITTY FUTURE...!

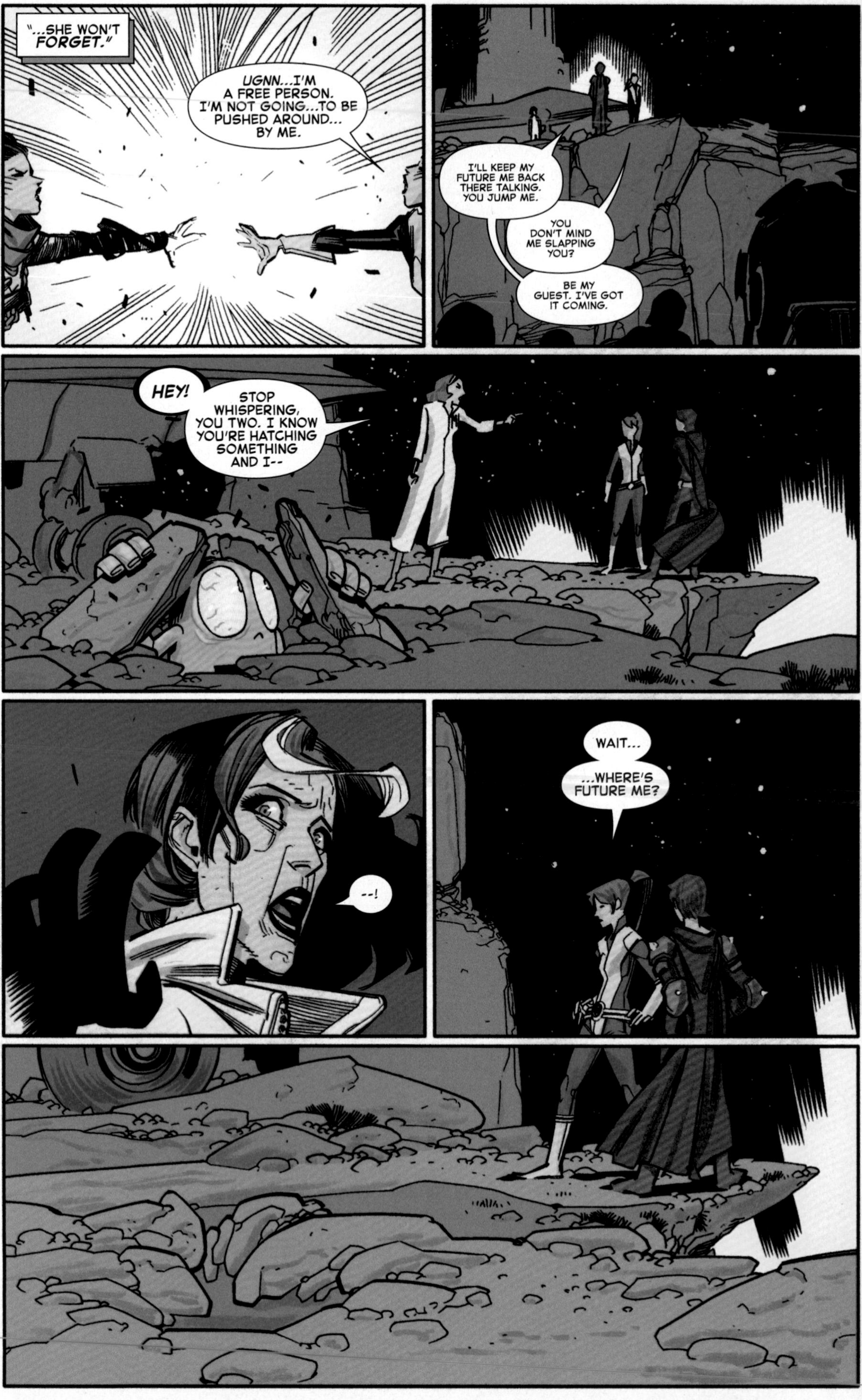
"...SHE WON'T FORGET."
UGNN...I'M A FREE PERSON. I'M NOT GOING...TO BE PUSHED AROUND... BY ME.
I'LL KEEP MY FUTURE ME BACK THERE TALKING. YOU JUMP ME.
YOU DON'T MIND ME SLAPPING YOU?
BE MY GUEST. I'VE GOT IT COMING.
HEY!
STOP WHISPERING, YOU TWO. I KNOW YOU'RE HATCHING SOMETHING AND I--
--!
WAIT...
...WHERE'S FUTURE ME?

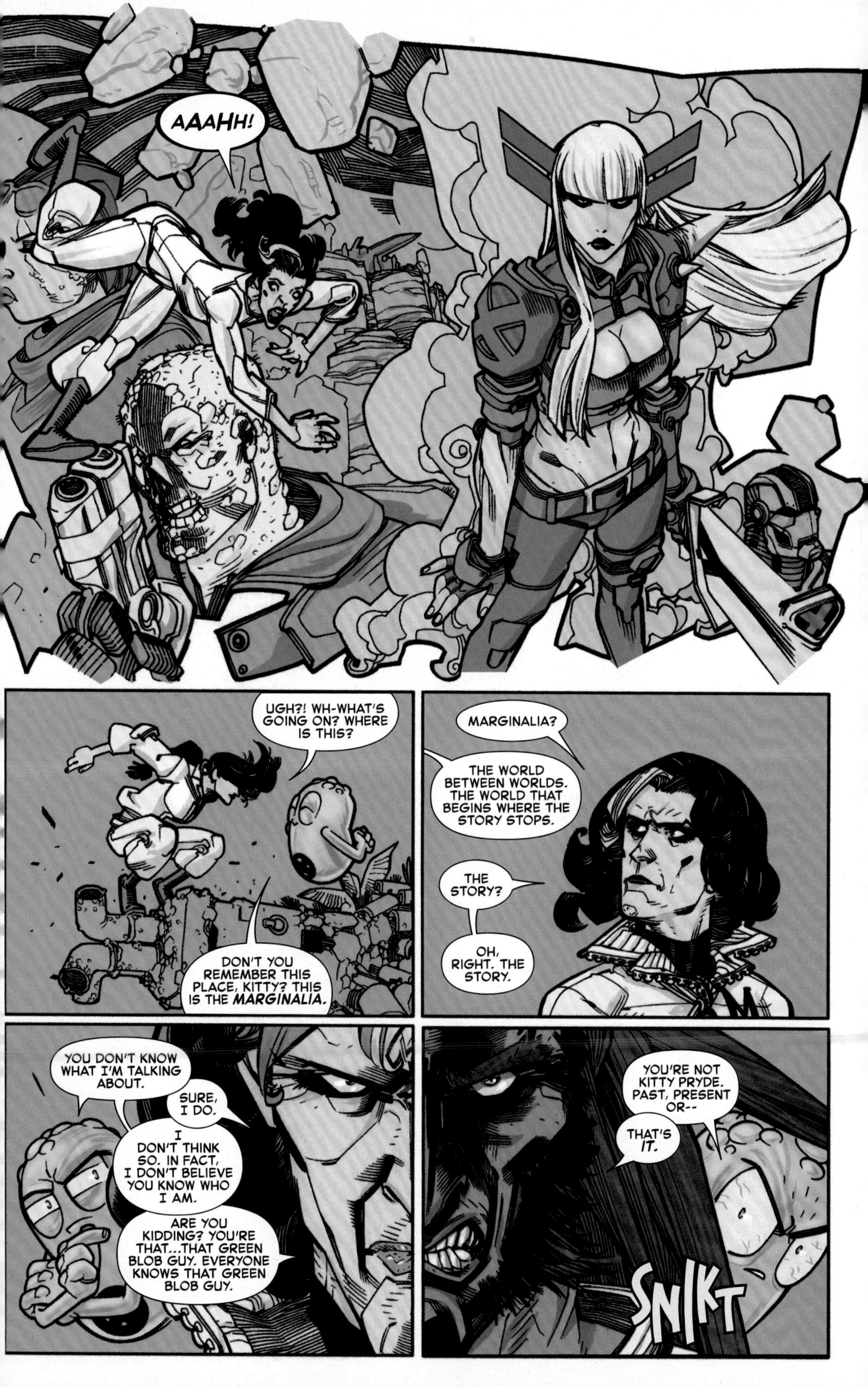
AAAHH!
UGH?! WH-WHAT'S GOING ON? WHERE IS THIS?
DON'T YOU REMEMBER THIS PLACE, KITTY? THIS IS THE MARGINALIA.
MARGINALIA?
THE WORLD BETWEEN WORLDS. THE WORLD THAT BEGINS WHERE THE STORY STOPS.
THE STORY?
OH, RIGHT. THE STORY.
YOU DON'T KNOW WHAT I'M TALKING ABOUT.
SURE, I DO.
I DON'T THINK SO. IN FACT, I DON'T BELIEVE YOU KNOW WHO I AM.
ARE YOU KIDDING? YOU'RE THAT...THAT GREEN BLOB GUY. EVERYONE KNOWS THAT GREEN BLOB GUY.
YOU'RE NOT KITTY PRYDE. PAST, PRESENT OR--
THAT'S IT.
SNIKT

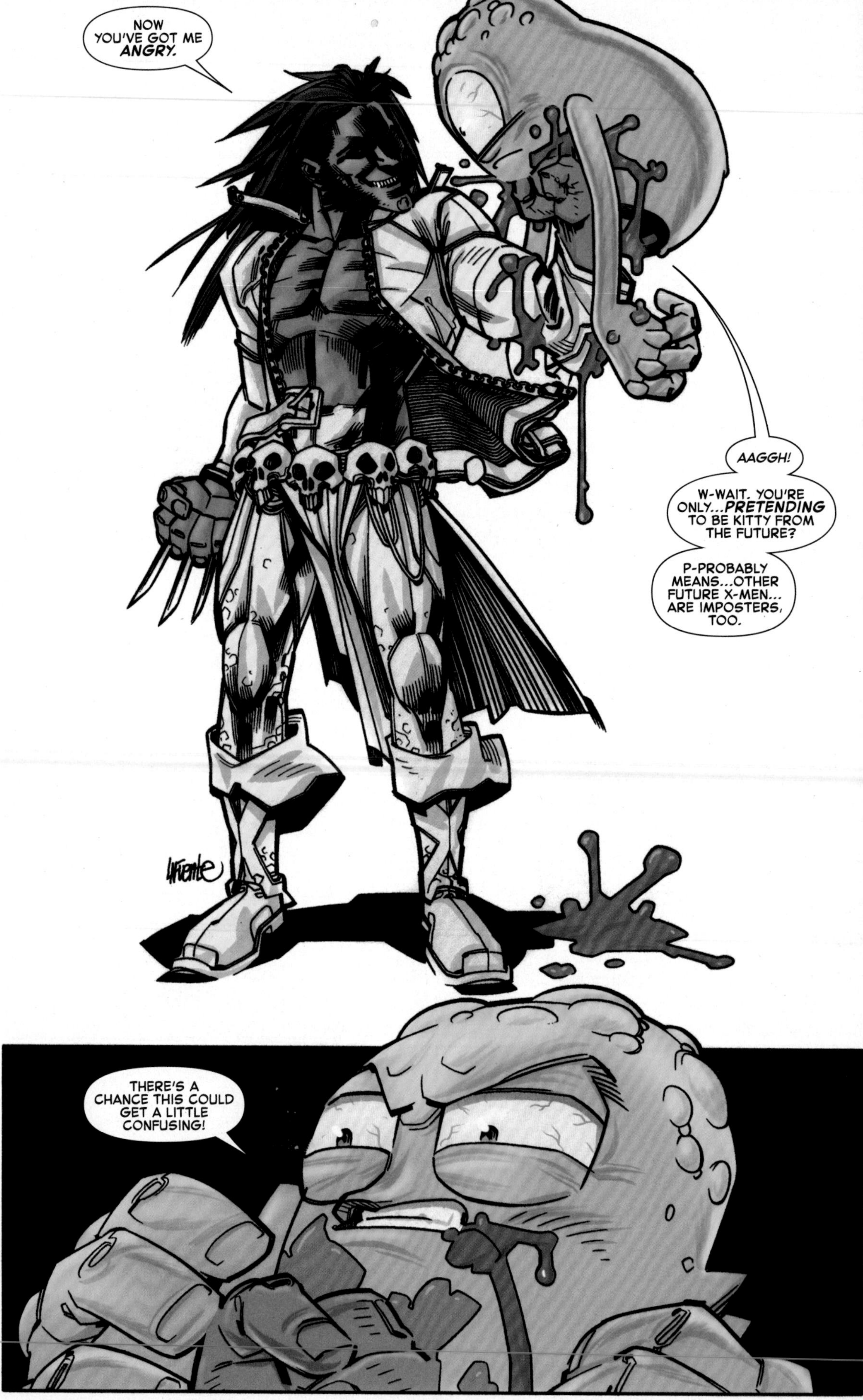

NOW YOU'VE GOT ME *ANGRY.*
AAGGH!
W-WAIT. YOU'RE ONLY...*PRETENDING* TO BE KITTY FROM THE FUTURE?
P-PROBABLY MEANS...OTHER FUTURE X-MEN... ARE IMPOSTERS, TOO.
THERE'S A CHANCE THIS COULD GET A LITTLE CONFUSING!

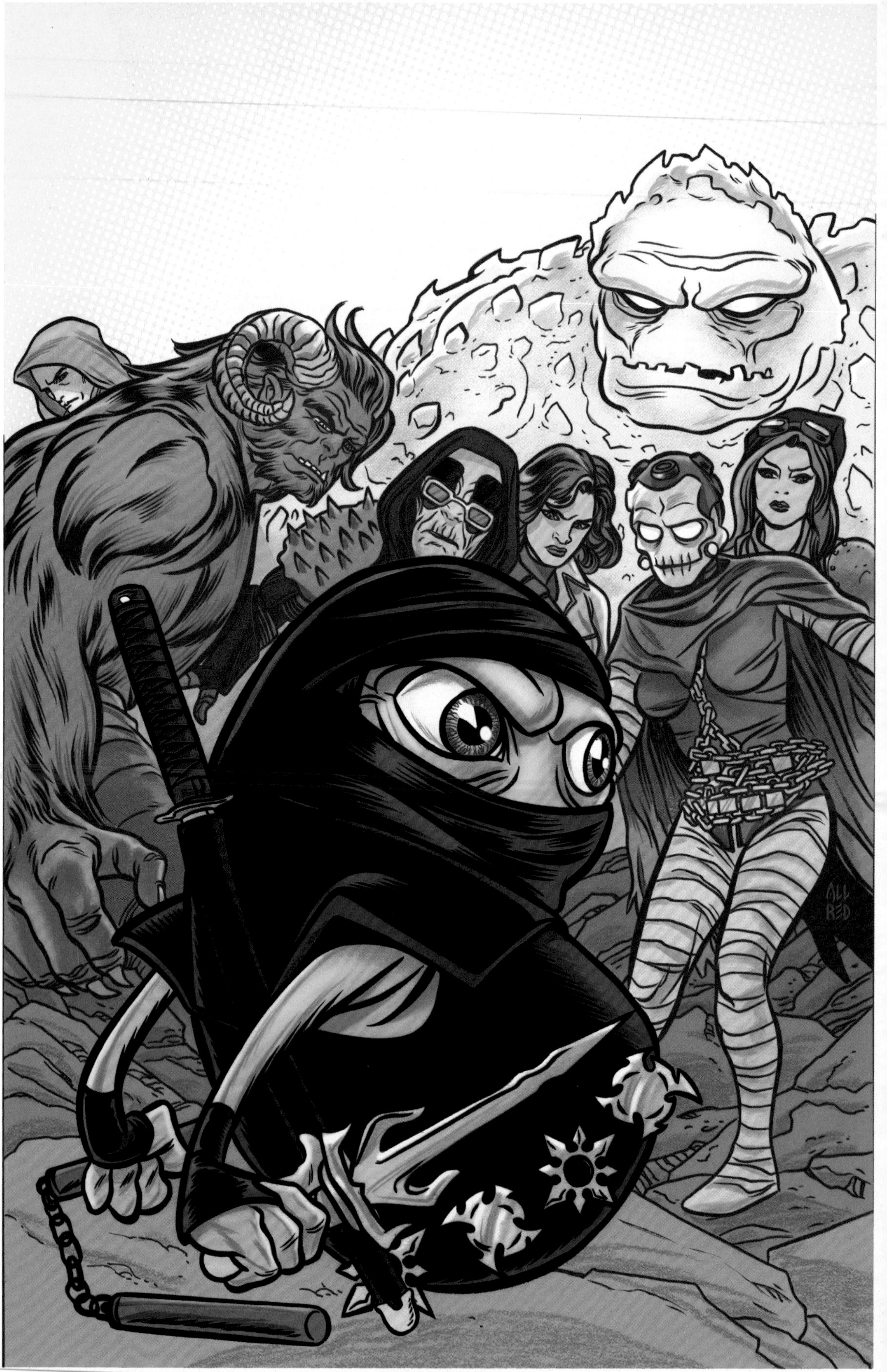
ALL RED

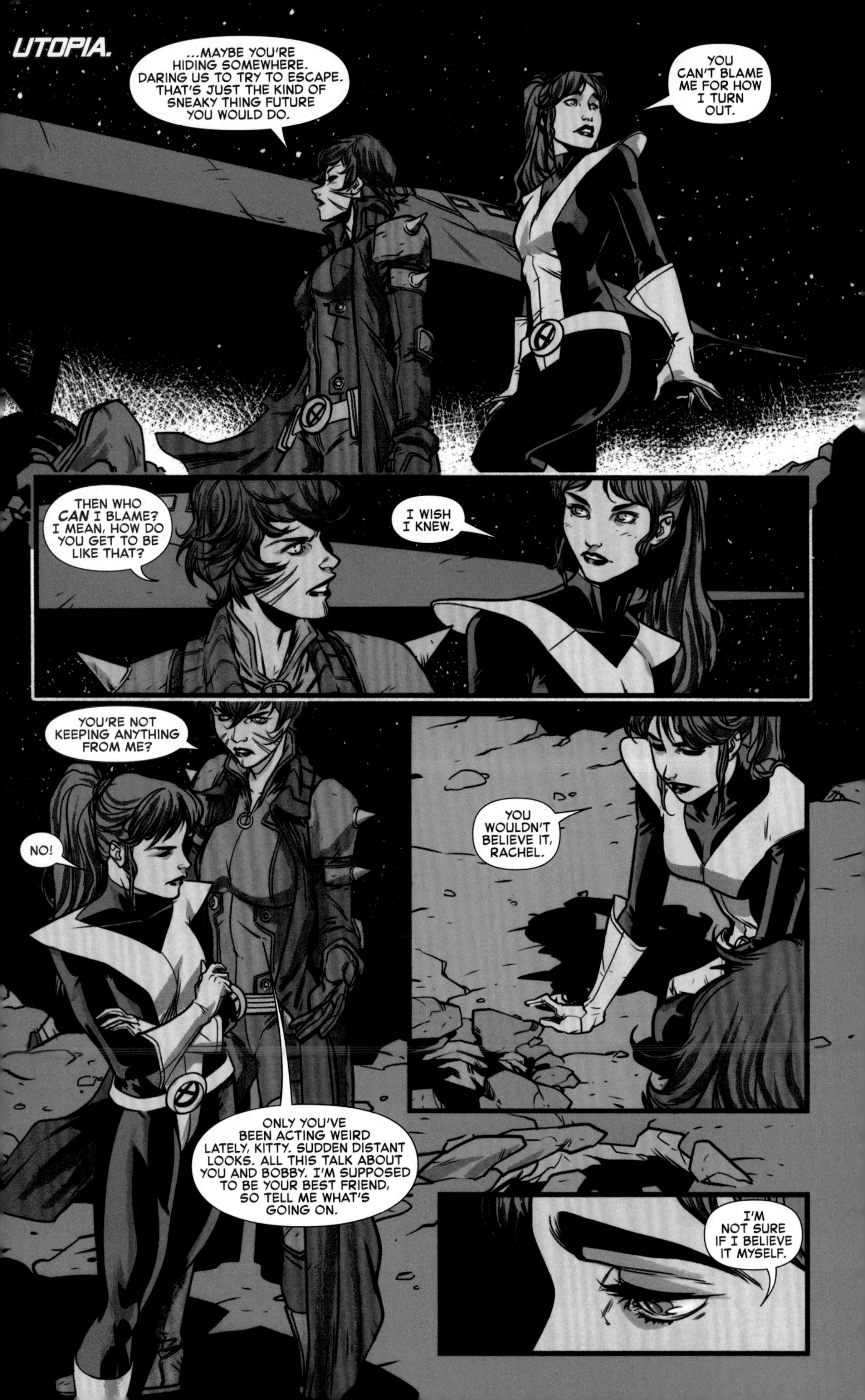

UTOPIA.
...MAYBE YOU'RE HIDING SOMEWHERE. DARING US TO TRY TO ESCAPE. THAT'S JUST THE KIND OF SNEAKY THING FUTURE YOU WOULD DO.
YOU CAN'T BLAME ME FOR HOW I TURN OUT.
THEN WHO CAN I BLAME? I MEAN, HOW DO YOU GET TO BE LIKE THAT?
I WISH I KNEW.
YOU'RE NOT KEEPING ANYTHING FROM ME?
NO!
ONLY YOU'VE BEEN ACTING WEIRD LATELY, KITTY. SUDDEN DISTANT LOOKS. ALL THIS TALK ABOUT YOU AND BOBBY. I'M SUPPOSED TO BE YOUR BEST FRIEND, SO TELL ME WHAT'S GOING ON.
YOU WOULDN'T BELIEVE IT, RACHEL.
I'M NOT SURE IF I BELIEVE IT MYSELF.

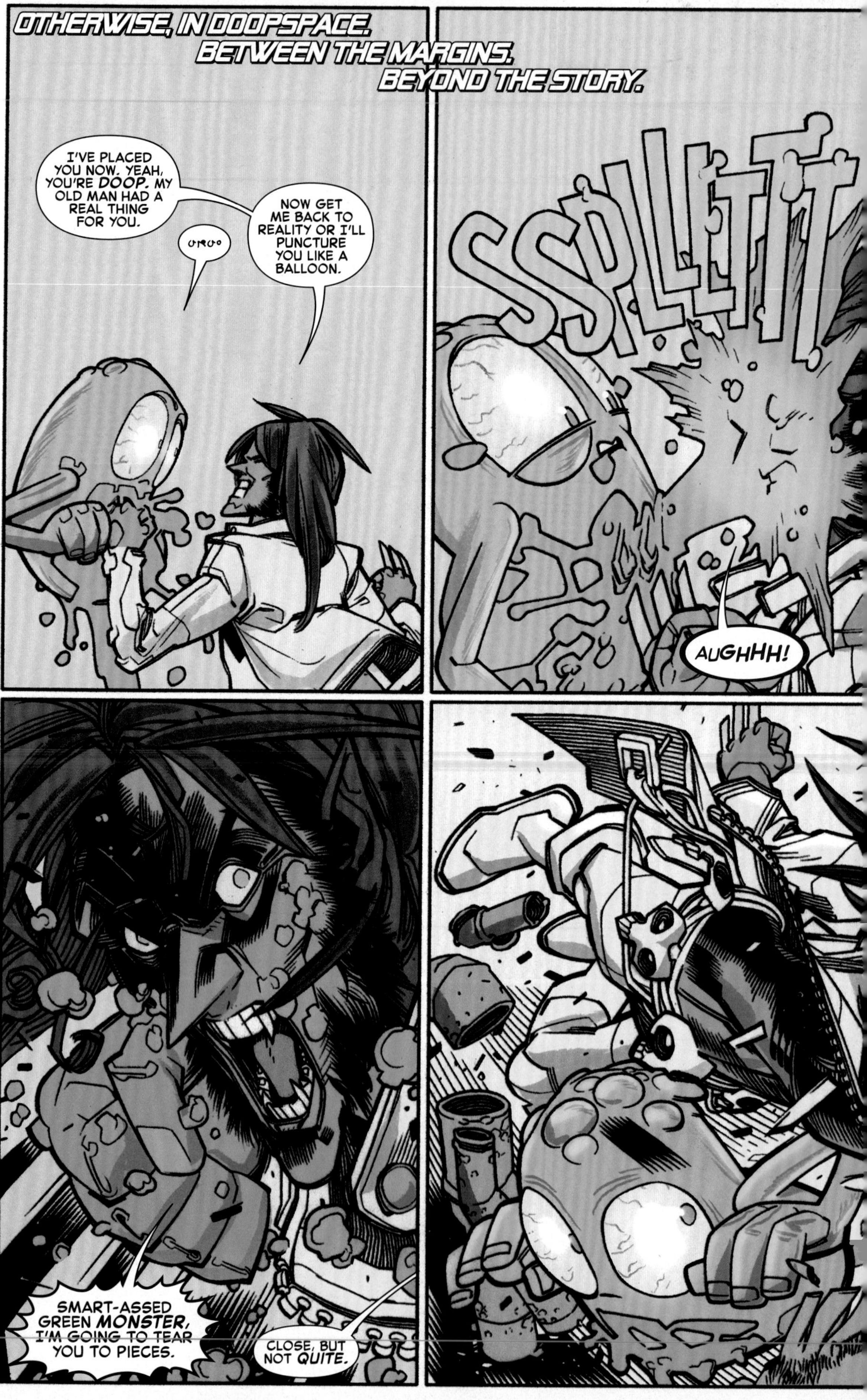
OTHERWISE, IN DOOPSPACE.
BETWEEN THE MARGINS.
BEYOND THE STORY.
I'VE PLACED YOU NOW. YEAH, YOU'RE DOOP. MY OLD MAN HAD A REAL THING FOR YOU.
NOW GET ME BACK TO REALITY OR I'LL PUNCTURE YOU LIKE A BALLOON.
SSPLLTT
AUGHHH!
SMART-ASSED GREEN MONSTER, I'M GOING TO TEAR YOU TO PIECES.
CLOSE, BUT NOT QUITE.

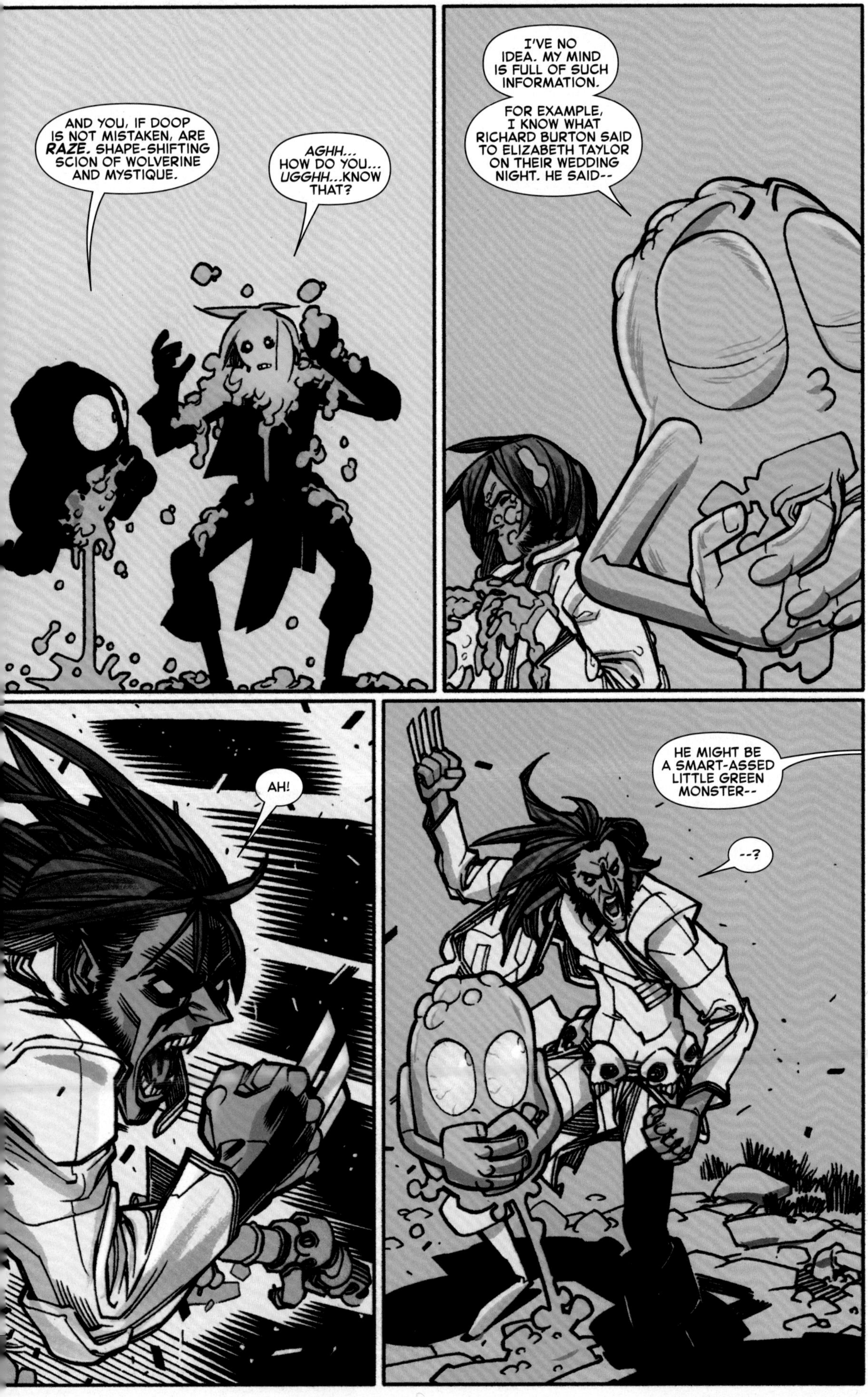
AND YOU, IF DOOP IS NOT MISTAKEN, ARE **RAZE.** SHAPE-SHIFTING SCION OF WOLVERINE AND MYSTIQUE.
AGHH... HOW DO YOU... *UGGHH...*KNOW THAT?
I'VE NO IDEA. MY MIND IS FULL OF SUCH INFORMATION.
FOR EXAMPLE, I KNOW WHAT RICHARD BURTON SAID TO ELIZABETH TAYLOR ON THEIR WEDDING NIGHT. HE SAID--
AH!
HE MIGHT BE A SMART-ASSED LITTLE GREEN MONSTER--
--?

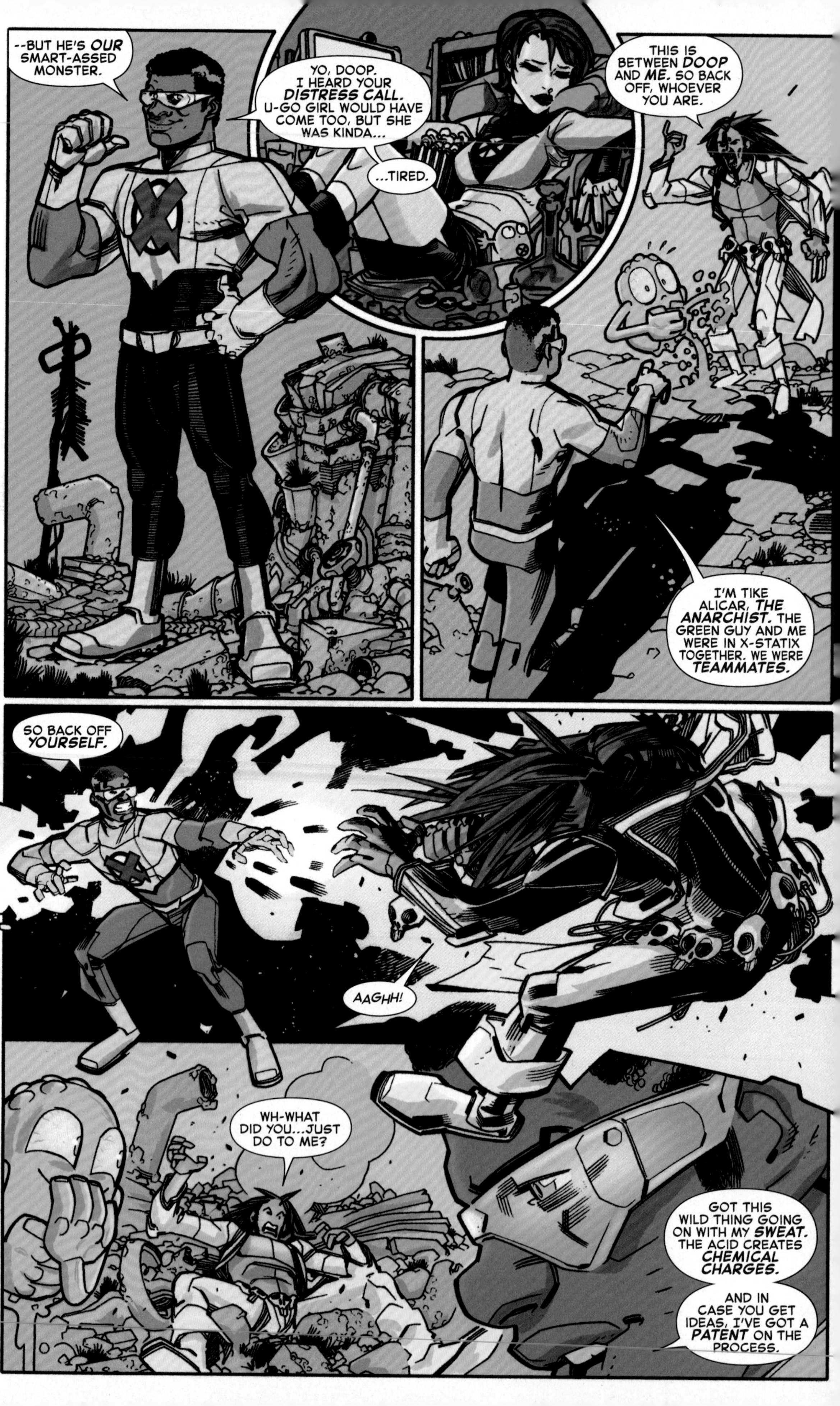
--BUT HE'S OUR SMART-ASSED MONSTER.
YO, DOOP. I HEARD YOUR DISTRESS CALL. U-GO GIRL WOULD HAVE COME TOO, BUT SHE WAS KINDA...
...TIRED.
THIS IS BETWEEN DOOP AND ME. SO BACK OFF, WHOEVER YOU ARE.
I'M TIKE ALICAR, THE ANARCHIST. THE GREEN GUY AND ME WERE IN X-STATIX TOGETHER. WE WERE TEAMMATES.
SO BACK OFF YOURSELF.
AAGHH!
WH-WHAT DID YOU...JUST DO TO ME?
GOT THIS WILD THING GOING ON WITH MY SWEAT. THE ACID CREATES CHEMICAL CHARGES.
AND IN CASE YOU GET IDEAS, I'VE GOT A PATENT ON THE PROCESS.

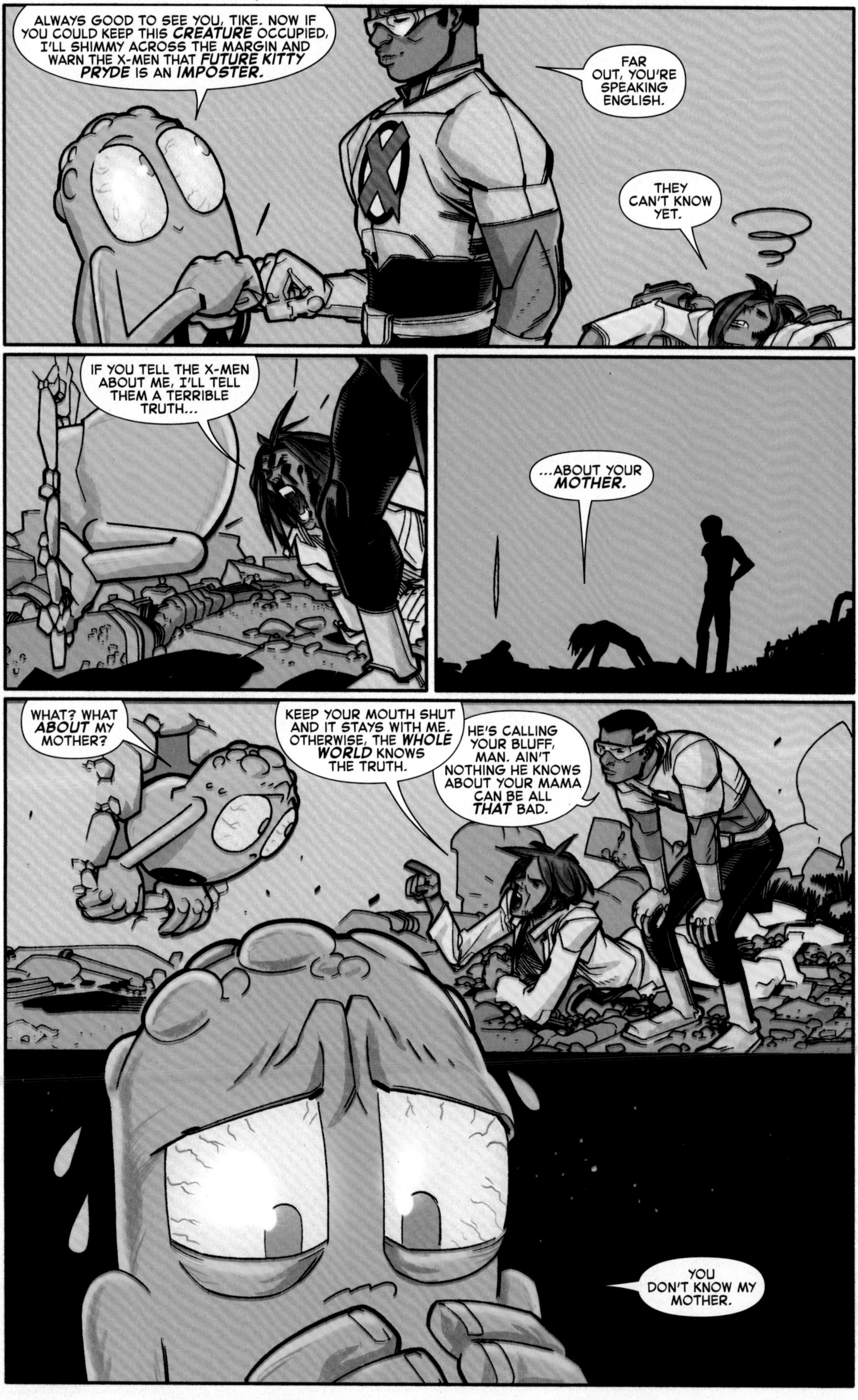
ALWAYS GOOD TO SEE YOU, TIKE. NOW IF YOU COULD KEEP THIS CREATURE OCCUPIED, I'LL SHIMMY ACROSS THE MARGIN AND WARN THE X-MEN THAT FUTURE KITTY PRYDE IS AN IMPOSTER.
FAR OUT, YOU'RE SPEAKING ENGLISH.
THEY CAN'T KNOW YET.
IF YOU TELL THE X-MEN ABOUT ME, I'LL TELL THEM A TERRIBLE TRUTH...
...ABOUT YOUR MOTHER.
WHAT? WHAT ABOUT MY MOTHER?
KEEP YOUR MOUTH SHUT AND IT STAYS WITH ME. OTHERWISE, THE WHOLE WORLD KNOWS THE TRUTH.
HE'S CALLING YOUR BLUFF, MAN. AIN'T NOTHING HE KNOWS ABOUT YOUR MAMA CAN BE ALL THAT BAD.
YOU DON'T KNOW MY MOTHER.

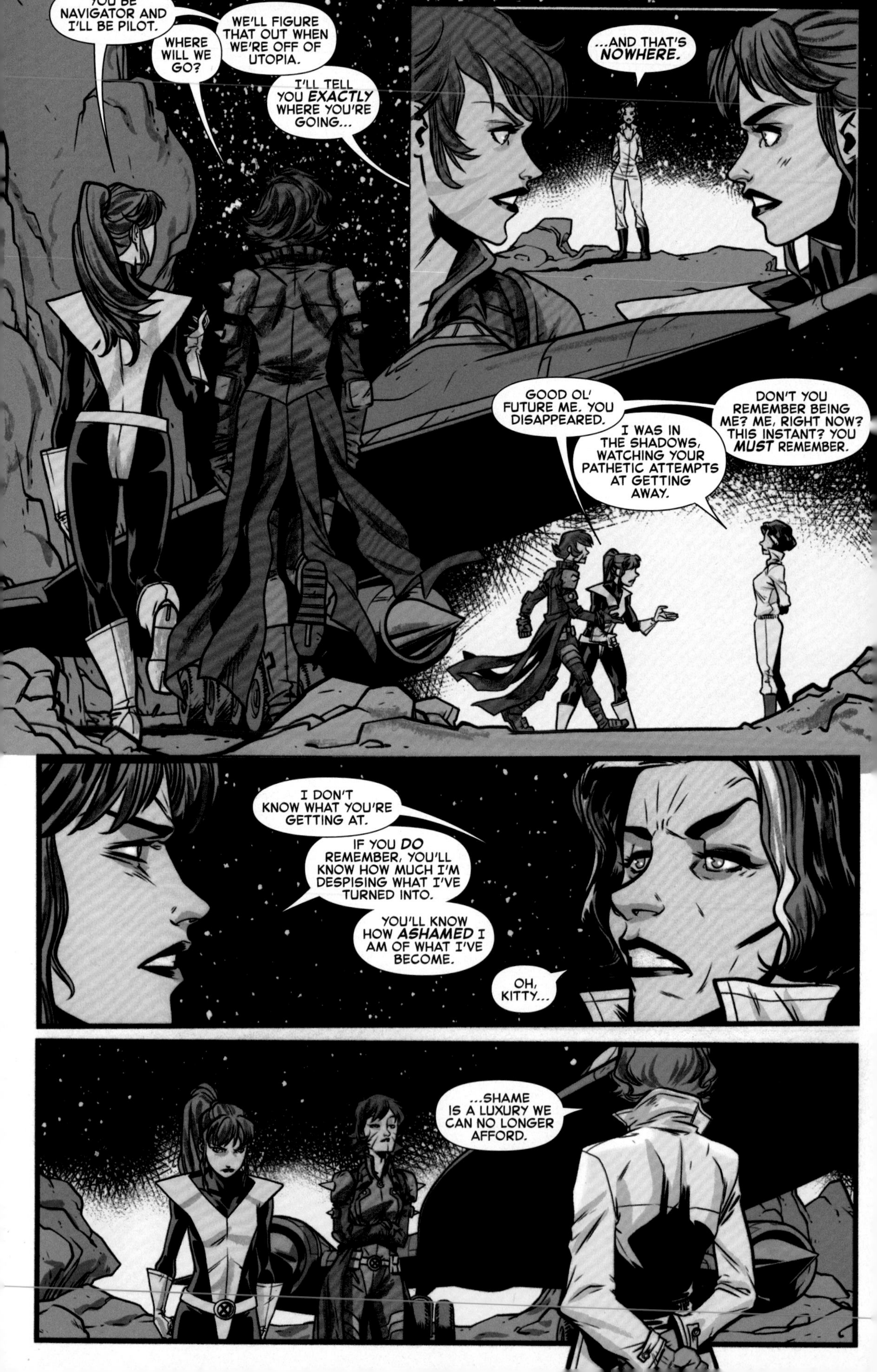
YOU BE NAVIGATOR AND I'LL BE PILOT.
WHERE WILL WE GO?
WE'LL FIGURE THAT OUT WHEN WE'RE OFF OF UTOPIA.
I'LL TELL YOU EXACTLY WHERE YOU'RE GOING...
...AND THAT'S NOWHERE.
GOOD OL' FUTURE ME. YOU DISAPPEARED.
I WAS IN THE SHADOWS, WATCHING YOUR PATHETIC ATTEMPTS AT GETTING AWAY.
DON'T YOU REMEMBER BEING ME? ME, RIGHT NOW? THIS INSTANT? YOU MUST REMEMBER.
I DON'T KNOW WHAT YOU'RE GETTING AT.
IF YOU DO REMEMBER, YOU'LL KNOW HOW MUCH I'M DESPISING WHAT I'VE TURNED INTO.
YOU'LL KNOW HOW ASHAMED I AM OF WHAT I'VE BECOME.
OH, KITTY...
...SHAME IS A LUXURY WE CAN NO LONGER AFFORD.

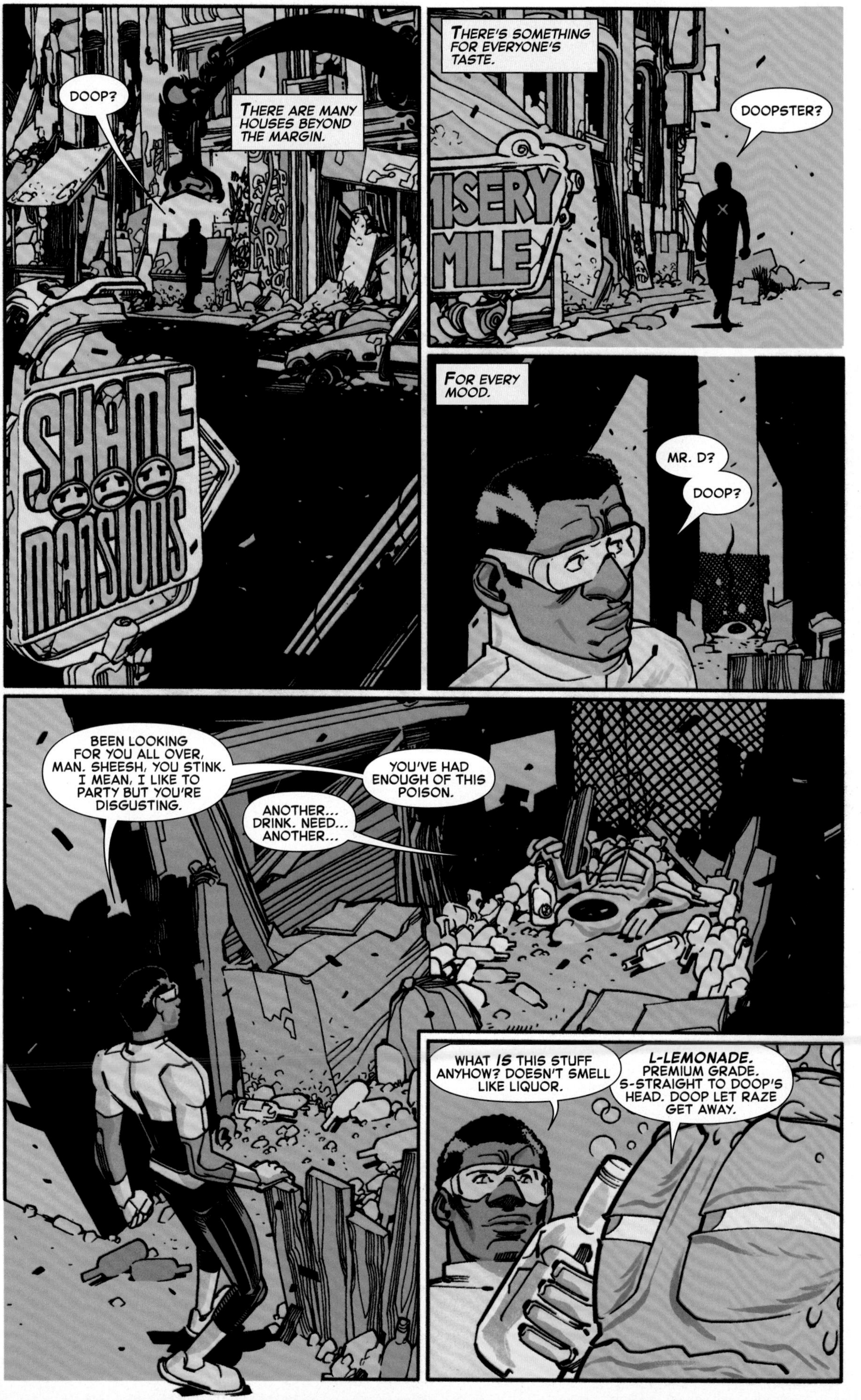
DOOP?
THERE ARE MANY HOUSES BEYOND THE MARGIN.
SHAME MANSIONS
THERE'S SOMETHING FOR EVERYONE'S TASTE.
DOOPSTER?
MISERY MILE
FOR EVERY MOOD.
MR. D?
DOOP?
BEEN LOOKING FOR YOU ALL OVER, MAN. SHEESH, YOU STINK. I MEAN, I LIKE TO PARTY BUT YOU'RE DISGUSTING.
YOU'VE HAD ENOUGH OF THIS POISON.
ANOTHER... DRINK. NEED... ANOTHER...
WHAT *IS* THIS STUFF ANYHOW? DOESN'T SMELL LIKE LIQUOR.
L-LEMONADE. PREMIUM GRADE. S-STRAIGHT TO DOOP'S HEAD. DOOP LET RAZE GET AWAY.

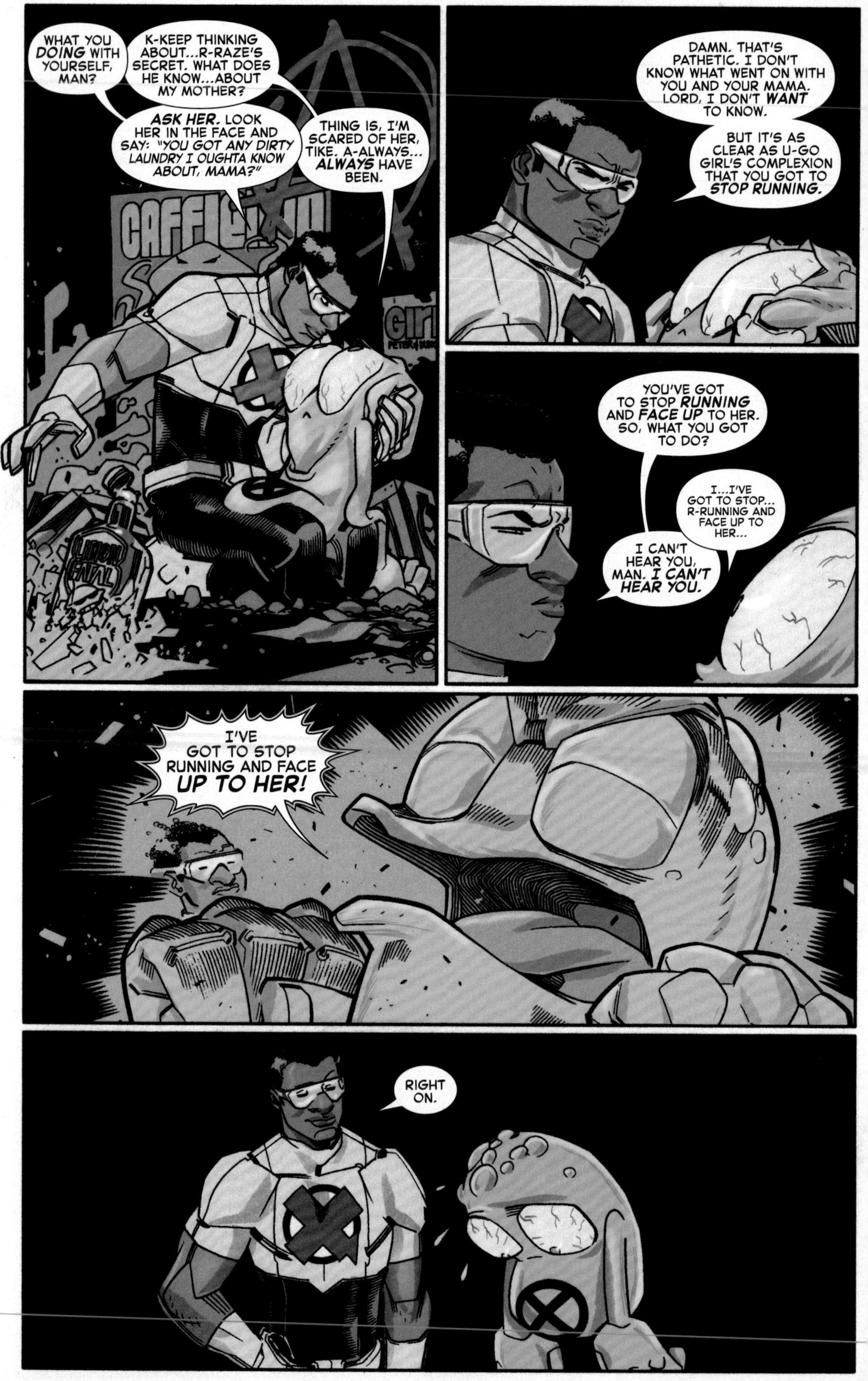
WHAT YOU DOING WITH YOURSELF, MAN?
K-KEEP THINKING ABOUT...R-RAZE'S SECRET. WHAT DOES HE KNOW...ABOUT MY MOTHER?
ASK HER. LOOK HER IN THE FACE AND SAY: "YOU GOT ANY DIRTY LAUNDRY I OUGHTA KNOW ABOUT, MAMA?"
THING IS, I'M SCARED OF HER, TIKE. A-ALWAYS... ALWAYS HAVE BEEN.
DAMN. THAT'S PATHETIC. I DON'T KNOW WHAT WENT ON WITH YOU AND YOUR MAMA. LORD, I DON'T WANT TO KNOW.
BUT IT'S AS CLEAR AS U-GO GIRL'S COMPLEXION THAT YOU GOT TO STOP RUNNING.
YOU'VE GOT TO STOP RUNNING AND FACE UP TO HER. SO, WHAT YOU GOT TO DO?
I...I'VE GOT TO STOP... R-RUNNING AND FACE UP TO HER...
I CAN'T HEAR YOU, MAN. I CAN'T HEAR YOU.
I'VE GOT TO STOP RUNNING AND FACE UP TO HER!
RIGHT ON.

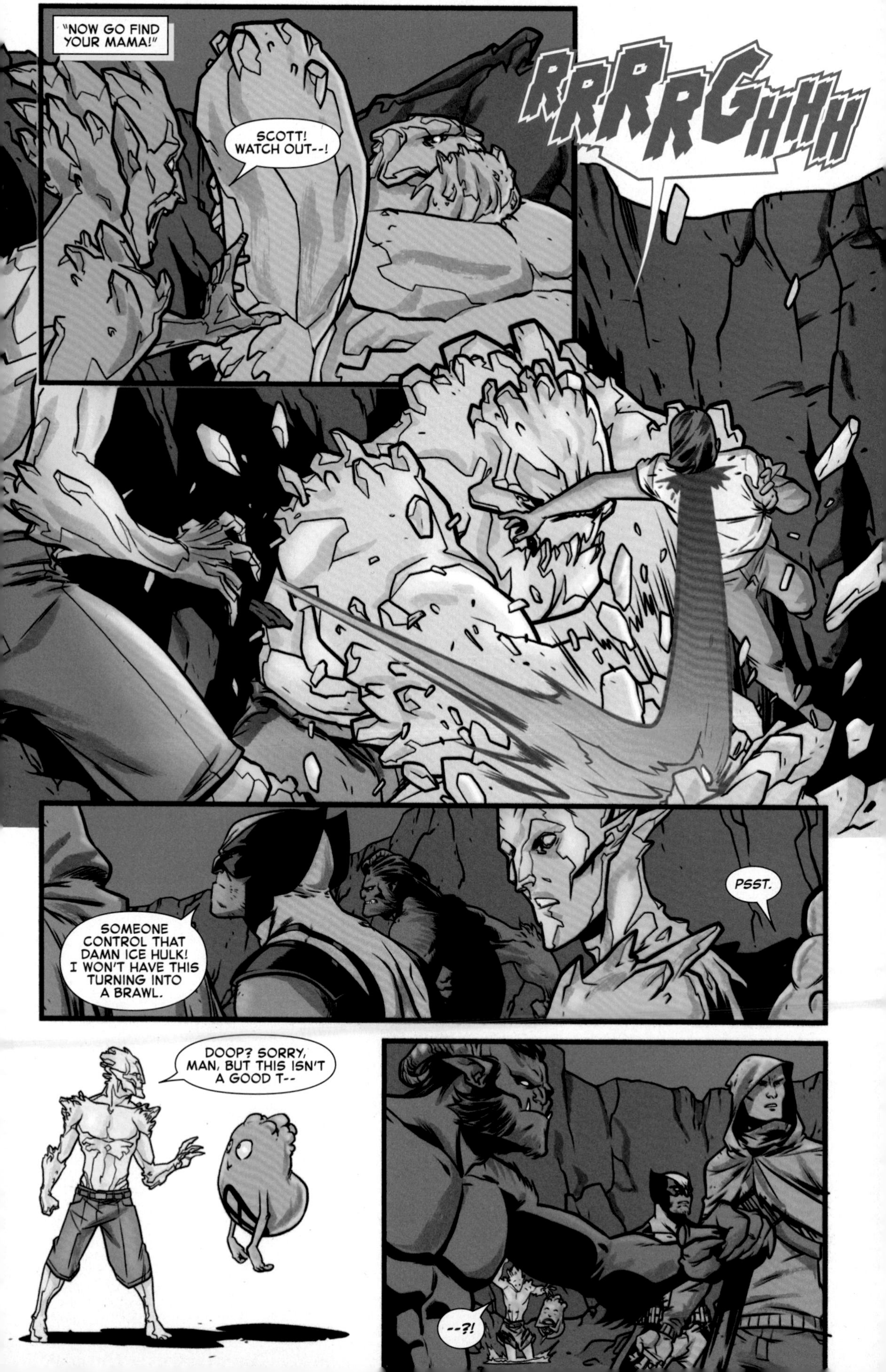
"NOW GO FIND YOUR MAMA!"
SCOTT! WATCH OUT--!
RRRRGHHH
SOMEONE CONTROL THAT DAMN ICE HULK! I WON'T HAVE THIS TURNING INTO A BRAWL.
PSST.
DOOP? SORRY, MAN, BUT THIS ISN'T A GOOD T--
--?!

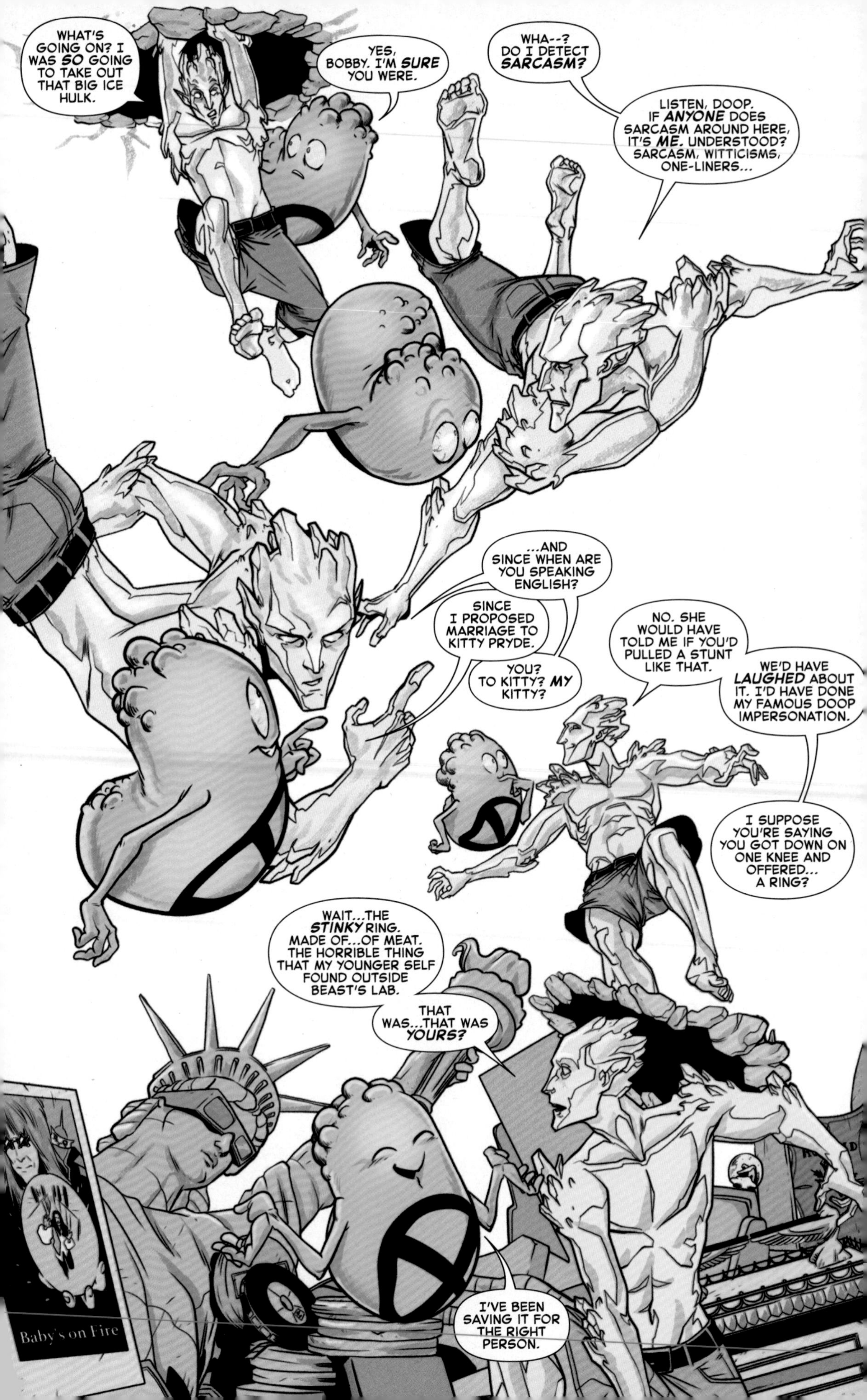
WHAT'S GOING ON? I WAS SO GOING TO TAKE OUT THAT BIG ICE HULK.
YES, BOBBY. I'M SURE YOU WERE.
WHA--? DO I DETECT SARCASM?
LISTEN, DOOP. IF ANYONE DOES SARCASM AROUND HERE, IT'S ME. UNDERSTOOD? SARCASM, WITTICISMS, ONE-LINERS...
...AND SINCE WHEN ARE YOU SPEAKING ENGLISH?
SINCE I PROPOSED MARRIAGE TO KITTY PRYDE.
YOU? TO KITTY? MY KITTY?
NO. SHE WOULD HAVE TOLD ME IF YOU'D PULLED A STUNT LIKE THAT.
WE'D HAVE LAUGHED ABOUT IT. I'D HAVE DONE MY FAMOUS DOOP IMPERSONATION.
I SUPPOSE YOU'RE SAYING YOU GOT DOWN ON ONE KNEE AND OFFERED... A RING?
WAIT...THE STINKY RING. MADE OF...OF MEAT. THE HORRIBLE THING THAT MY YOUNGER SELF FOUND OUTSIDE BEAST'S LAB.
THAT WAS...THAT WAS YOURS?
I'VE BEEN SAVING IT FOR THE RIGHT PERSON.
Baby's on Fire

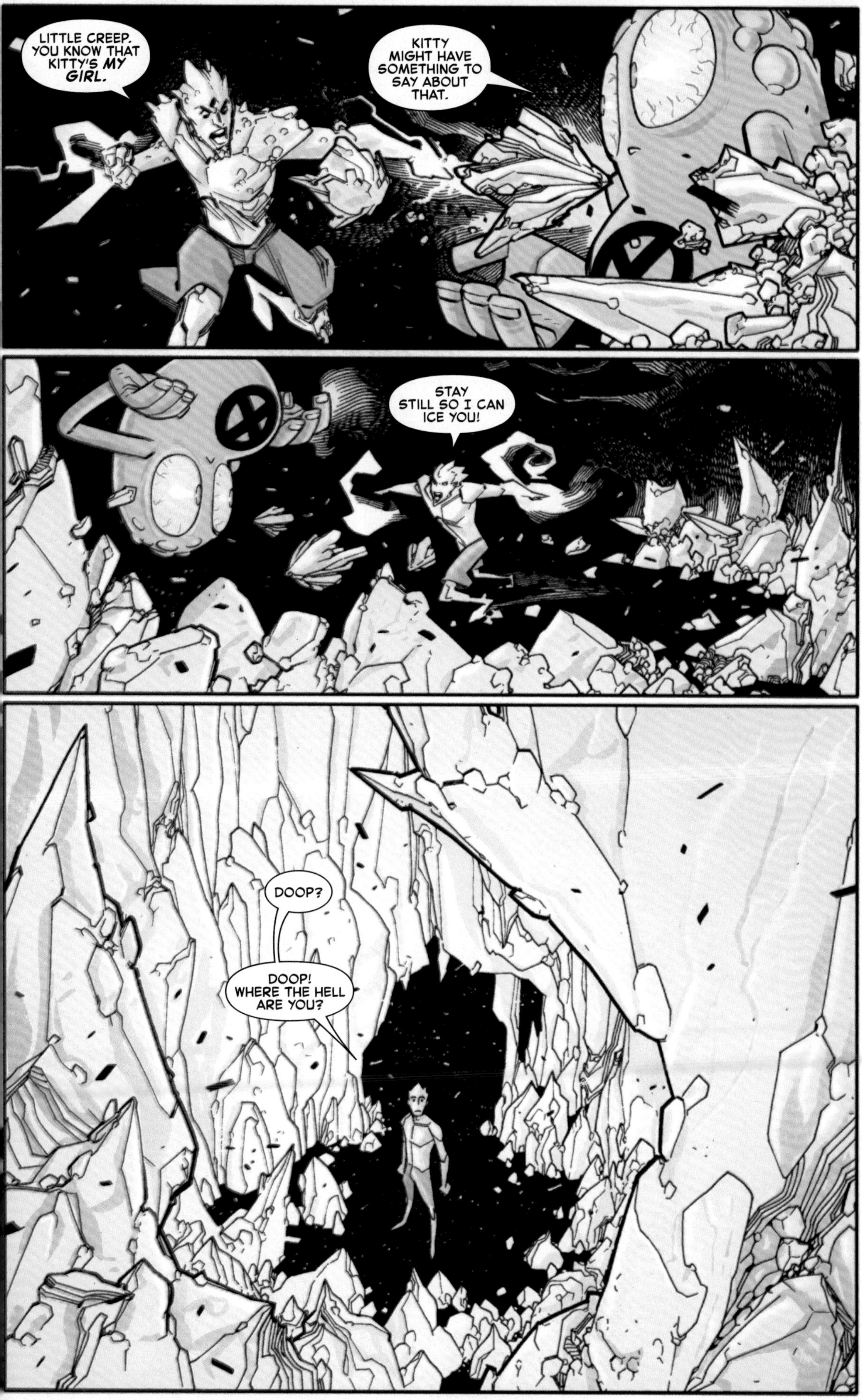
LITTLE CREEP. YOU KNOW THAT KITTY'S MY GIRL.
KITTY MIGHT HAVE SOMETHING TO SAY ABOUT THAT.
STAY STILL SO I CAN ICE YOU!
DOOP?
DOOP! WHERE THE HELL ARE YOU?

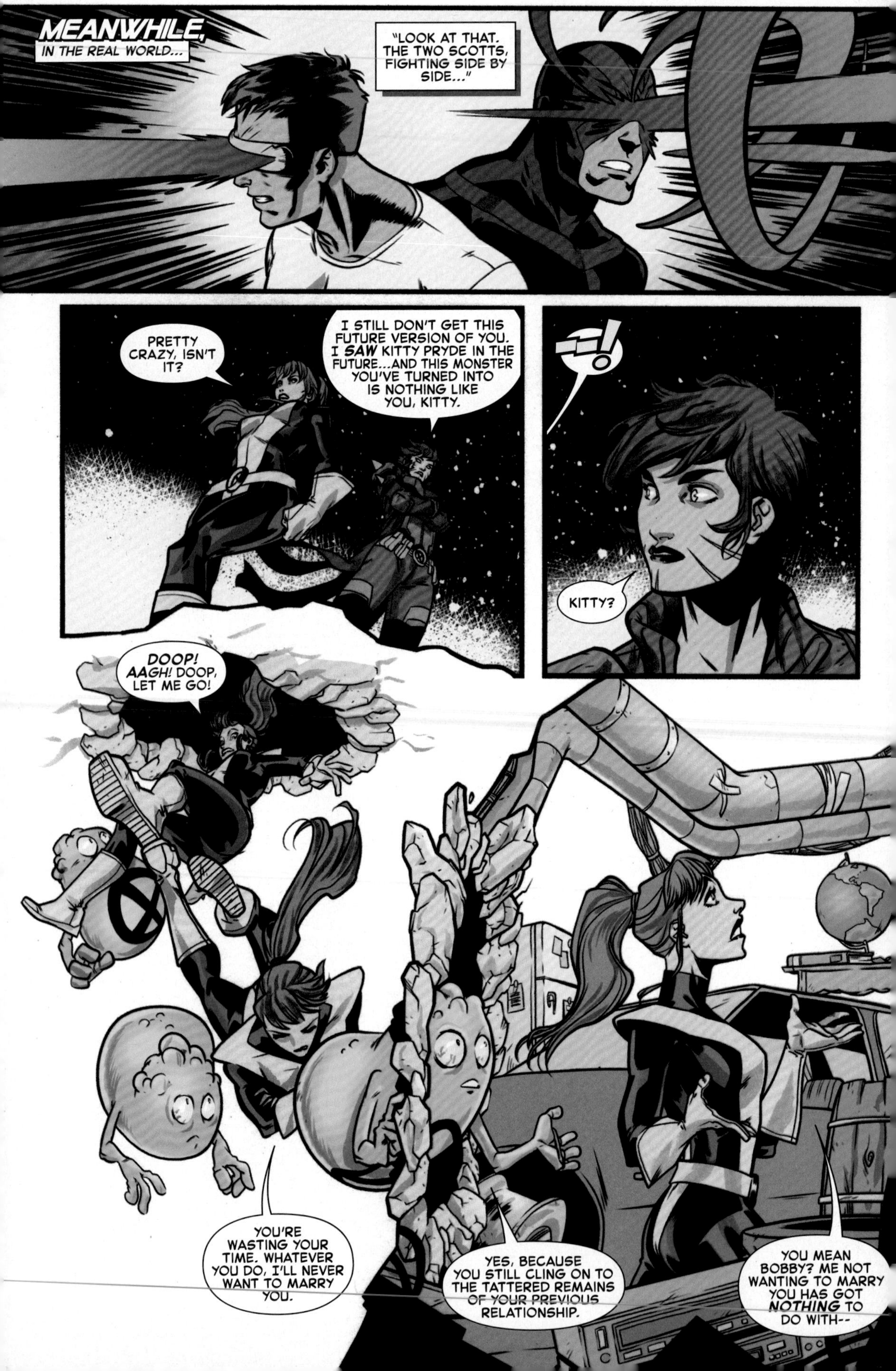
MEANWHILE, IN THE REAL WORLD...
"LOOK AT THAT. THE TWO SCOTTS, FIGHTING SIDE BY SIDE..."
PRETTY CRAZY, ISN'T IT?
I STILL DON'T GET THIS FUTURE VERSION OF YOU. I SAW KITTY PRYDE IN THE FUTURE...AND THIS MONSTER YOU'VE TURNED INTO IS NOTHING LIKE YOU, KITTY.
--!
KITTY?
DOOP! AAGH! DOOP, LET ME GO!
YOU'RE WASTING YOUR TIME. WHATEVER YOU DO, I'LL NEVER WANT TO MARRY YOU.
YES, BECAUSE YOU STILL CLING ON TO THE TATTERED REMAINS OF YOUR PREVIOUS RELATIONSHIP.
YOU MEAN BOBBY? ME NOT WANTING TO MARRY YOU HAS GOT NOTHING TO DO WITH--

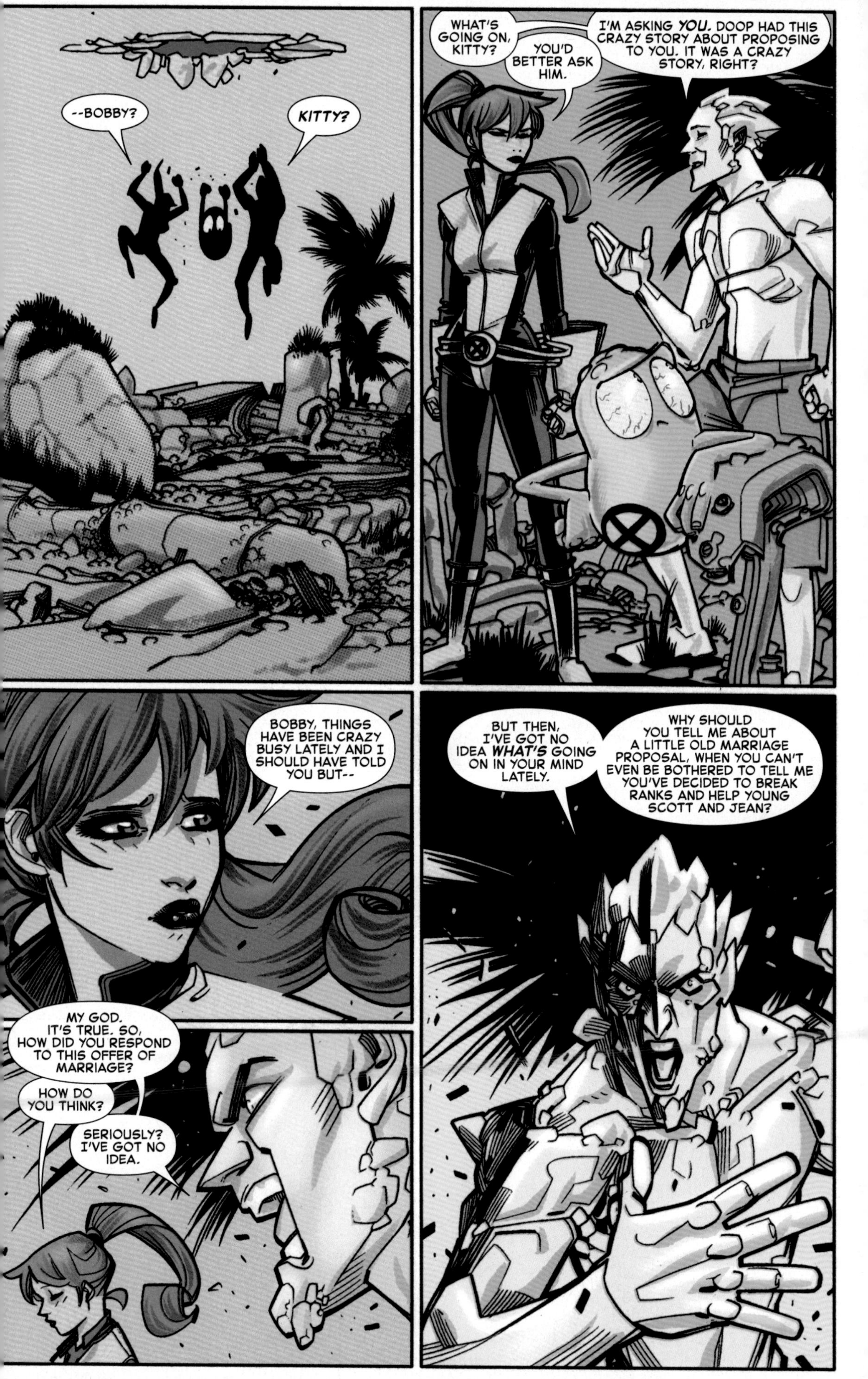
--BOBBY?
KITTY?
WHAT'S GOING ON, KITTY?
YOU'D BETTER ASK HIM.
I'M ASKING YOU. DOOP HAD THIS CRAZY STORY ABOUT PROPOSING TO YOU. IT WAS A CRAZY STORY, RIGHT?
BOBBY, THINGS HAVE BEEN CRAZY BUSY LATELY AND I SHOULD HAVE TOLD YOU BUT--
MY GOD. IT'S TRUE. SO, HOW DID YOU RESPOND TO THIS OFFER OF MARRIAGE?
HOW DO YOU THINK?
SERIOUSLY? I'VE GOT NO IDEA.
BUT THEN, I'VE GOT NO IDEA WHAT'S GOING ON IN YOUR MIND LATELY.
WHY SHOULD YOU TELL ME ABOUT A LITTLE OLD MARRIAGE PROPOSAL, WHEN YOU CAN'T EVEN BE BOTHERED TO TELL ME YOU'VE DECIDED TO BREAK RANKS AND HELP YOUNG SCOTT AND JEAN?

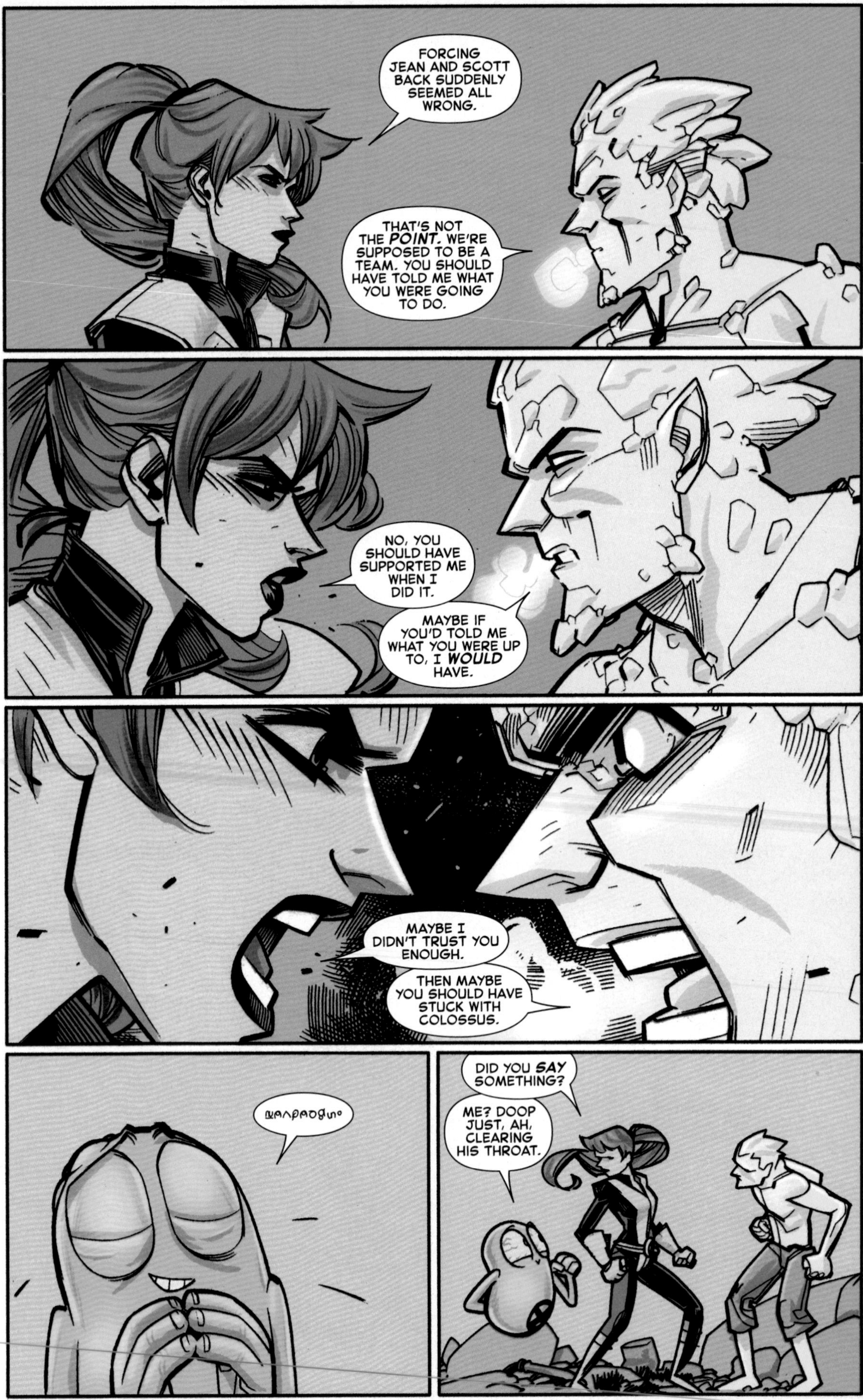
FORCING JEAN AND SCOTT BACK SUDDENLY SEEMED ALL WRONG.
THAT'S NOT THE POINT. WE'RE SUPPOSED TO BE A TEAM. YOU SHOULD HAVE TOLD ME WHAT YOU WERE GOING TO DO.
NO, YOU SHOULD HAVE SUPPORTED ME WHEN I DID IT.
MAYBE IF YOU'D TOLD ME WHAT YOU WERE UP TO, I WOULD HAVE.
MAYBE I DIDN'T TRUST YOU ENOUGH.
THEN MAYBE YOU SHOULD HAVE STUCK WITH COLOSSUS.
DID YOU SAY SOMETHING?
ME? DOOP JUST, AH, CLEARING HIS THROAT.

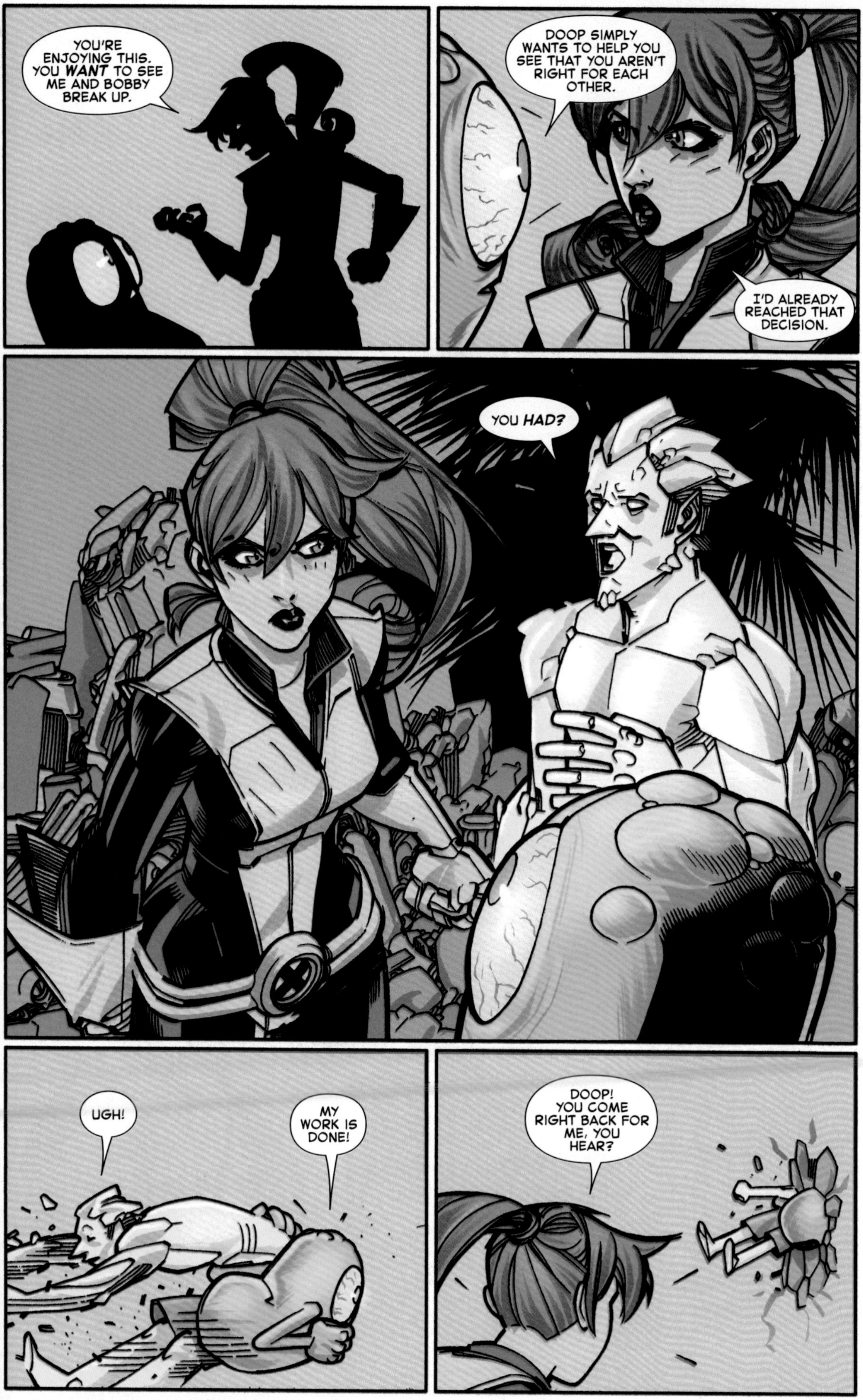
YOU'RE ENJOYING THIS. YOU WANT TO SEE ME AND BOBBY BREAK UP.
DOOP SIMPLY WANTS TO HELP YOU SEE THAT YOU AREN'T RIGHT FOR EACH OTHER.
I'D ALREADY REACHED THAT DECISION.
YOU HAD?
UGH!
MY WORK IS DONE!
DOOP! YOU COME RIGHT BACK FOR ME, YOU HEAR?

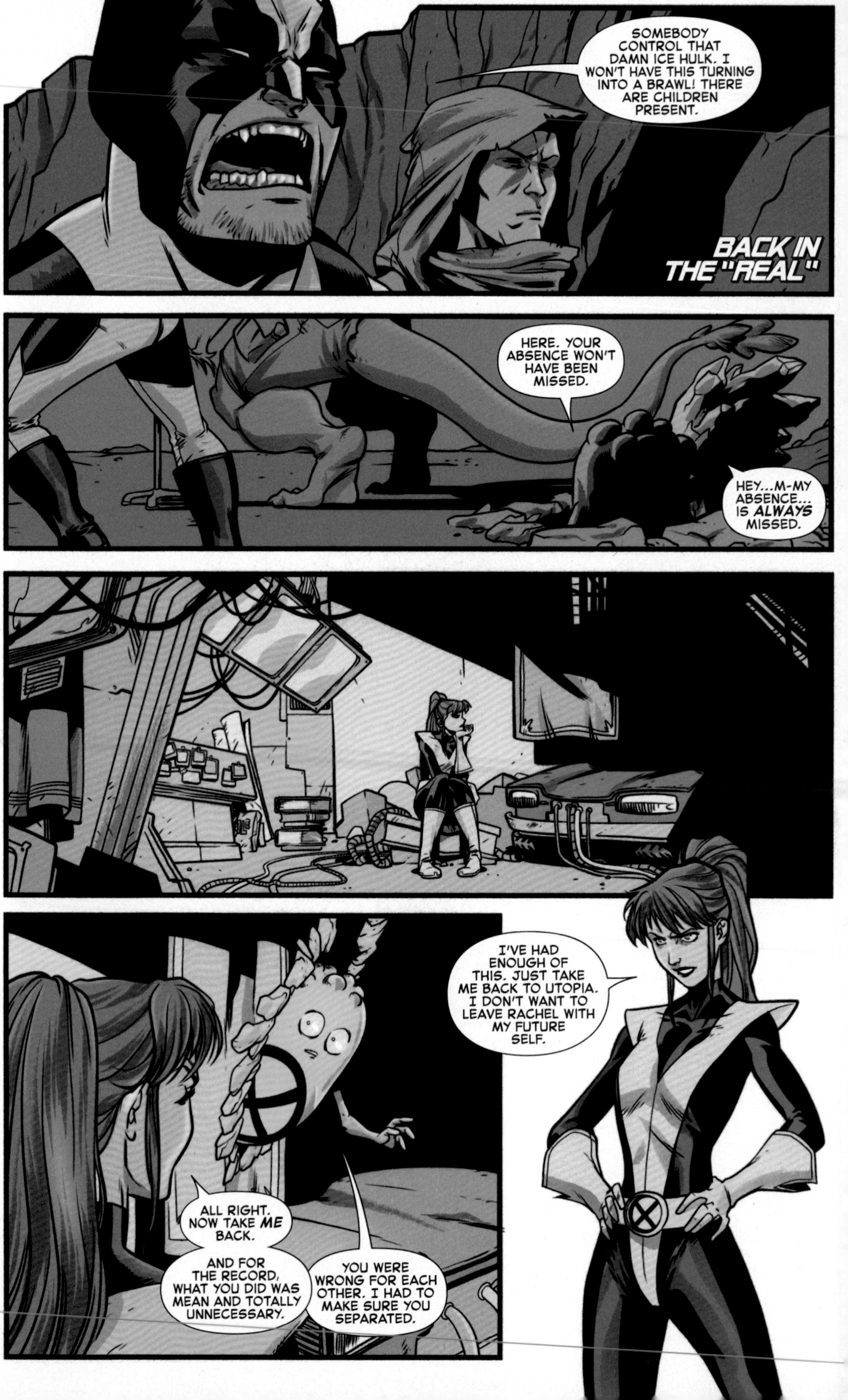
SOMEBODY CONTROL THAT DAMN ICE HULK. I WON'T HAVE THIS TURNING INTO A BRAWL! THERE ARE CHILDREN PRESENT.
BACK IN THE "REAL"
HERE. YOUR ABSENCE WON'T HAVE BEEN MISSED.
HEY...M-MY ABSENCE... IS *ALWAYS* MISSED.
I'VE HAD ENOUGH OF THIS. JUST TAKE ME BACK TO UTOPIA. I DON'T WANT TO LEAVE RACHEL WITH MY FUTURE SELF.
ALL RIGHT. NOW TAKE *ME* BACK.
AND FOR THE RECORD, WHAT YOU DID WAS MEAN AND TOTALLY UNNECESSARY.
YOU WERE WRONG FOR EACH OTHER. I HAD TO MAKE SURE YOU SEPARATED.

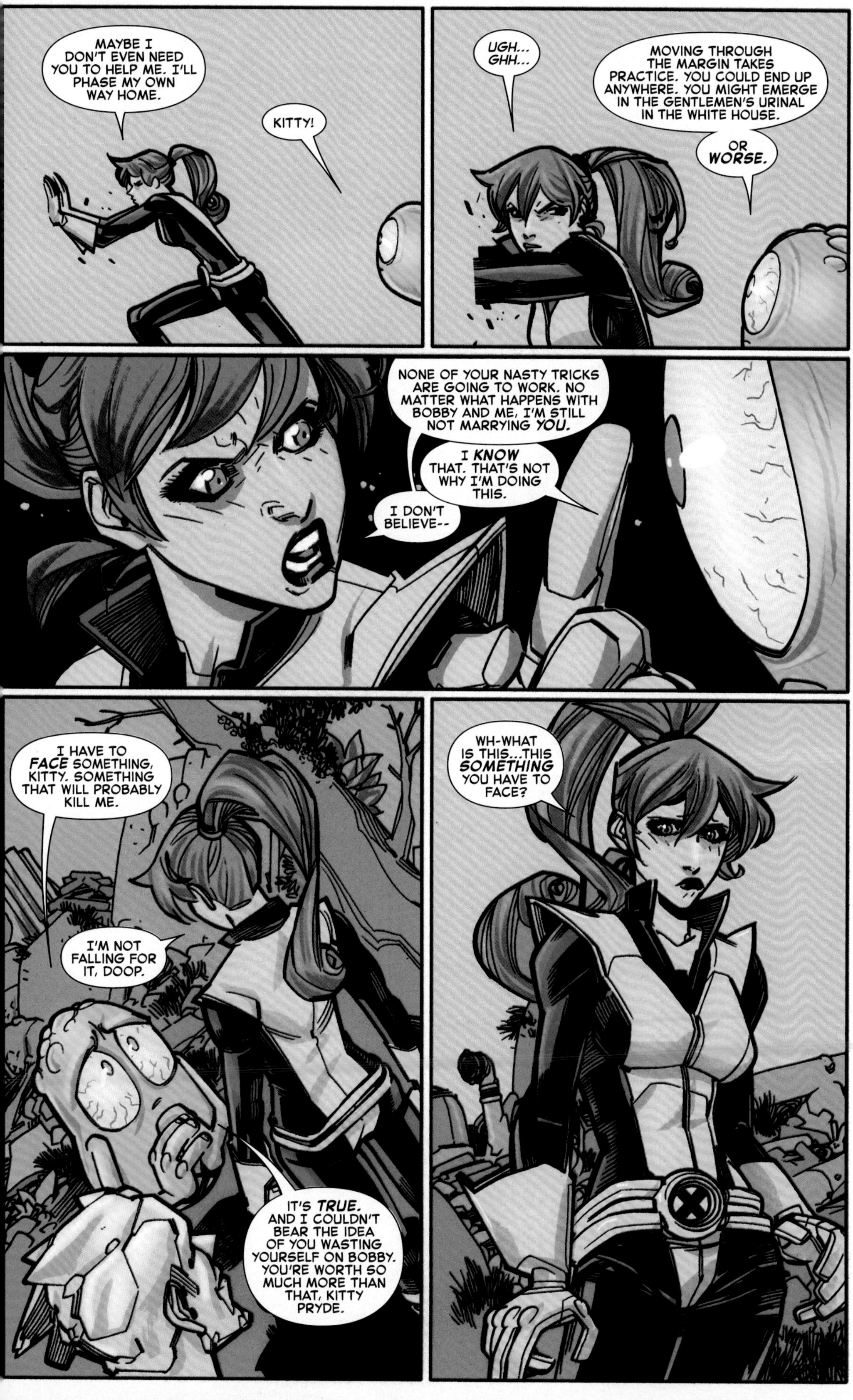
MAYBE I DON'T EVEN NEED YOU TO HELP ME. I'LL PHASE MY OWN WAY HOME.
KITTY!
UGH... GHH...
MOVING THROUGH THE MARGIN TAKES PRACTICE. YOU COULD END UP ANYWHERE. YOU MIGHT EMERGE IN THE GENTLEMEN'S URINAL IN THE WHITE HOUSE.
OR WORSE.
NONE OF YOUR NASTY TRICKS ARE GOING TO WORK. NO MATTER WHAT HAPPENS WITH BOBBY AND ME, I'M STILL NOT MARRYING YOU.
I KNOW THAT. THAT'S NOT WHY I'M DOING THIS.
I DON'T BELIEVE--
I HAVE TO FACE SOMETHING, KITTY. SOMETHING THAT WILL PROBABLY KILL ME.
I'M NOT FALLING FOR IT, DOOP.
IT'S TRUE. AND I COULDN'T BEAR THE IDEA OF YOU WASTING YOURSELF ON BOBBY. YOU'RE WORTH SO MUCH MORE THAN THAT, KITTY PRYDE.
WH-WHAT IS THIS...THIS SOMETHING YOU HAVE TO FACE?

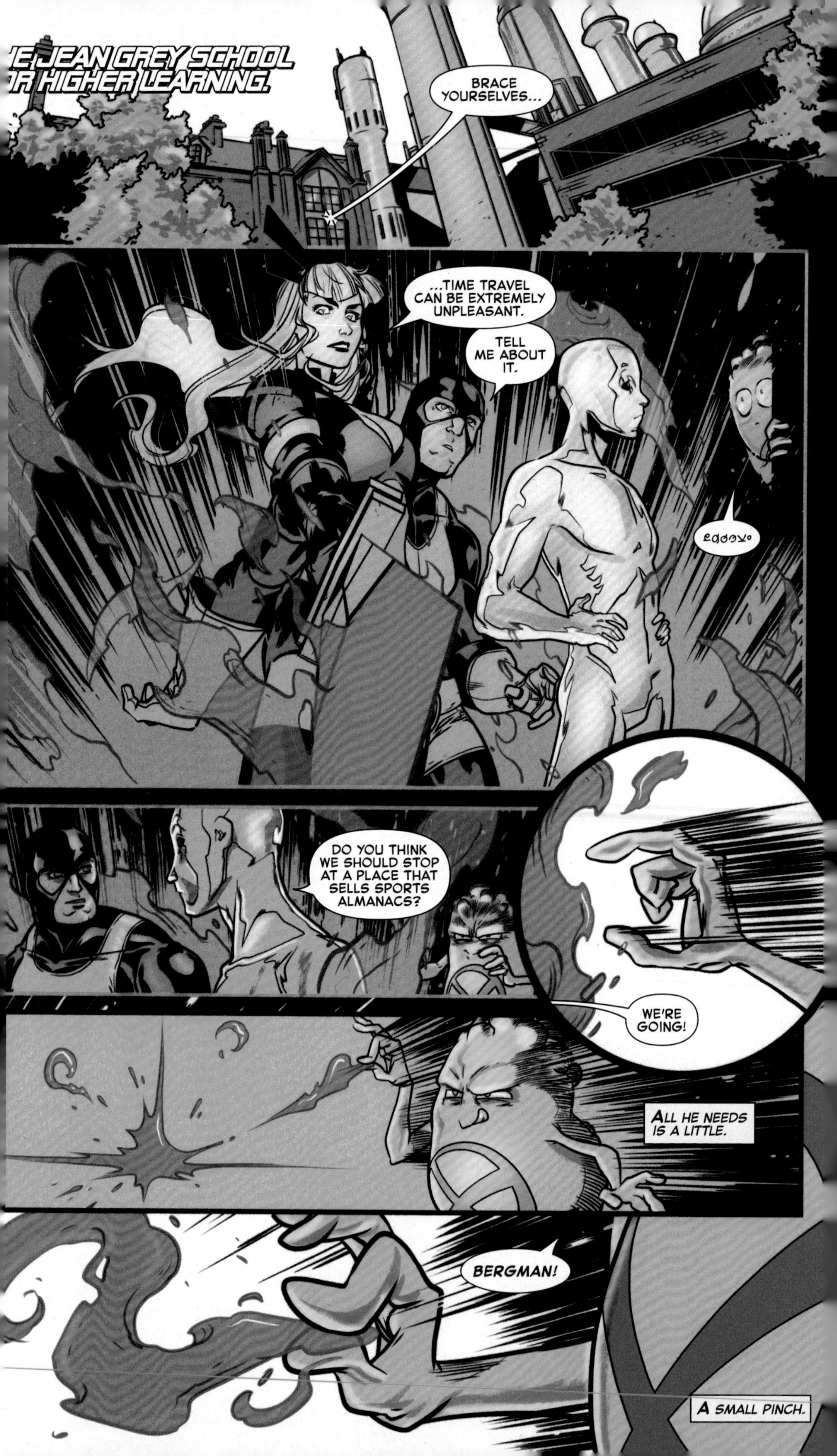

E JEAN GREY SCHOOL
R HIGHER LEARNING.
BRACE YOURSELVES...
...TIME TRAVEL CAN BE EXTREMELY UNPLEASANT.
TELL ME ABOUT IT.
DO YOU THINK WE SHOULD STOP AT A PLACE THAT SELLS SPORTS ALMANACS?
WE'RE GOING!
ALL HE NEEDS IS A LITTLE.
BERGMAN!
A SMALL PINCH.

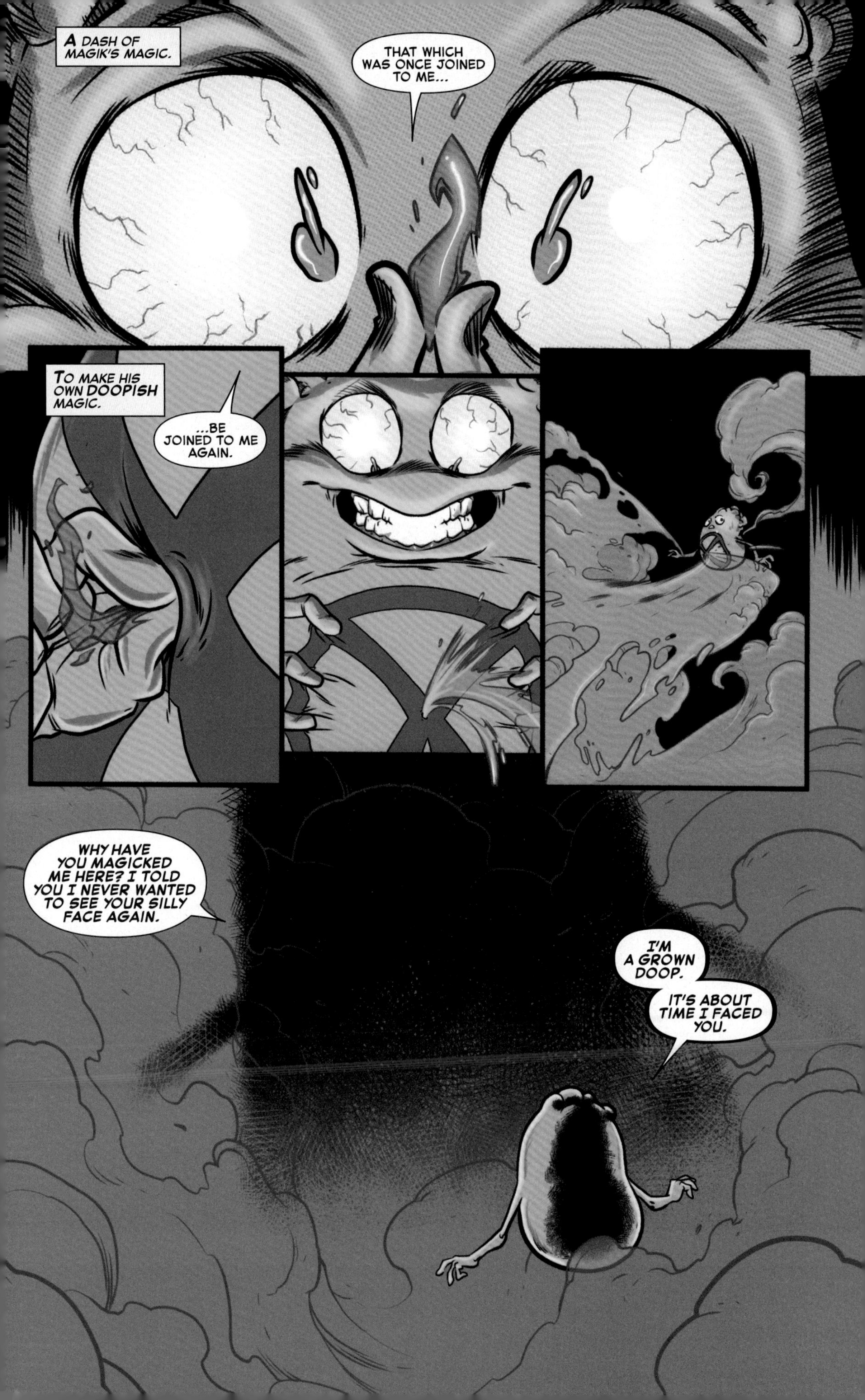
A DASH OF MAGIK'S MAGIC.
THAT WHICH WAS ONCE JOINED TO ME...
TO MAKE HIS OWN DOOPISH MAGIC.
...BE JOINED TO ME AGAIN.
WHY HAVE YOU MAGICKED ME HERE? I TOLD YOU I NEVER WANTED TO SEE YOUR SILLY FACE AGAIN.
I'M A GROWN DOOP.
IT'S ABOUT TIME I FACED YOU.

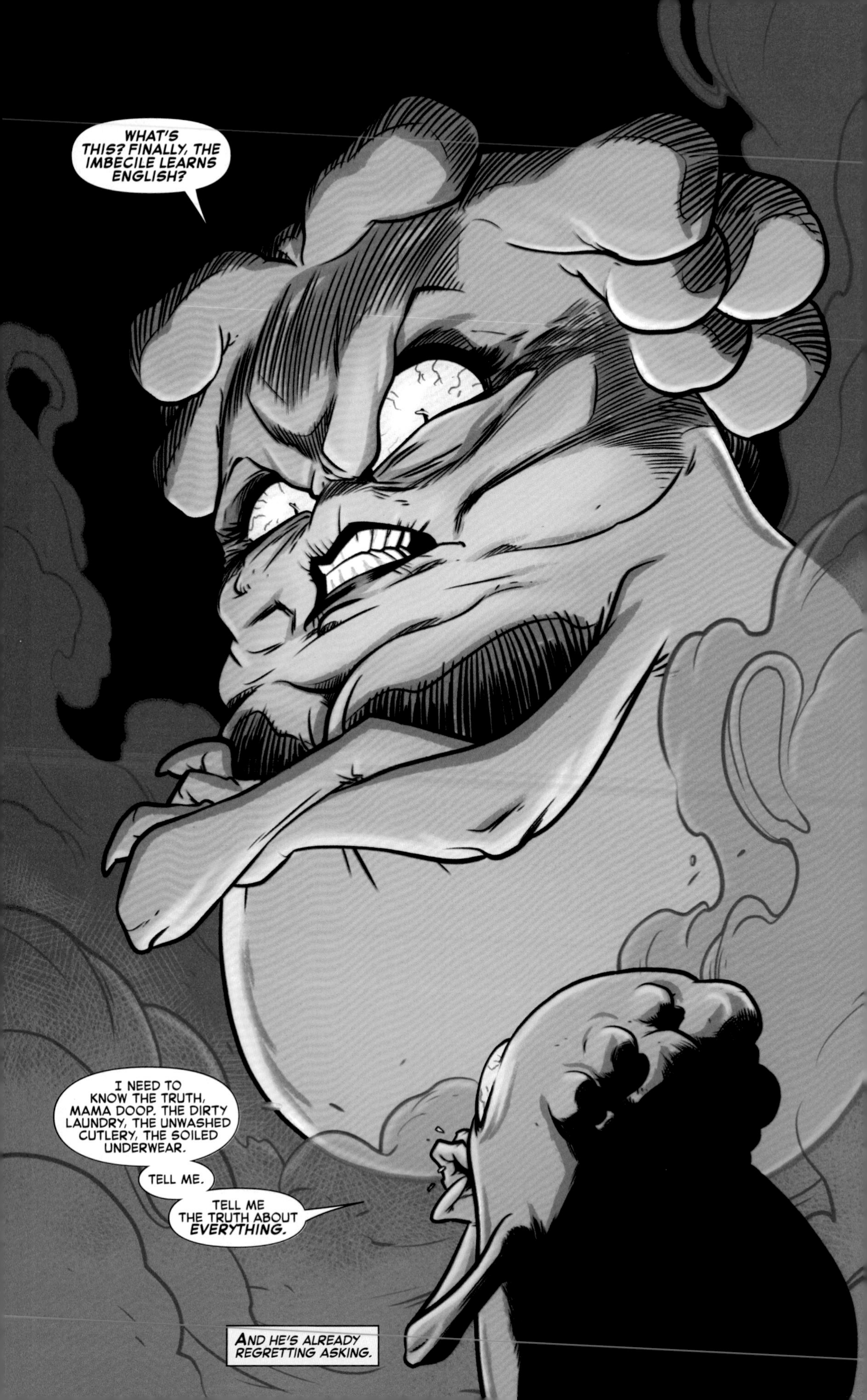
WHAT'S THIS? FINALLY, THE IMBECILE LEARNS ENGLISH?
I NEED TO KNOW THE TRUTH, MAMA DOOP. THE DIRTY LAUNDRY, THE UNWASHED CUTLERY, THE SOILED UNDERWEAR.
TELL ME.
TELL ME THE TRUTH ABOUT EVERYTHING.
AND HE'S ALREADY REGRETTING ASKING.

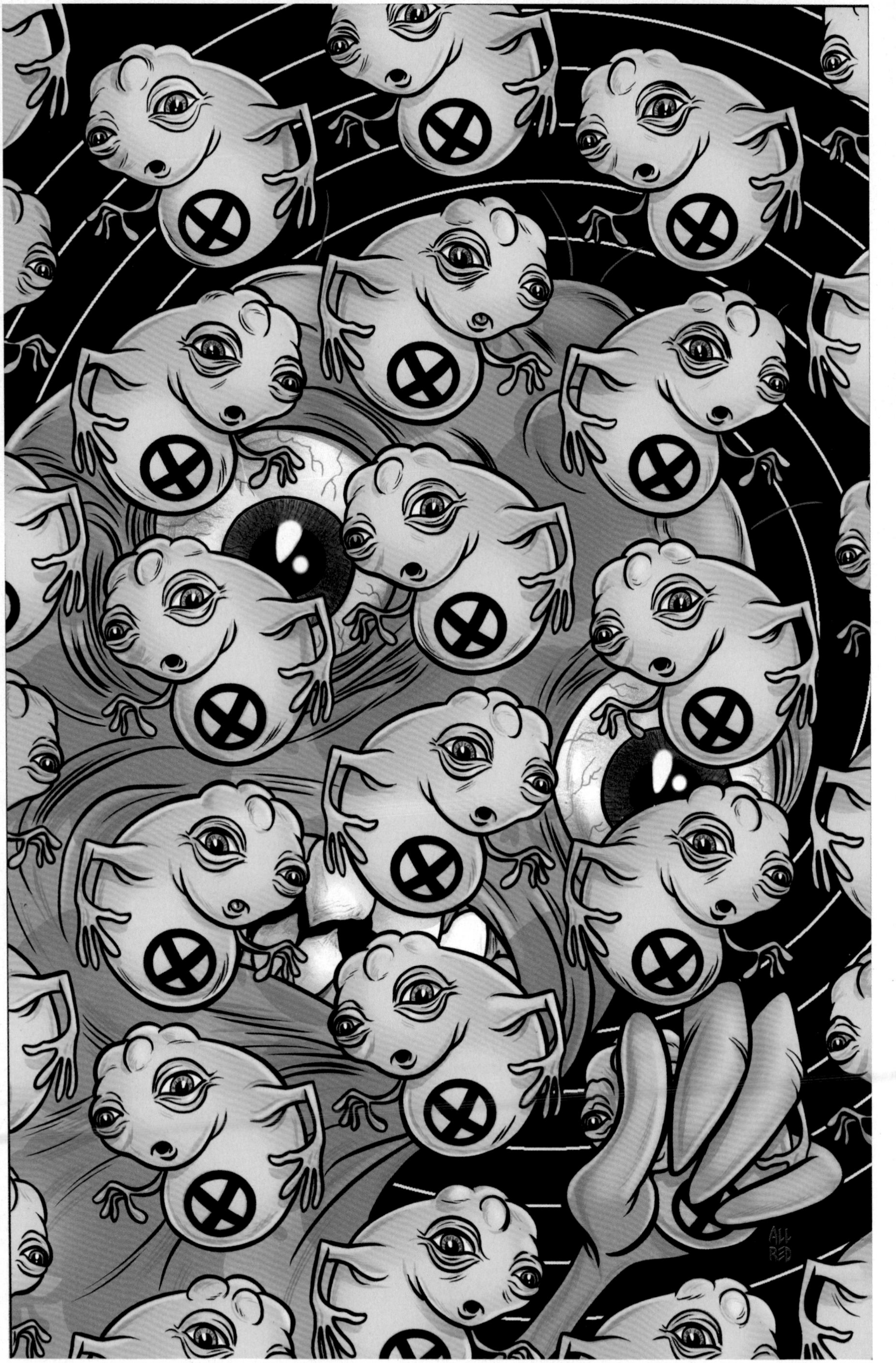
ALL
RED

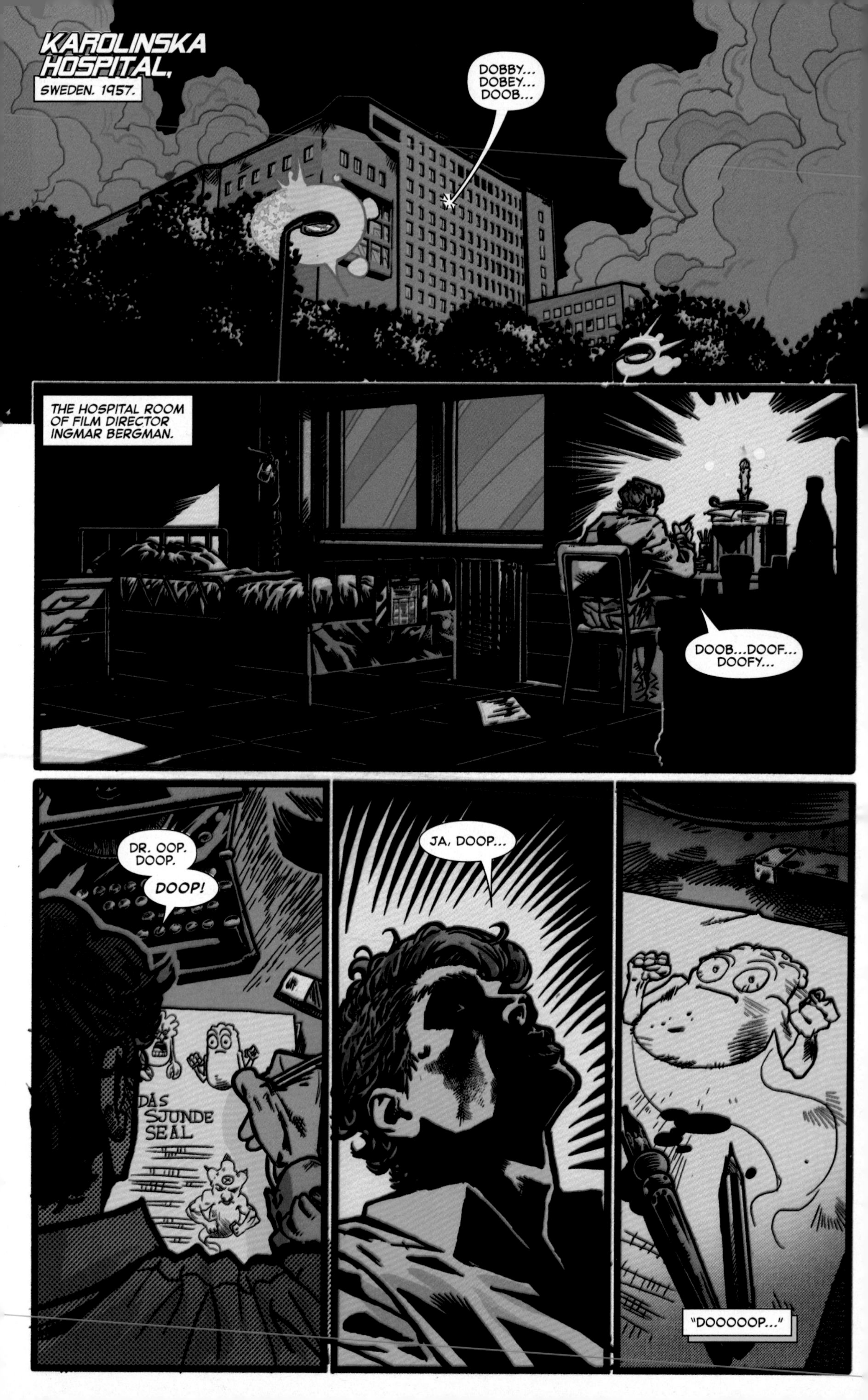
KAROLINSKA HOSPITAL,
SWEDEN. 1957.
DOBBY... DOBEY... DOOB...
THE HOSPITAL ROOM OF FILM DIRECTOR INGMAR BERGMAN.
DOOB...DOOF... DOOFY...
DR. OOP. DOOP.
DOOP!
DÅS SJUNDE SEAL
JA, DOOP...
"DOOOOOP..."

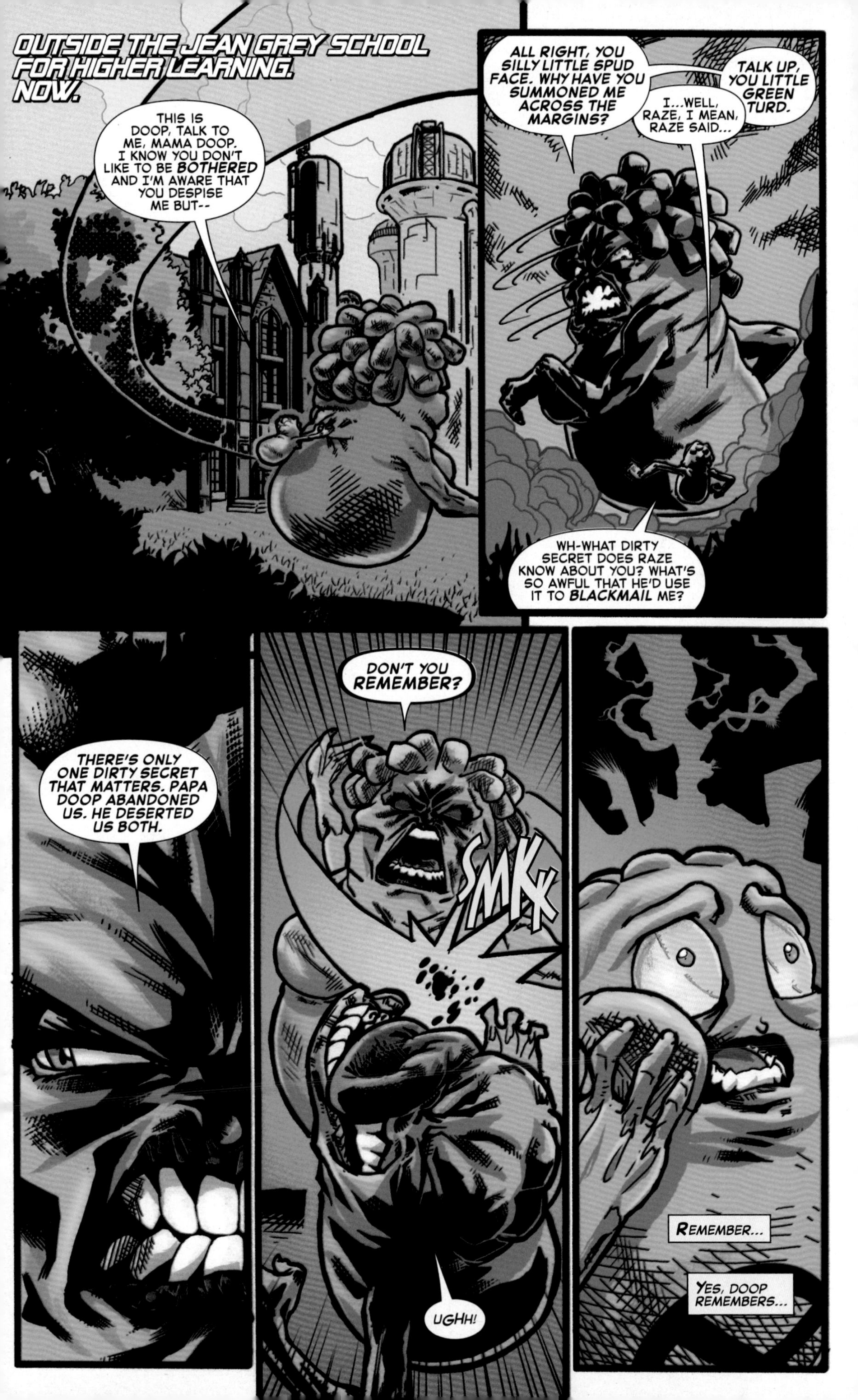
OUTSIDE THE JEAN GREY SCHOOL FOR HIGHER LEARNING. NOW.
THIS IS DOOP, TALK TO ME, MAMA DOOP. I KNOW YOU DON'T LIKE TO BE BOTHERED AND I'M AWARE THAT YOU DESPISE ME BUT--
ALL RIGHT, YOU SILLY LITTLE SPUD FACE. WHY HAVE YOU SUMMONED ME ACROSS THE MARGINS?
TALK UP, YOU LITTLE GREEN TURD.
I...WELL, RAZE, I MEAN, RAZE SAID...
WH-WHAT DIRTY SECRET DOES RAZE KNOW ABOUT YOU? WHAT'S SO AWFUL THAT HE'D USE IT TO BLACKMAIL ME?
THERE'S ONLY ONE DIRTY SECRET THAT MATTERS. PAPA DOOP ABANDONED US. HE DESERTED US BOTH.
DON'T YOU REMEMBER?
SMKK
UGHH!
REMEMBER...
YES, DOOP REMEMBERS...

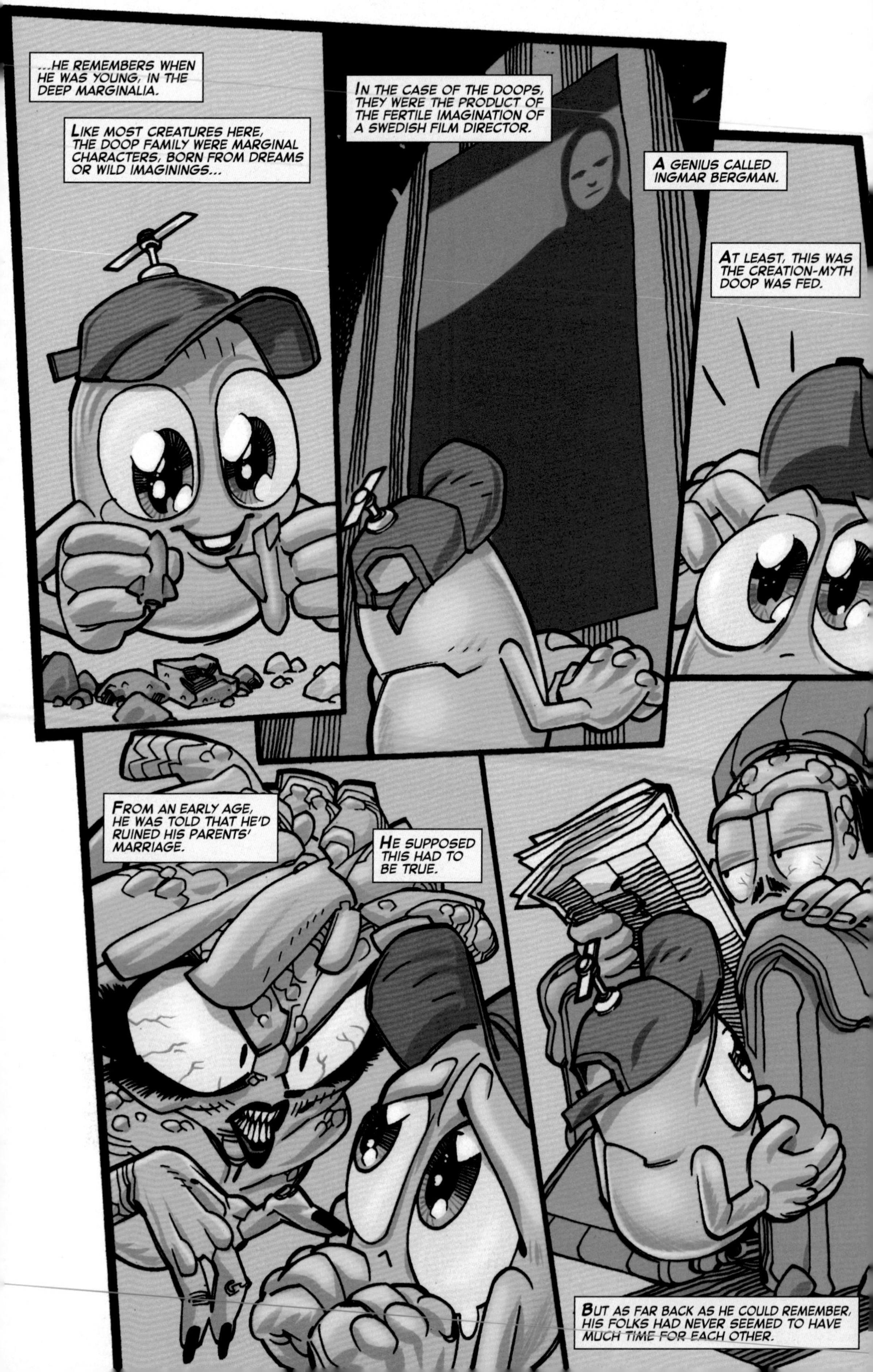
...HE REMEMBERS WHEN HE WAS YOUNG, IN THE DEEP MARGINALIA.
LIKE MOST CREATURES HERE, THE DOOP FAMILY WERE MARGINAL CHARACTERS, BORN FROM DREAMS OR WILD IMAGININGS...
IN THE CASE OF THE DOOPS, THEY WERE THE PRODUCT OF THE FERTILE IMAGINATION OF A SWEDISH FILM DIRECTOR.
A GENIUS CALLED INGMAR BERGMAN.
AT LEAST, THIS WAS THE CREATION-MYTH DOOP WAS FED.
FROM AN EARLY AGE, HE WAS TOLD THAT HE'D RUINED HIS PARENTS' MARRIAGE.
HE SUPPOSED THIS HAD TO BE TRUE.
BUT AS FAR BACK AS HE COULD REMEMBER, HIS FOLKS HAD NEVER SEEMED TO HAVE MUCH TIME FOR EACH OTHER.

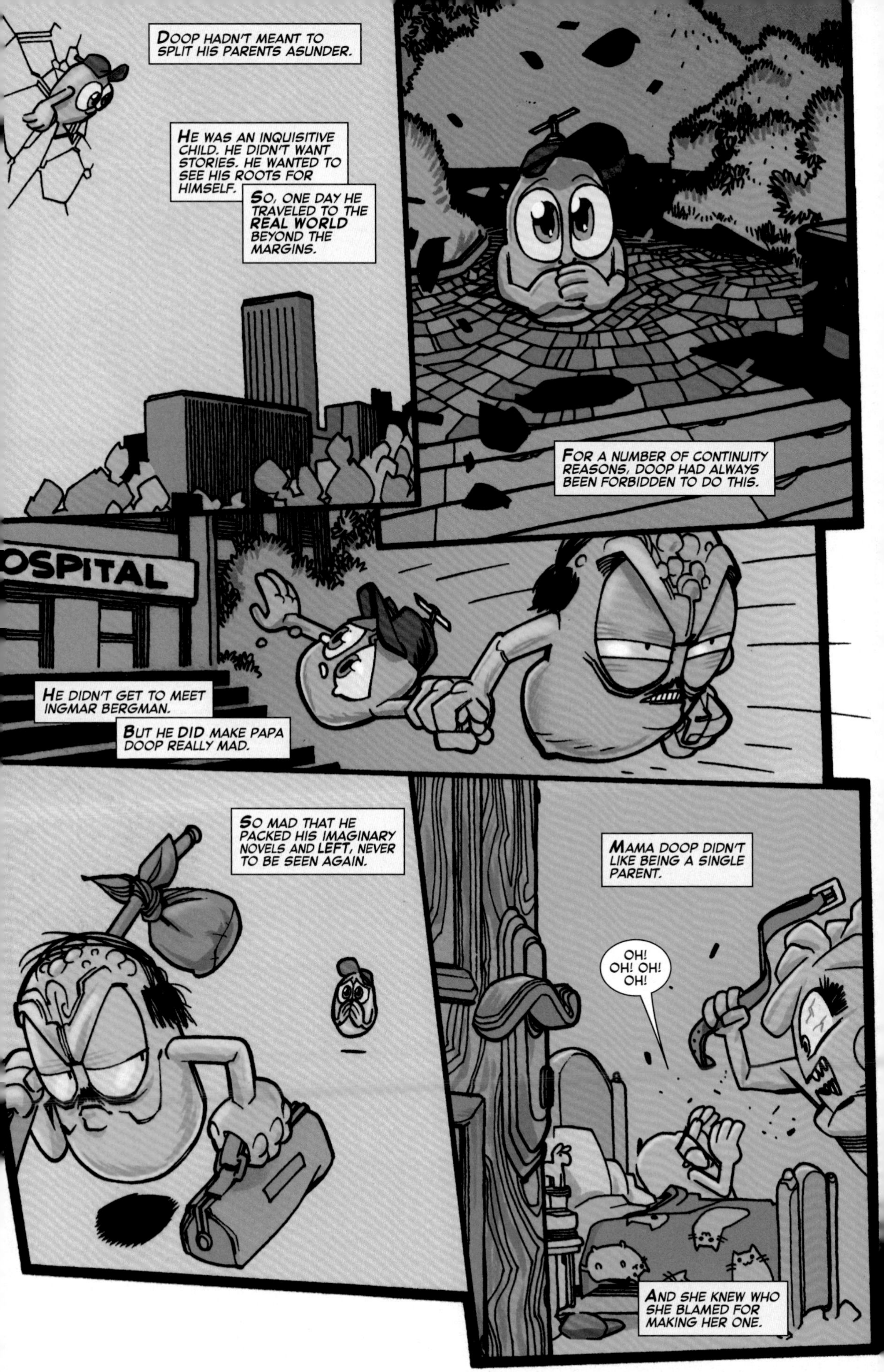
DOOP HADN'T MEANT TO SPLIT HIS PARENTS ASUNDER.
HE WAS AN INQUISITIVE CHILD. HE DIDN'T WANT STORIES. HE WANTED TO SEE HIS ROOTS FOR HIMSELF.
SO, ONE DAY HE TRAVELED TO THE REAL WORLD BEYOND THE MARGINS.
FOR A NUMBER OF CONTINUITY REASONS, DOOP HAD ALWAYS BEEN FORBIDDEN TO DO THIS.
OSPITAL
HE DIDN'T GET TO MEET INGMAR BERGMAN.
BUT HE DID MAKE PAPA DOOP REALLY MAD.
SO MAD THAT HE PACKED HIS IMAGINARY NOVELS AND LEFT, NEVER TO BE SEEN AGAIN.
MAMA DOOP DIDN'T LIKE BEING A SINGLE PARENT.
OH! OH! OH! OH!
AND SHE KNEW WHO SHE BLAMED FOR MAKING HER ONE.

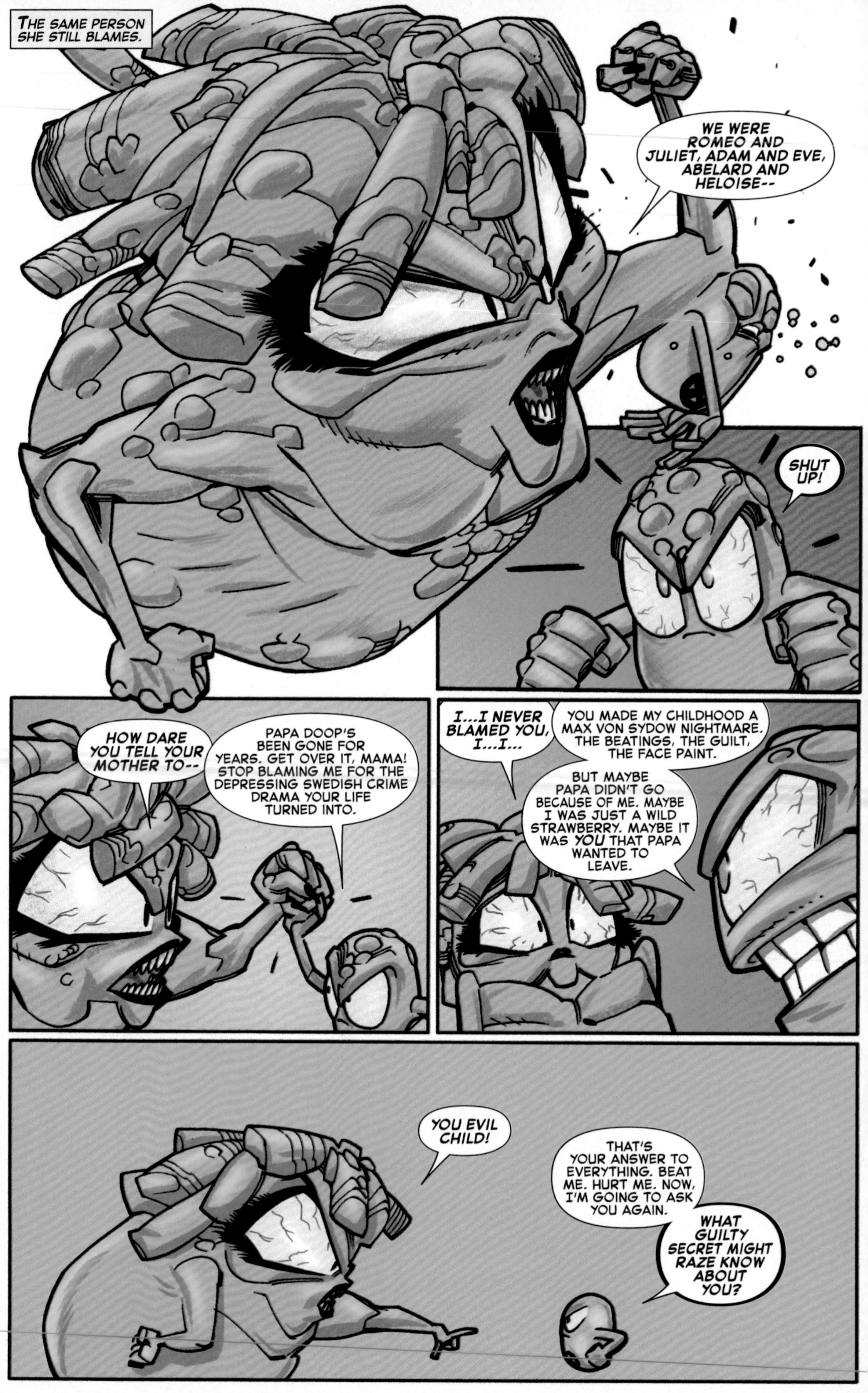
THE SAME PERSON SHE STILL BLAMES.
WE WERE ROMEO AND JULIET, ADAM AND EVE, ABELARD AND HELOISE--
SHUT UP!
HOW DARE YOU TELL YOUR MOTHER TO--
PAPA DOOP'S BEEN GONE FOR YEARS. GET OVER IT, MAMA! STOP BLAMING ME FOR THE DEPRESSING SWEDISH CRIME DRAMA YOUR LIFE TURNED INTO.
I...I NEVER BLAMED YOU, I...I...
YOU MADE MY CHILDHOOD A MAX VON SYDOW NIGHTMARE. THE BEATINGS, THE GUILT, THE FACE PAINT.
BUT MAYBE PAPA DIDN'T GO BECAUSE OF ME. MAYBE I WAS JUST A WILD STRAWBERRY. MAYBE IT WAS YOU THAT PAPA WANTED TO LEAVE.
YOU EVIL CHILD!
THAT'S YOUR ANSWER TO EVERYTHING. BEAT ME. HURT ME. NOW, I'M GOING TO ASK YOU AGAIN.
WHAT GUILTY SECRET MIGHT RAZE KNOW ABOUT YOU?

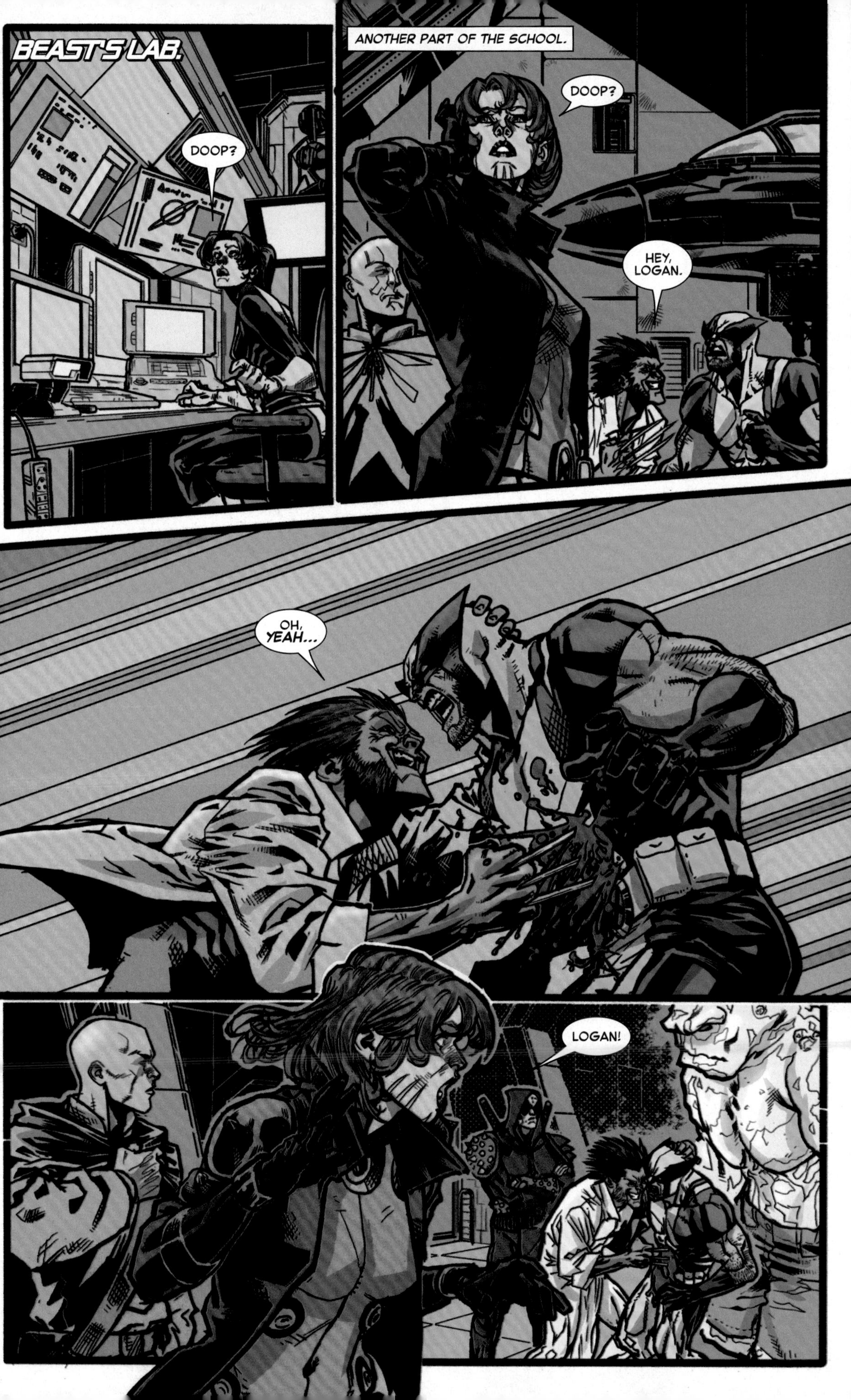
BEAST'S LAB.
DOOP?
ANOTHER PART OF THE SCHOOL.
DOOP?
HEY, LOGAN.
OH, YEAH...
LOGAN!

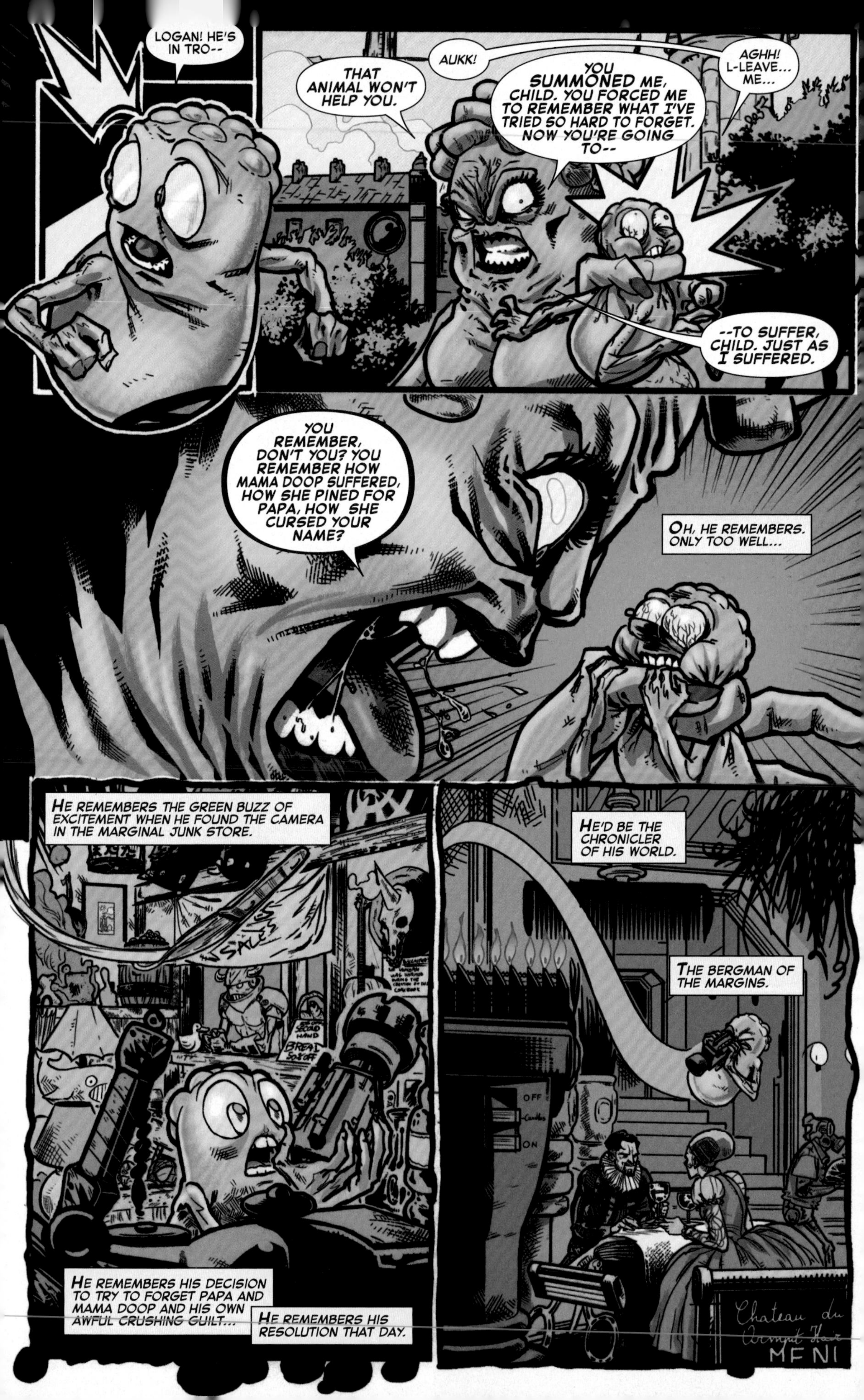
LOGAN! HE'S IN TRO--
THAT ANIMAL WON'T HELP YOU.
AUKK!
YOU SUMMONED ME, CHILD. YOU FORCED ME TO REMEMBER WHAT I'VE TRIED SO HARD TO FORGET. NOW YOU'RE GOING TO--
AGHH! L-LEAVE... ME...
--TO SUFFER, CHILD. JUST AS I SUFFERED.
YOU REMEMBER, DON'T YOU? YOU REMEMBER HOW MAMA DOOP SUFFERED, HOW SHE PINED FOR PAPA, HOW SHE CURSED YOUR NAME?
OH, HE REMEMBERS. ONLY TOO WELL...
HE REMEMBERS THE GREEN BUZZ OF EXCITEMENT WHEN HE FOUND THE CAMERA IN THE MARGINAL JUNK STORE.
SALE
SECOND HAND
BREAD 50% OFF
HE REMEMBERS HIS DECISION TO TRY TO FORGET PAPA AND MAMA DOOP AND HIS OWN AWFUL CRUSHING GUILT...
HE REMEMBERS HIS RESOLUTION THAT DAY.
HE'D BE THE CHRONICLER OF HIS WORLD.
THE BERGMAN OF THE MARGINS.
OFF
ON
MENI

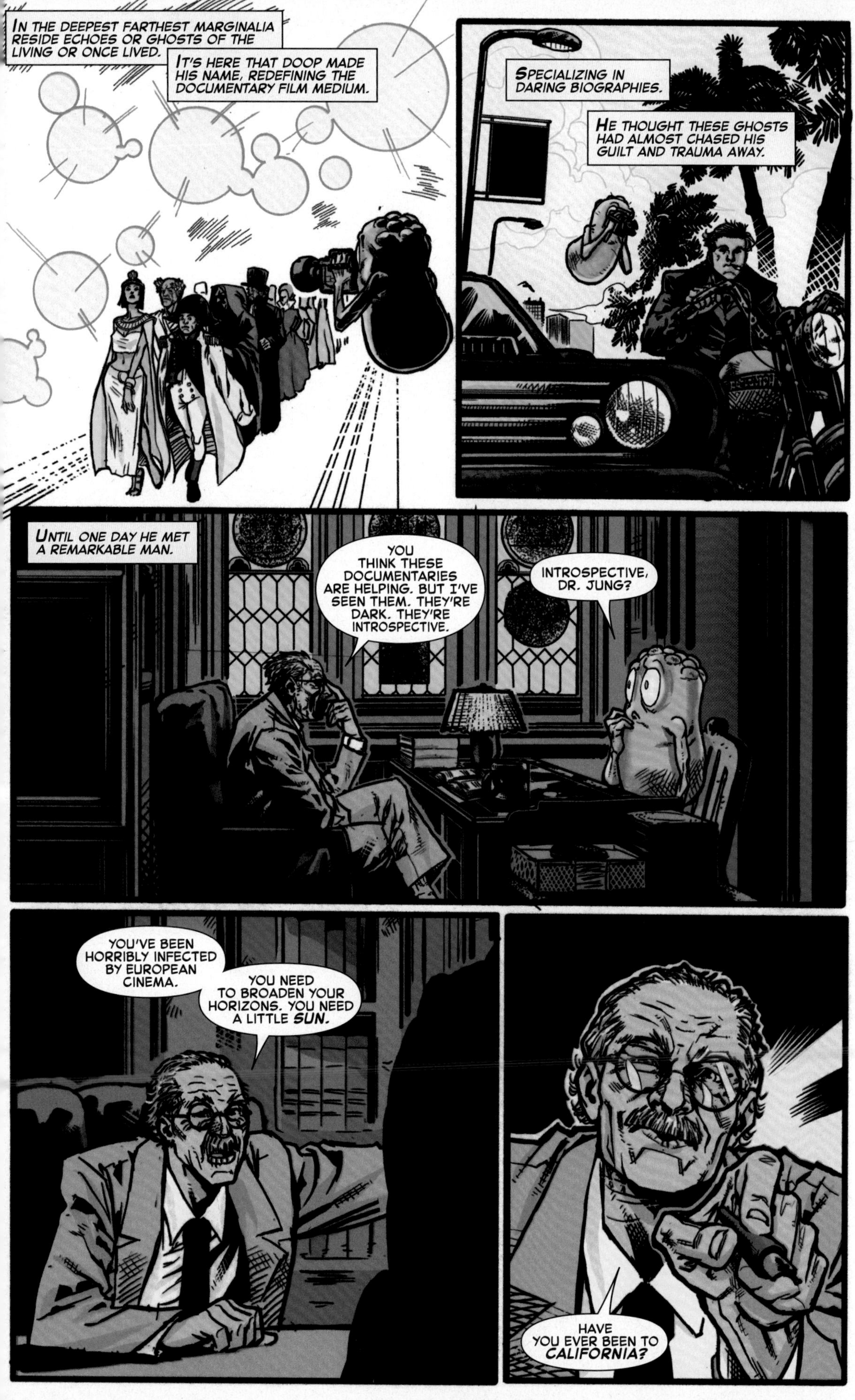
IN THE DEEPEST FARTHEST MARGINALIA RESIDE ECHOES OR GHOSTS OF THE LIVING OR ONCE LIVED.
IT'S HERE THAT DOOP MADE HIS NAME, REDEFINING THE DOCUMENTARY FILM MEDIUM.
SPECIALIZING IN DARING BIOGRAPHIES.
HE THOUGHT THESE GHOSTS HAD ALMOST CHASED HIS GUILT AND TRAUMA AWAY.
UNTIL ONE DAY HE MET A REMARKABLE MAN.
YOU THINK THESE DOCUMENTARIES ARE HELPING. BUT I'VE SEEN THEM. THEY'RE DARK. THEY'RE INTROSPECTIVE.
INTROSPECTIVE, DR. JUNG?
YOU'VE BEEN HORRIBLY INFECTED BY EUROPEAN CINEMA.
YOU NEED TO BROADEN YOUR HORIZONS. YOU NEED A LITTLE SUN.
HAVE YOU EVER BEEN TO CALIFORNIA?

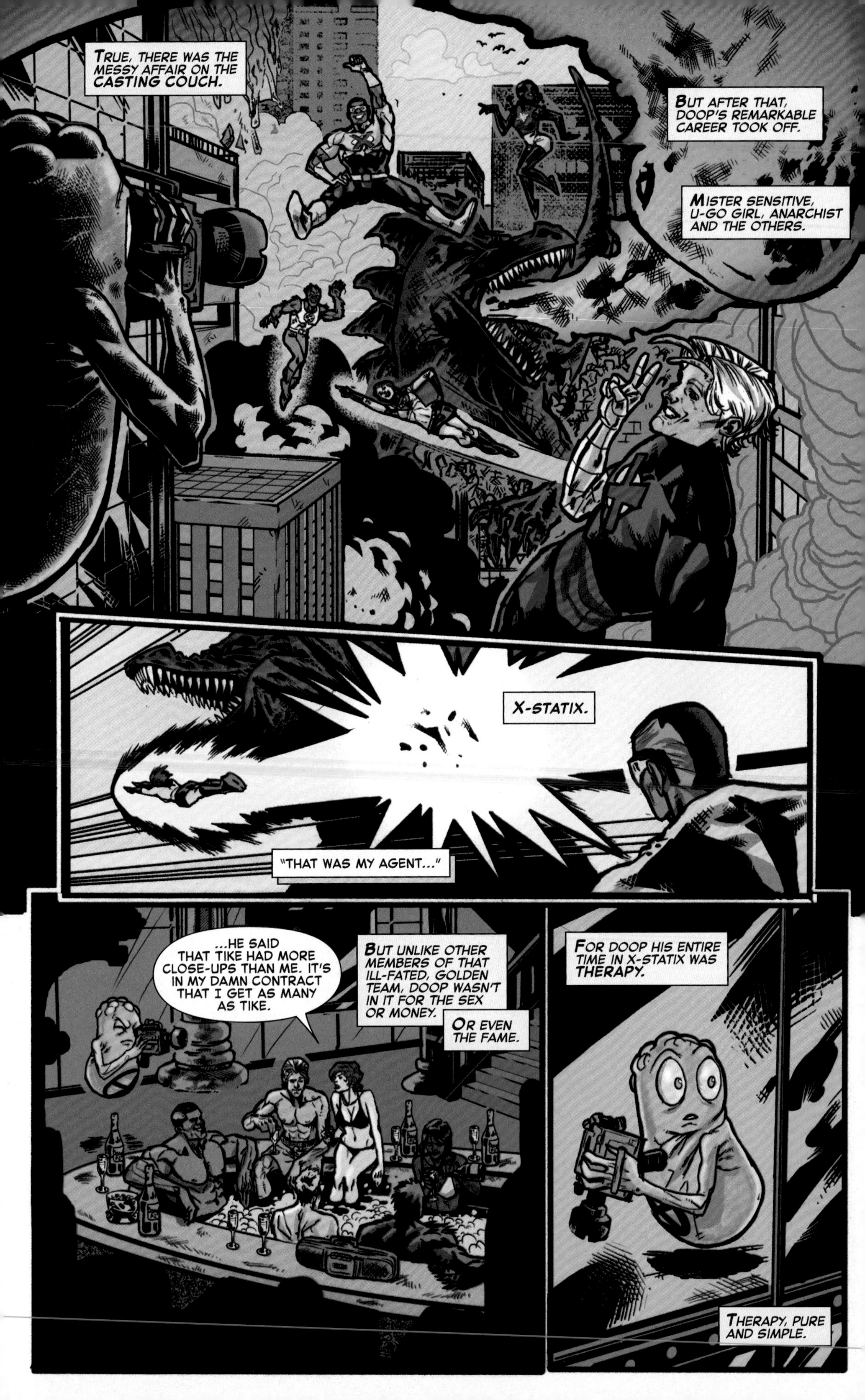
TRUE, THERE WAS THE MESSY AFFAIR ON THE CASTING COUCH.
BUT AFTER THAT, DOOP'S REMARKABLE CAREER TOOK OFF.
MISTER SENSITIVE, U-GO GIRL, ANARCHIST AND THE OTHERS.
X-STATIX.
"THAT WAS MY AGENT..."
...HE SAID THAT TIKE HAD MORE CLOSE-UPS THAN ME. IT'S IN MY DAMN CONTRACT THAT I GET AS MANY AS TIKE.
BUT UNLIKE OTHER MEMBERS OF THAT ILL-FATED, GOLDEN TEAM, DOOP WASN'T IN IT FOR THE SEX OR MONEY.
OR EVEN THE FAME.
FOR DOOP HIS ENTIRE TIME IN X-STATIX WAS THERAPY.
THERAPY, PURE AND SIMPLE.

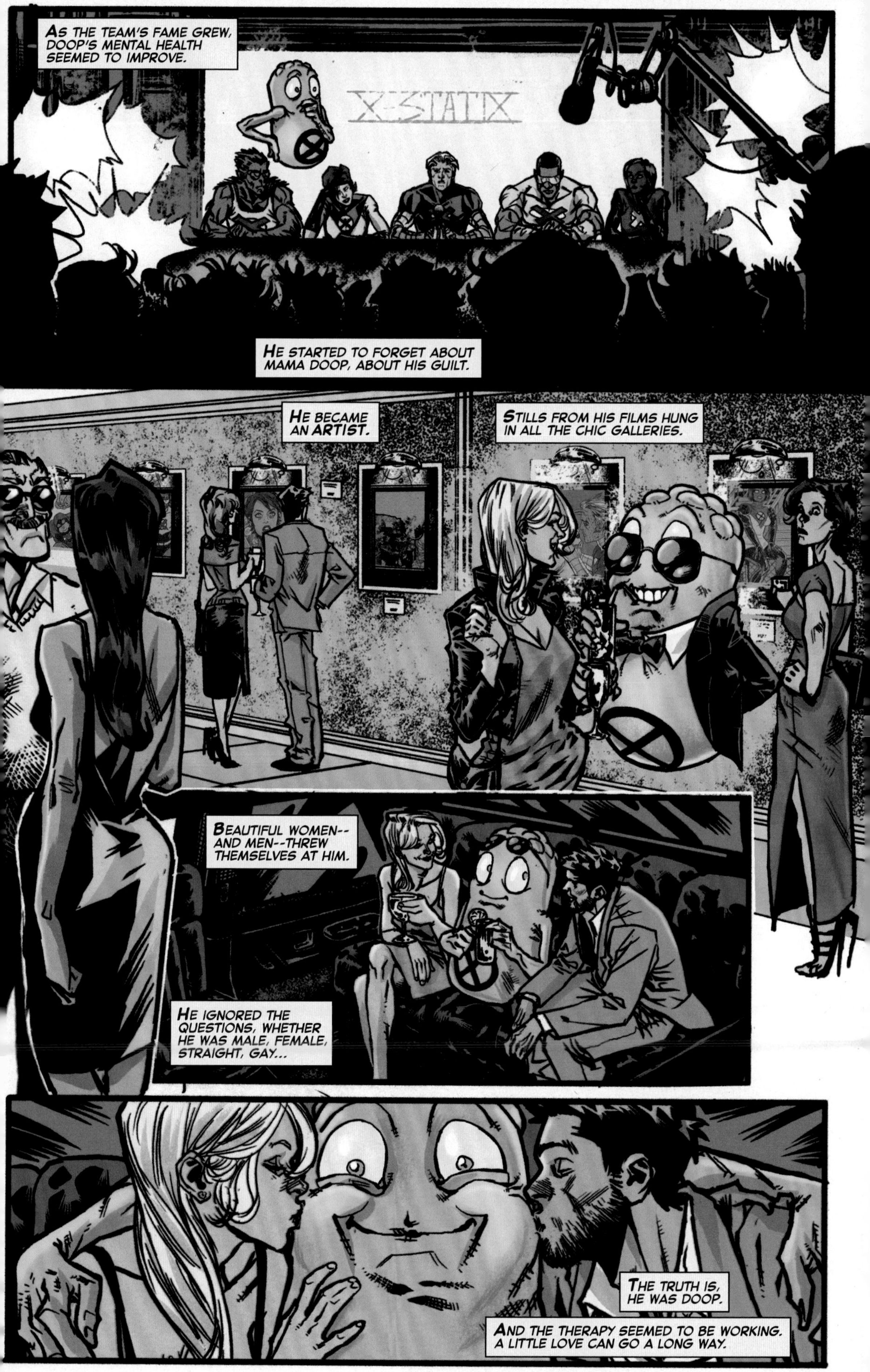
As the team's fame grew, Doop's mental health seemed to improve.
X-STATIX
He started to forget about Mama Doop, about his guilt.
He became an ARTIST.
Stills from his films hung in all the chic galleries.
Beautiful women--and men--threw themselves at him.
He ignored the questions, whether he was male, female, straight, gay...
The truth is, he was Doop.
And the therapy seemed to be working. A little love can go a long way.

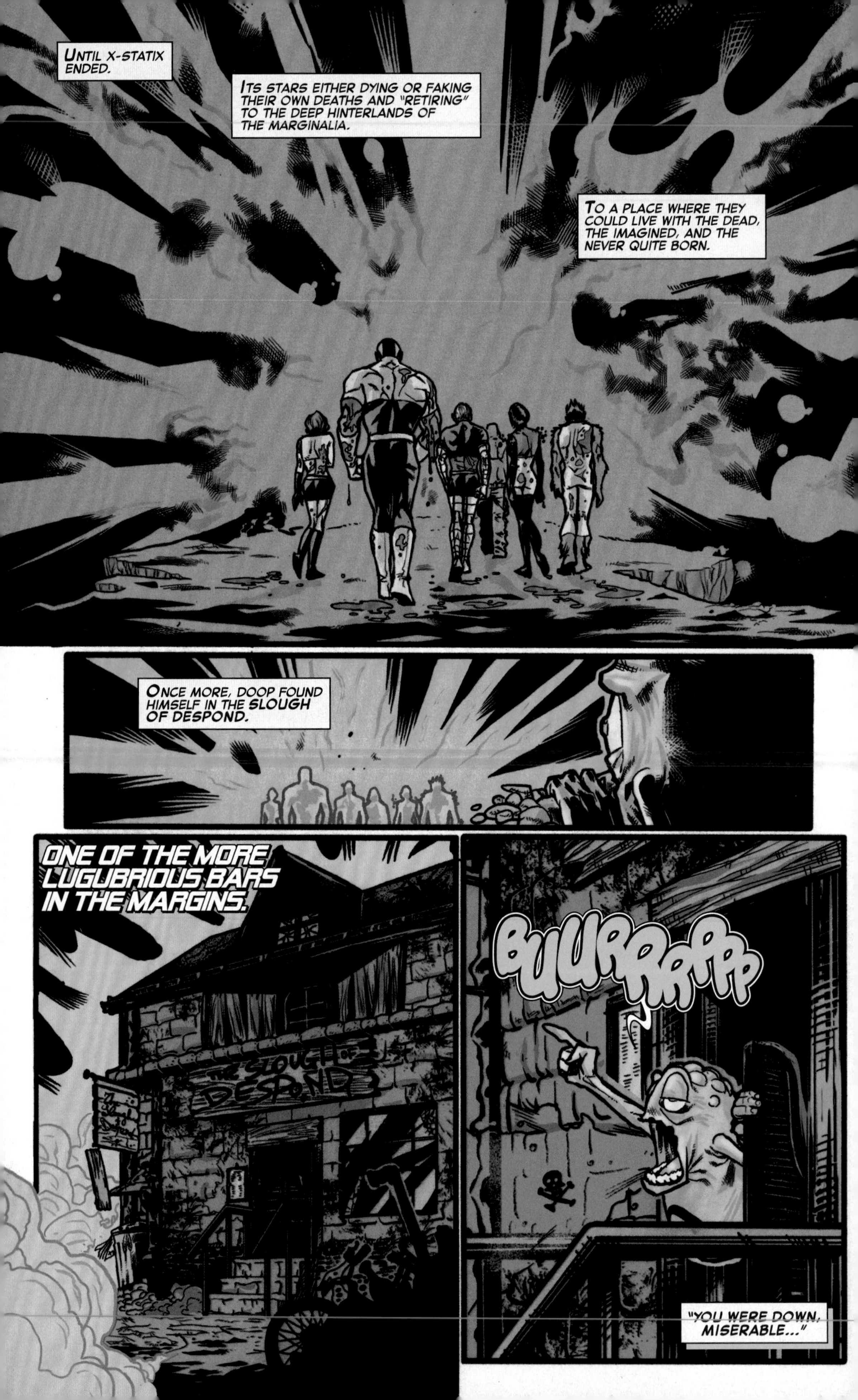
UNTIL X-STATIX ENDED.
ITS STARS EITHER DYING OR FAKING THEIR OWN DEATHS AND "RETIRING" TO THE DEEP HINTERLANDS OF THE MARGINALIA.
TO A PLACE WHERE THEY COULD LIVE WITH THE DEAD, THE IMAGINED, AND THE NEVER QUITE BORN.
ONCE MORE, DOOP FOUND HIMSELF IN THE SLOUGH OF DESPOND.
ONE OF THE MORE LUGUBRIOUS BARS IN THE MARGINS.
THE SLOUGH OF DESPOND
BUURRRPPP
"YOU WERE DOWN, MISERABLE..."

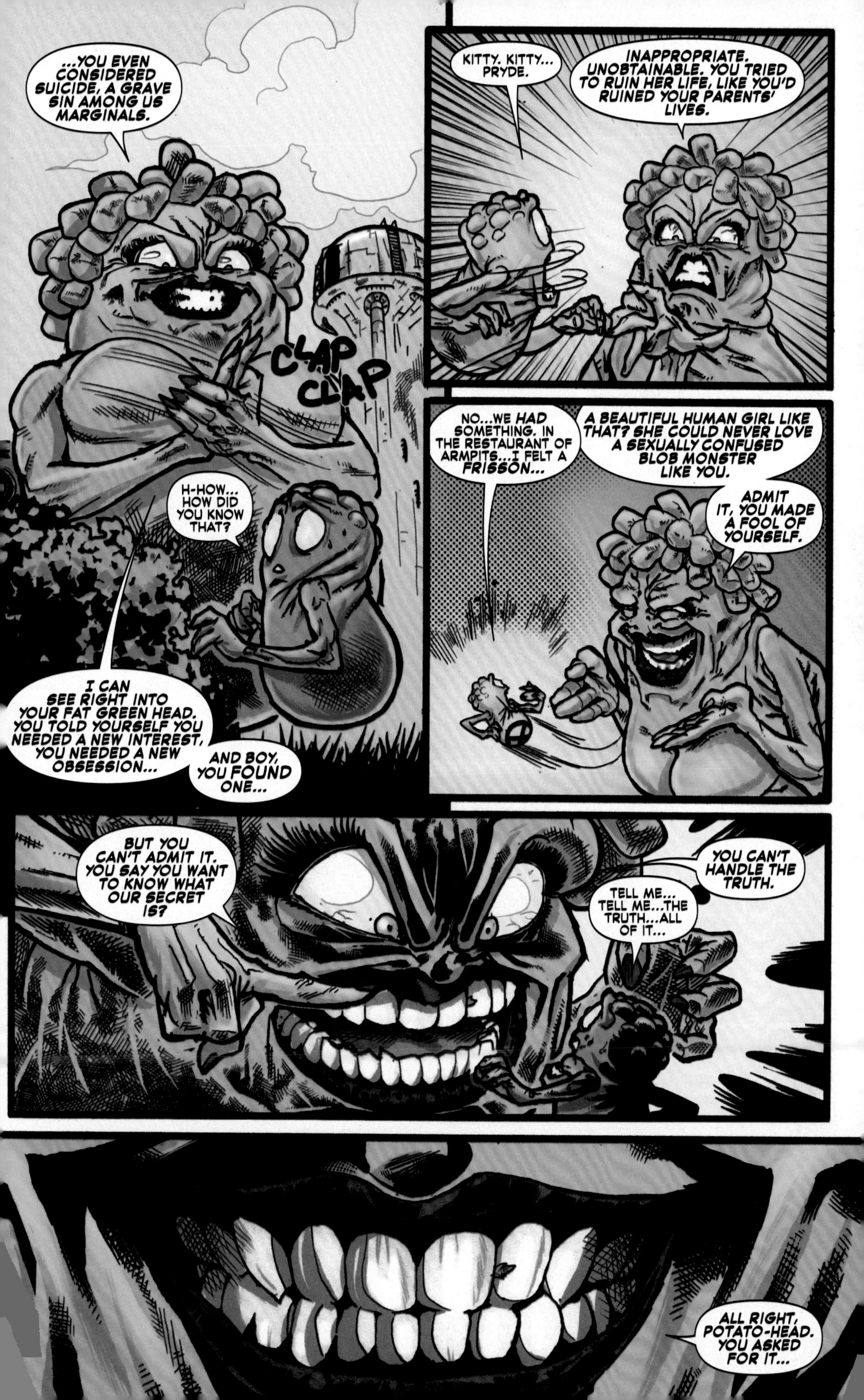
...YOU EVEN CONSIDERED SUICIDE, A GRAVE SIN AMONG US MARGINALS.
CLAP CLAP
H-HOW... HOW DID YOU KNOW THAT?
I CAN SEE RIGHT INTO YOUR FAT GREEN HEAD. YOU TOLD YOURSELF YOU NEEDED A NEW INTEREST, YOU NEEDED A NEW OBSESSION...
AND BOY, YOU FOUND ONE...
KITTY. KITTY... PRYDE.
INAPPROPRIATE. UNOBTAINABLE. YOU TRIED TO RUIN HER LIFE, LIKE YOU'D RUINED YOUR PARENTS' LIVES.
NO...WE HAD SOMETHING. IN THE RESTAURANT OF ARMPITS...I FELT A FRISSON...
A BEAUTIFUL HUMAN GIRL LIKE THAT? SHE COULD NEVER LOVE A SEXUALLY CONFUSED BLOB MONSTER LIKE YOU.
ADMIT IT, YOU MADE A FOOL OF YOURSELF.
BUT YOU CAN'T ADMIT IT. YOU SAY YOU WANT TO KNOW WHAT OUR SECRET IS?
YOU CAN'T HANDLE THE TRUTH.
TELL ME... TELL ME...THE TRUTH...ALL OF IT...
ALL RIGHT, POTATO-HEAD. YOU ASKED FOR IT...

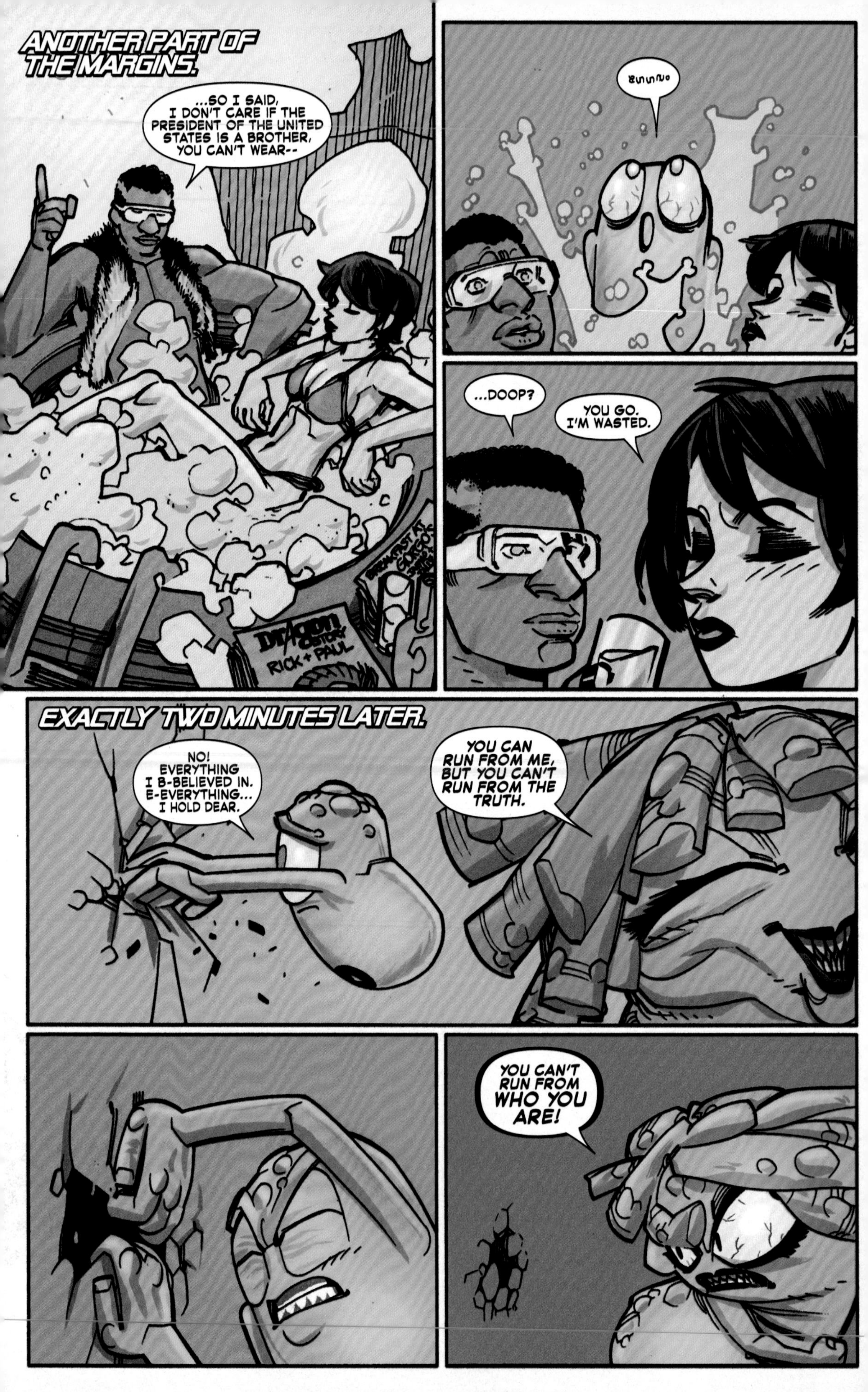
ANOTHER PART OF THE MARGINS.
...SO I SAID, I DON'T CARE IF THE PRESIDENT OF THE UNITED STATES IS A BROTHER, YOU CAN'T WEAR--
DRAGON STORY
RICK + PAUL
...DOOP?
YOU GO. I'M WASTED.
EXACTLY TWO MINUTES LATER.
NO! EVERYTHING I B-BELIEVED IN. E-EVERYTHING... I HOLD DEAR.
YOU CAN RUN FROM ME, BUT YOU CAN'T RUN FROM THE TRUTH.
YOU CAN'T RUN FROM WHO YOU ARE!

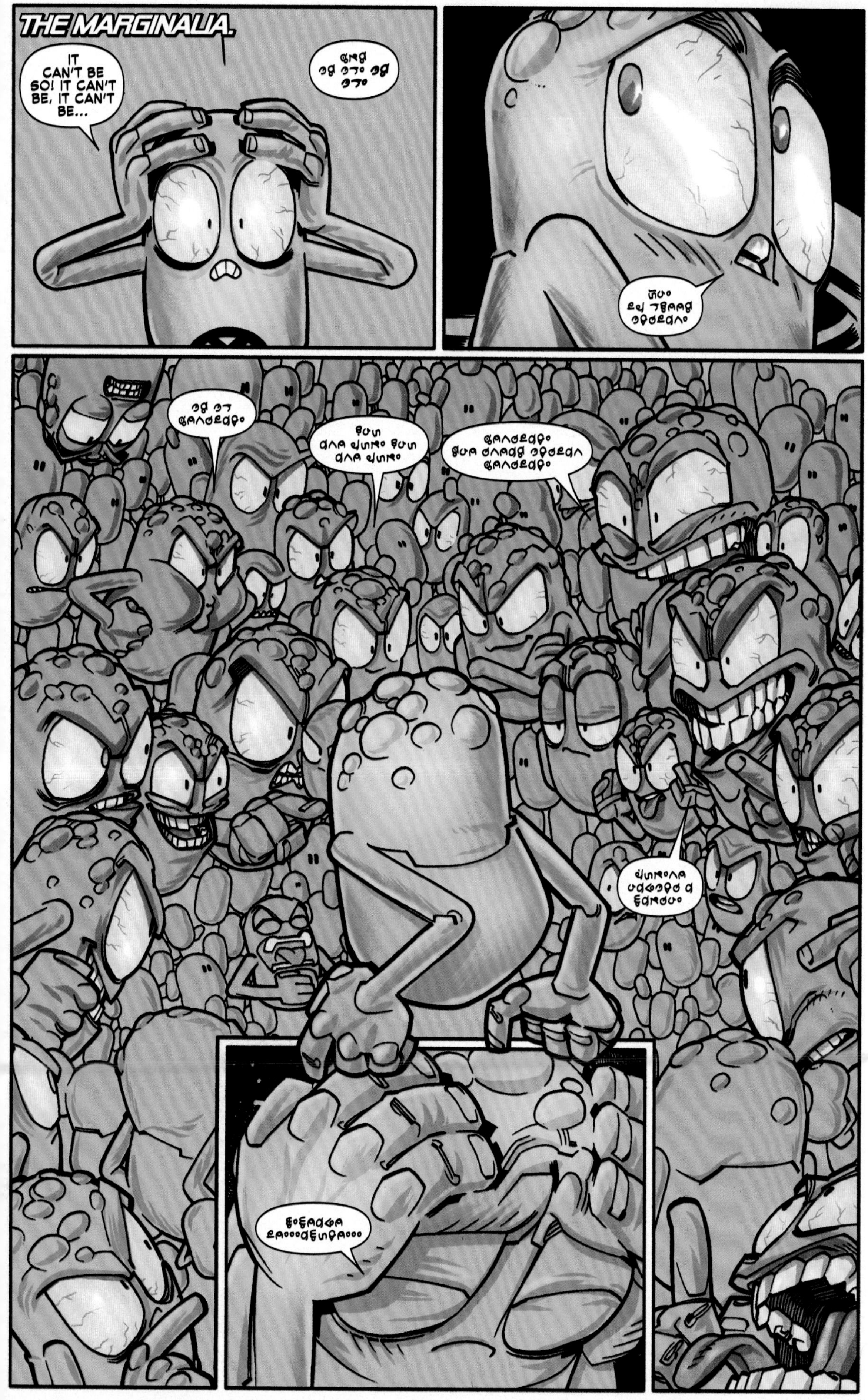
THE MARGINALIA.
IT CAN'T BE SO! IT CAN'T BE, IT CAN'T BE...

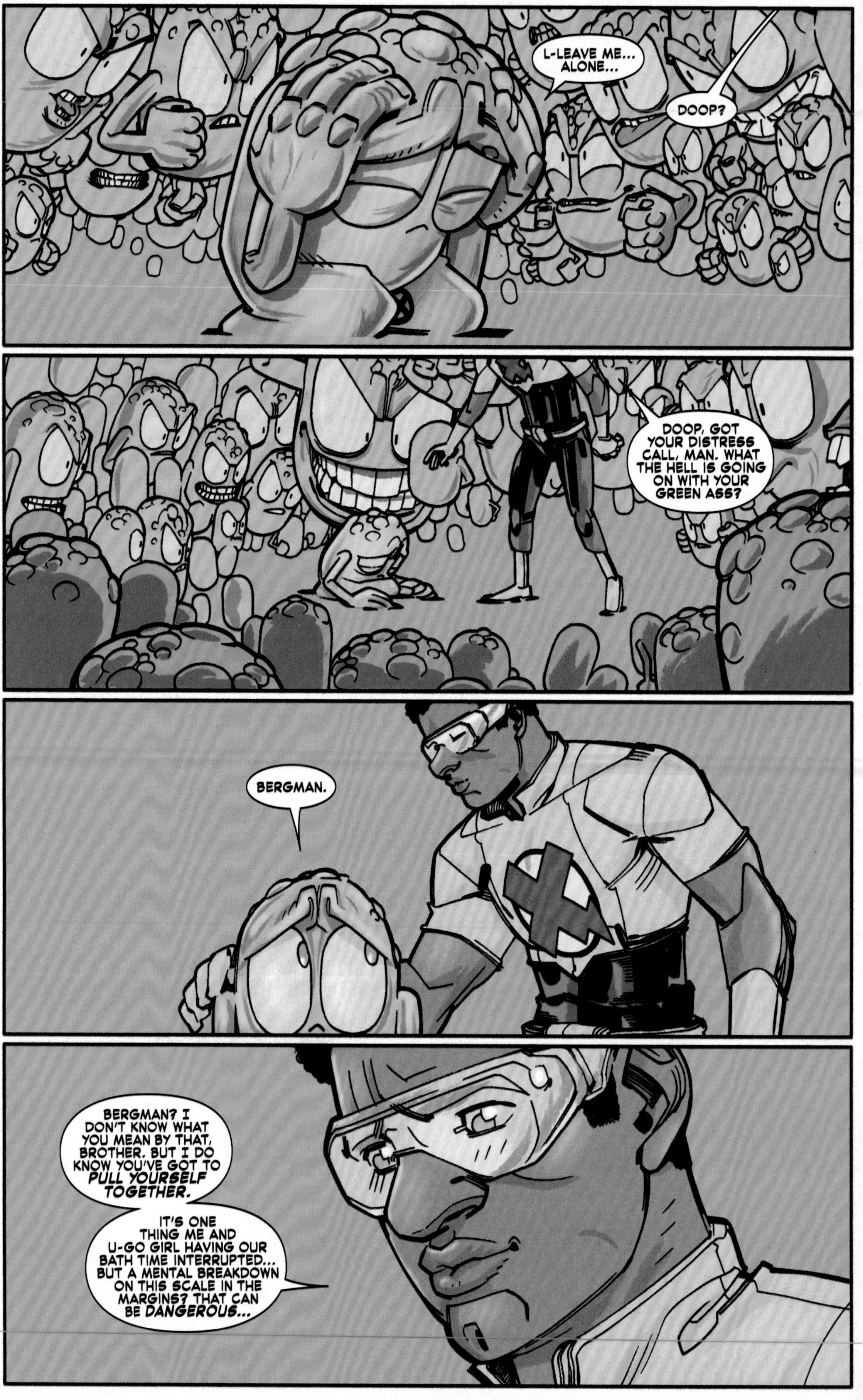
L-LEAVE ME... ALONE...
DOOP?
DOOP, GOT YOUR DISTRESS CALL, MAN. WHAT THE HELL IS GOING ON WITH YOUR GREEN ASS?
BERGMAN.
BERGMAN? I DON'T KNOW WHAT YOU MEAN BY THAT, BROTHER. BUT I DO KNOW YOU'VE GOT TO *PULL YOURSELF TOGETHER.*
IT'S ONE THING ME AND U-GO GIRL HAVING OUR BATH TIME INTERRUPTED... BUT A MENTAL BREAKDOWN ON THIS SCALE IN THE MARGINS? THAT CAN BE *DANGEROUS...*

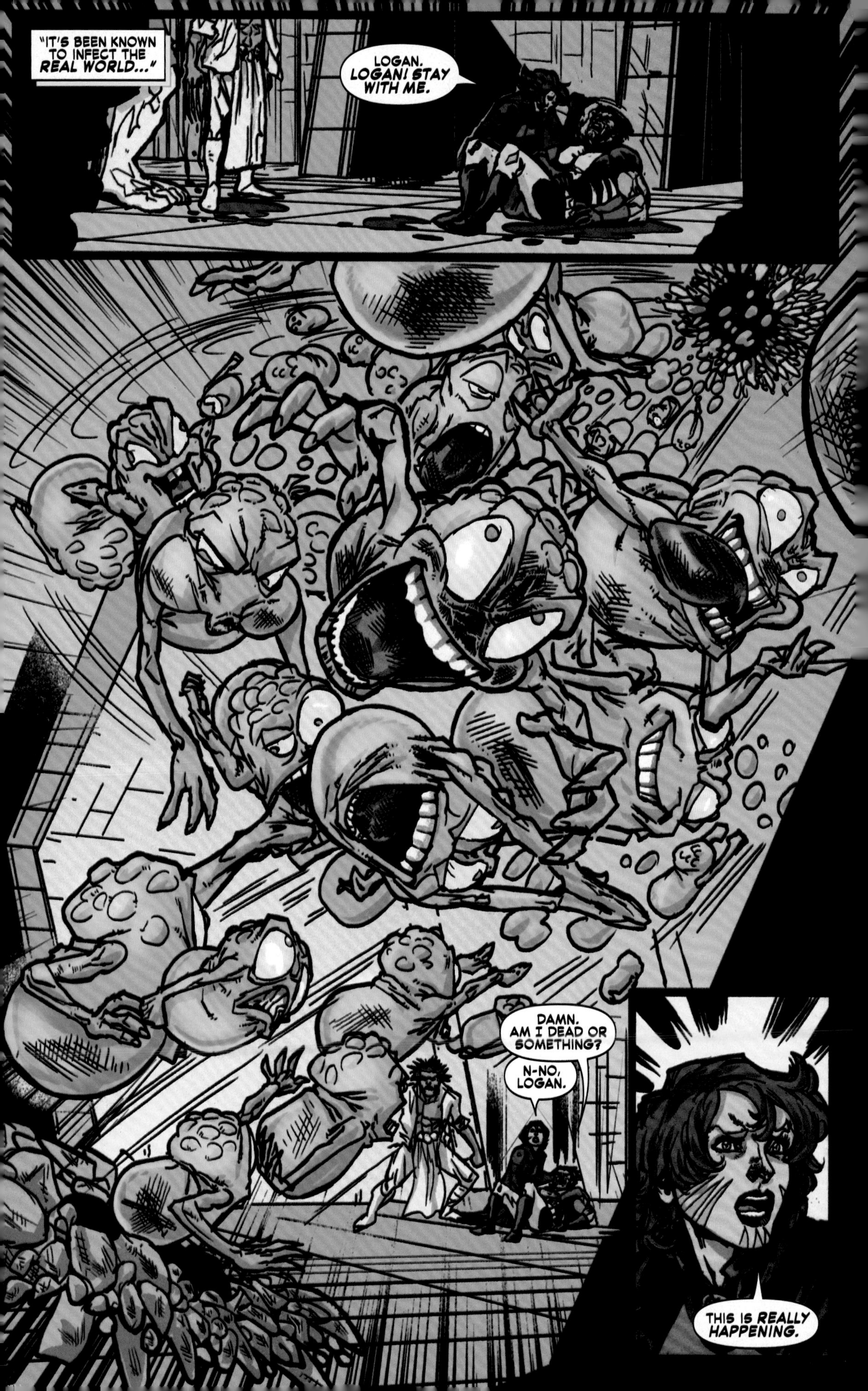
"IT'S BEEN KNOWN TO INFECT THE REAL WORLD..."
LOGAN. LOGAN! STAY WITH ME.
DAMN. AM I DEAD OR SOMETHING?
N-NO, LOGAN.
THIS IS REALLY HAPPENING.

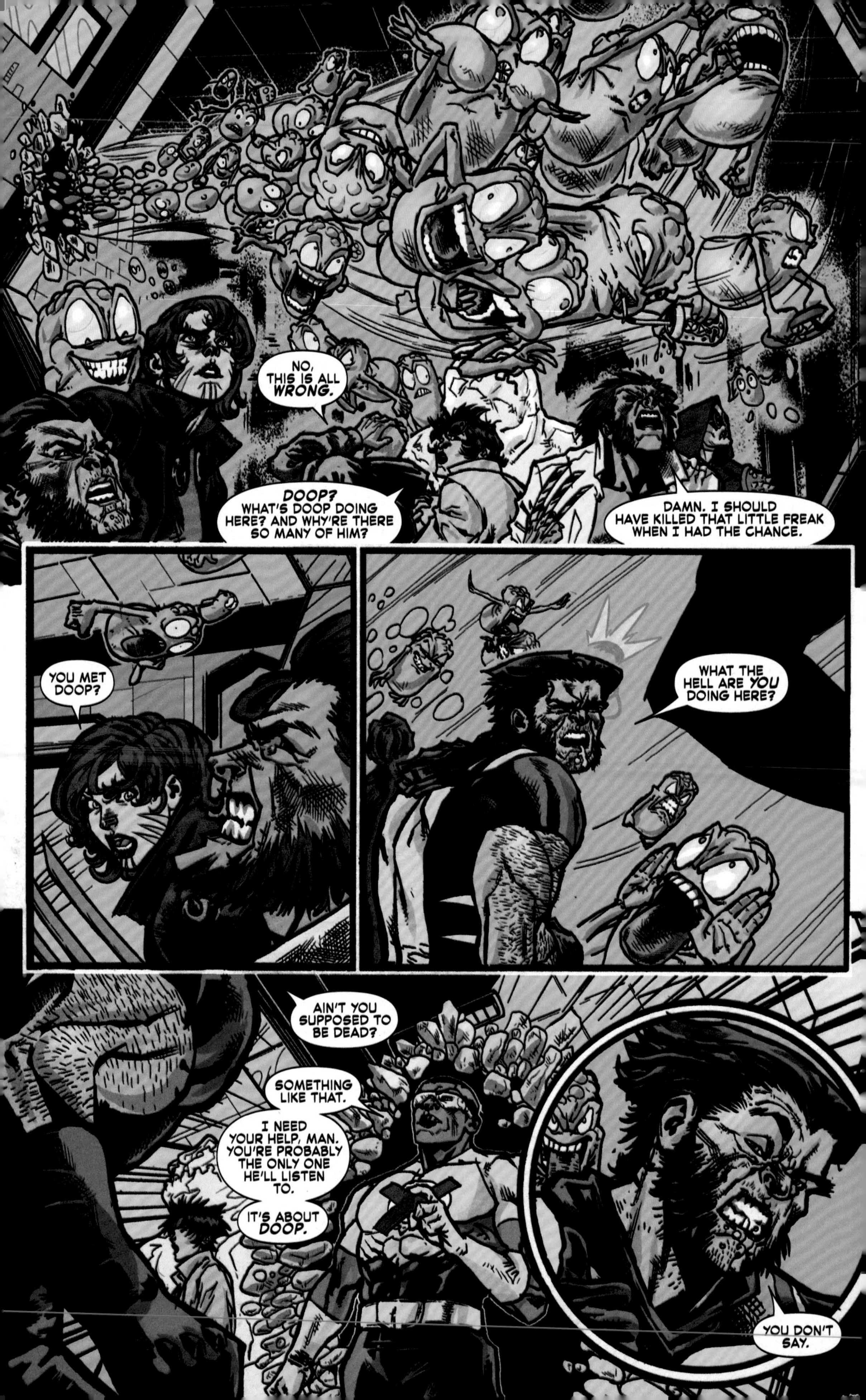
NO, THIS IS ALL *WRONG.*
DOOP? WHAT'S DOOP DOING HERE? AND WHY'RE THERE SO MANY OF HIM?
DAMN. I SHOULD HAVE KILLED THAT LITTLE FREAK WHEN I HAD THE CHANCE.
YOU MET DOOP?
WHAT THE HELL ARE *YOU* DOING HERE?
AIN'T YOU SUPPOSED TO BE DEAD?
SOMETHING LIKE THAT.
I NEED YOUR HELP, MAN. YOU'RE PROBABLY THE ONLY ONE HE'LL LISTEN TO.
IT'S ABOUT *DOOP.*
YOU DON'T SAY.

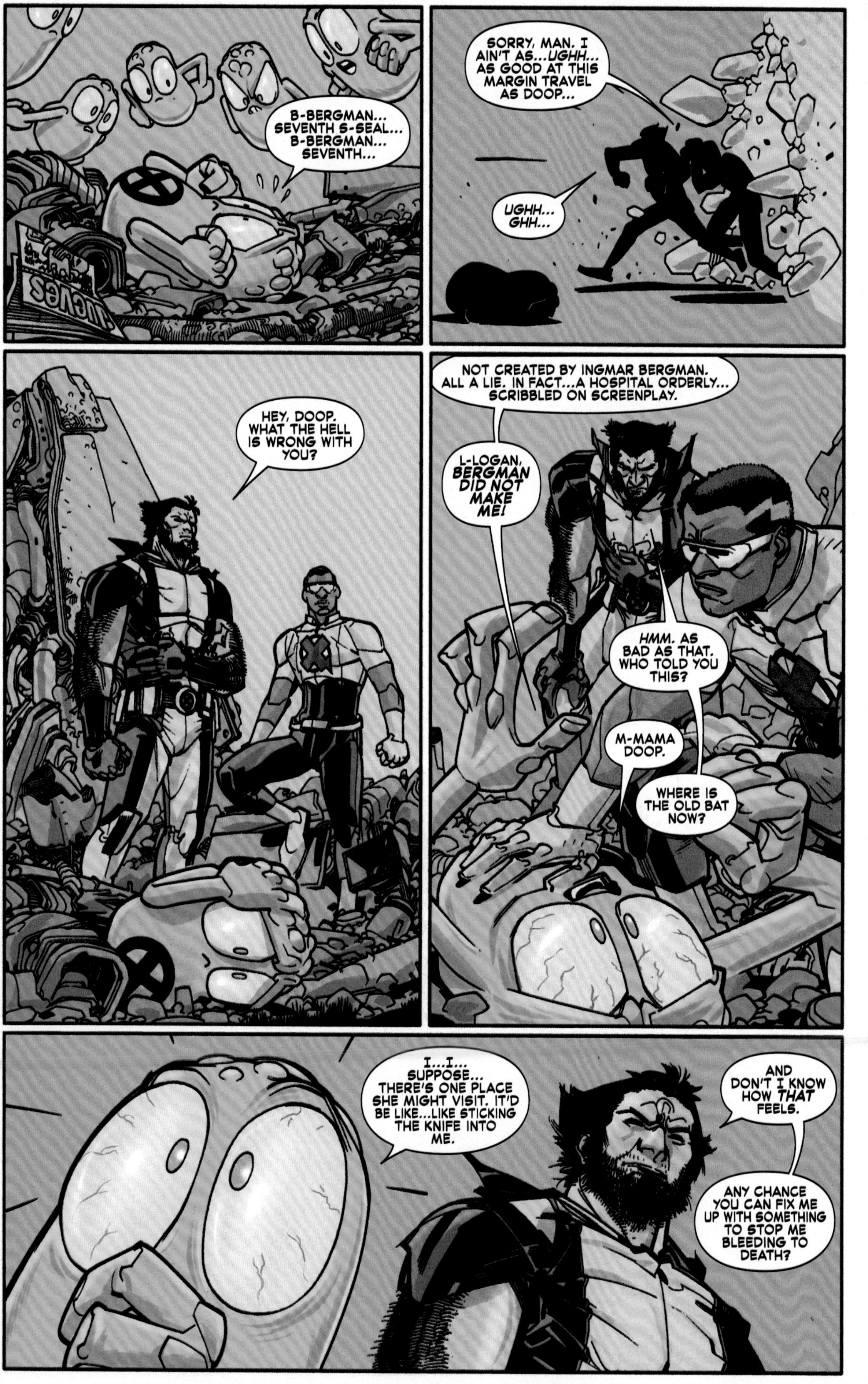
B-BERGMAN... SEVENTH S-SEAL... B-BERGMAN... SEVENTH...
SORRY, MAN. I AIN'T AS...UGHH... AS GOOD AT THIS MARGIN TRAVEL AS DOOP...
UGHH... GHH...
HEY, DOOP. WHAT THE HELL IS WRONG WITH YOU?
NOT CREATED BY INGMAR BERGMAN. ALL A LIE. IN FACT...A HOSPITAL ORDERLY... SCRIBBLED ON SCREENPLAY.
L-LOGAN, BERGMAN DID NOT MAKE ME!
HMM. AS BAD AS THAT. WHO TOLD YOU THIS?
M-MAMA DOOP.
WHERE IS THE OLD BAT NOW?
I...I... SUPPOSE... THERE'S ONE PLACE SHE MIGHT VISIT. IT'D BE LIKE...LIKE STICKING THE KNIFE INTO ME.
AND DON'T I KNOW HOW THAT FEELS.
ANY CHANCE YOU CAN FIX ME UP WITH SOMETHING TO STOP ME BLEEDING TO DEATH?

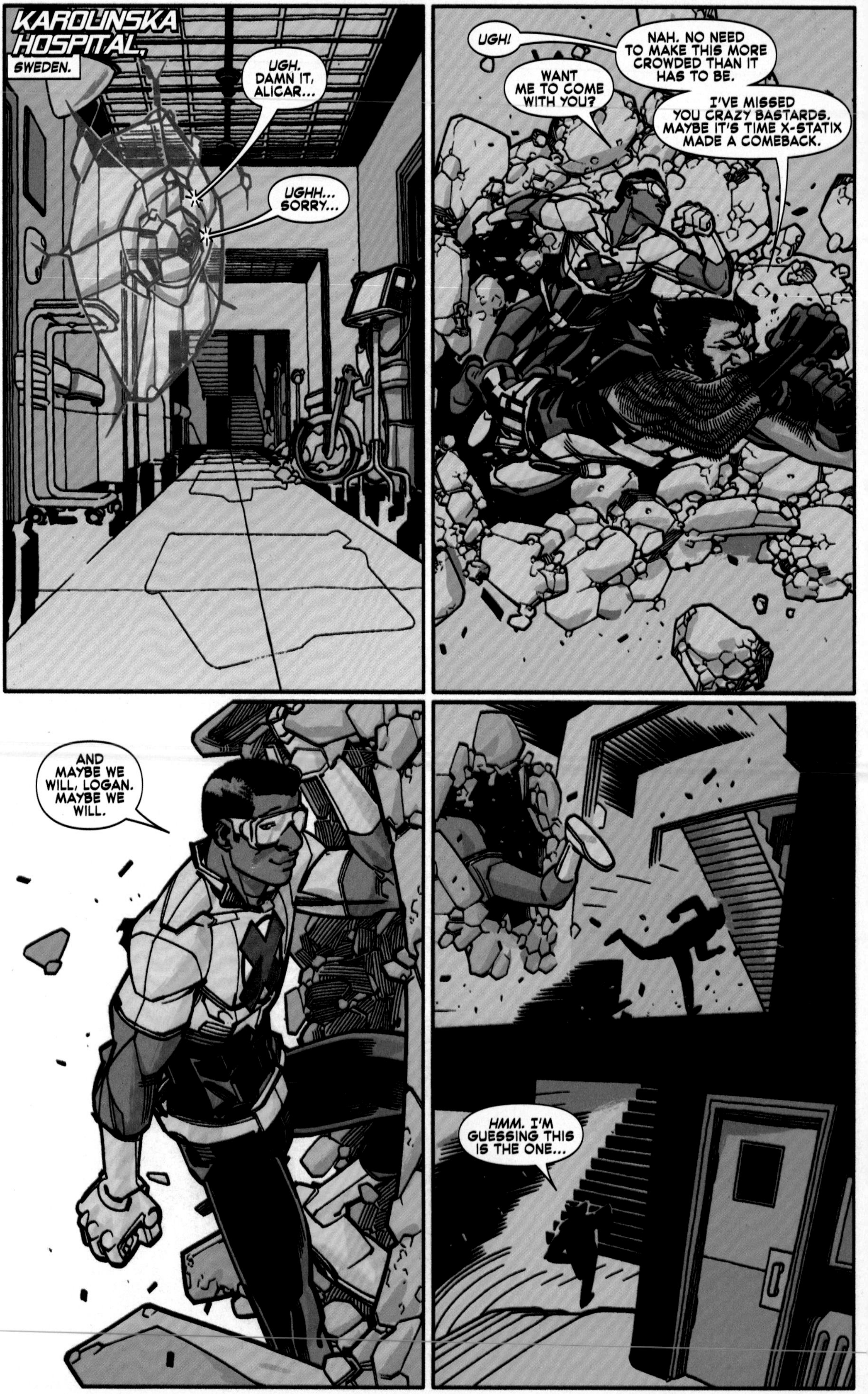
KAROLINSKA HOSPITAL,
SWEDEN.
UGH. DAMN IT, ALICAR...
UGHH... SORRY...
UGH!
WANT ME TO COME WITH YOU?
NAH. NO NEED TO MAKE THIS MORE CROWDED THAN IT HAS TO BE.
I'VE MISSED YOU CRAZY BASTARDS. MAYBE IT'S TIME X-STATIX MADE A COMEBACK.
AND MAYBE WE WILL, LOGAN. MAYBE WE WILL.
HMM. I'M GUESSING THIS IS THE ONE...

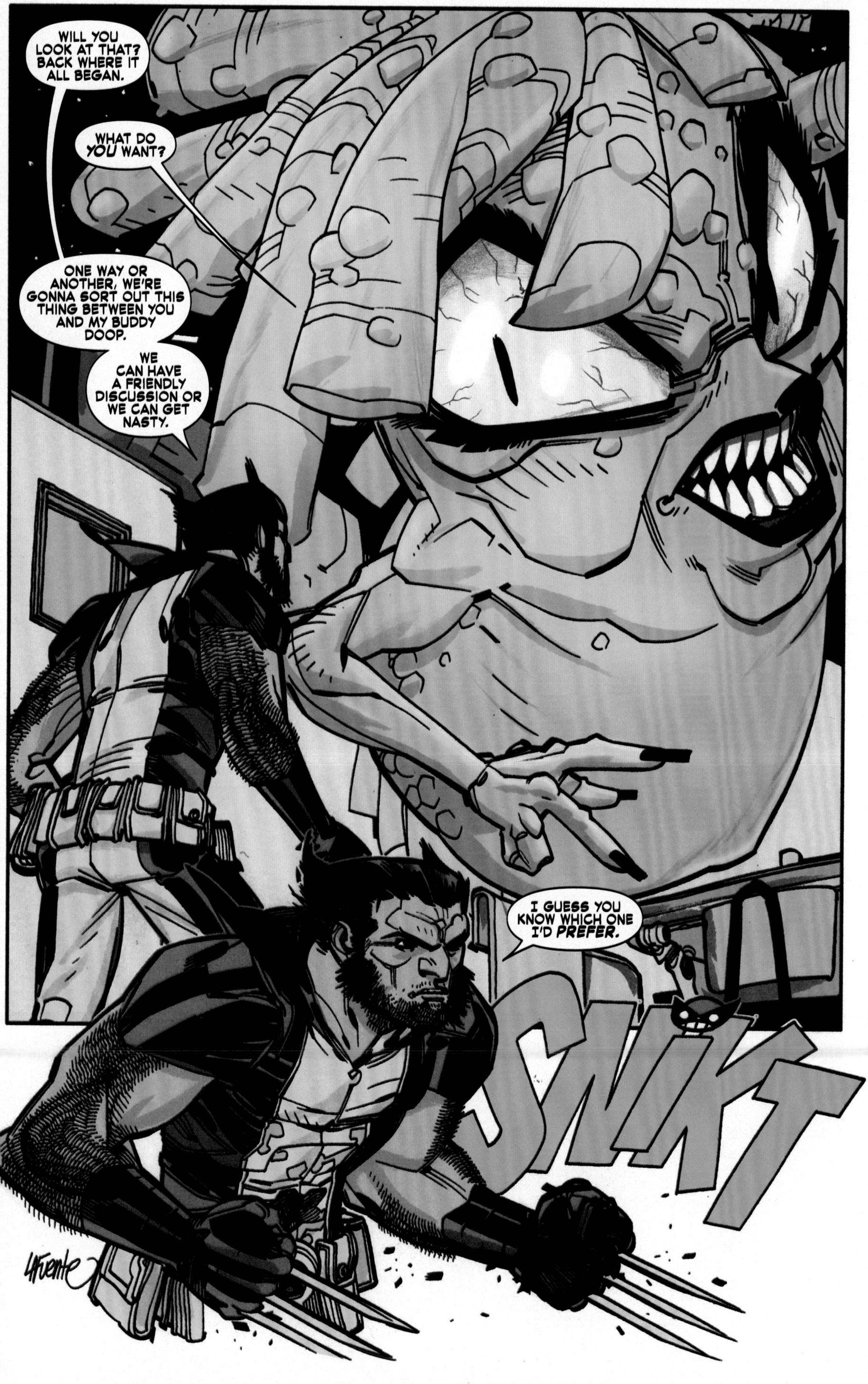

WILL YOU LOOK AT THAT? BACK WHERE IT ALL BEGAN.
WHAT DO *YOU* WANT?
ONE WAY OR ANOTHER, WE'RE GONNA SORT OUT THIS THING BETWEEN YOU AND MY BUDDY DOOP.
WE CAN HAVE A FRIENDLY DISCUSSION OR WE CAN GET NASTY.
I GUESS YOU KNOW WHICH ONE I'D *PREFER.*
SNIKT

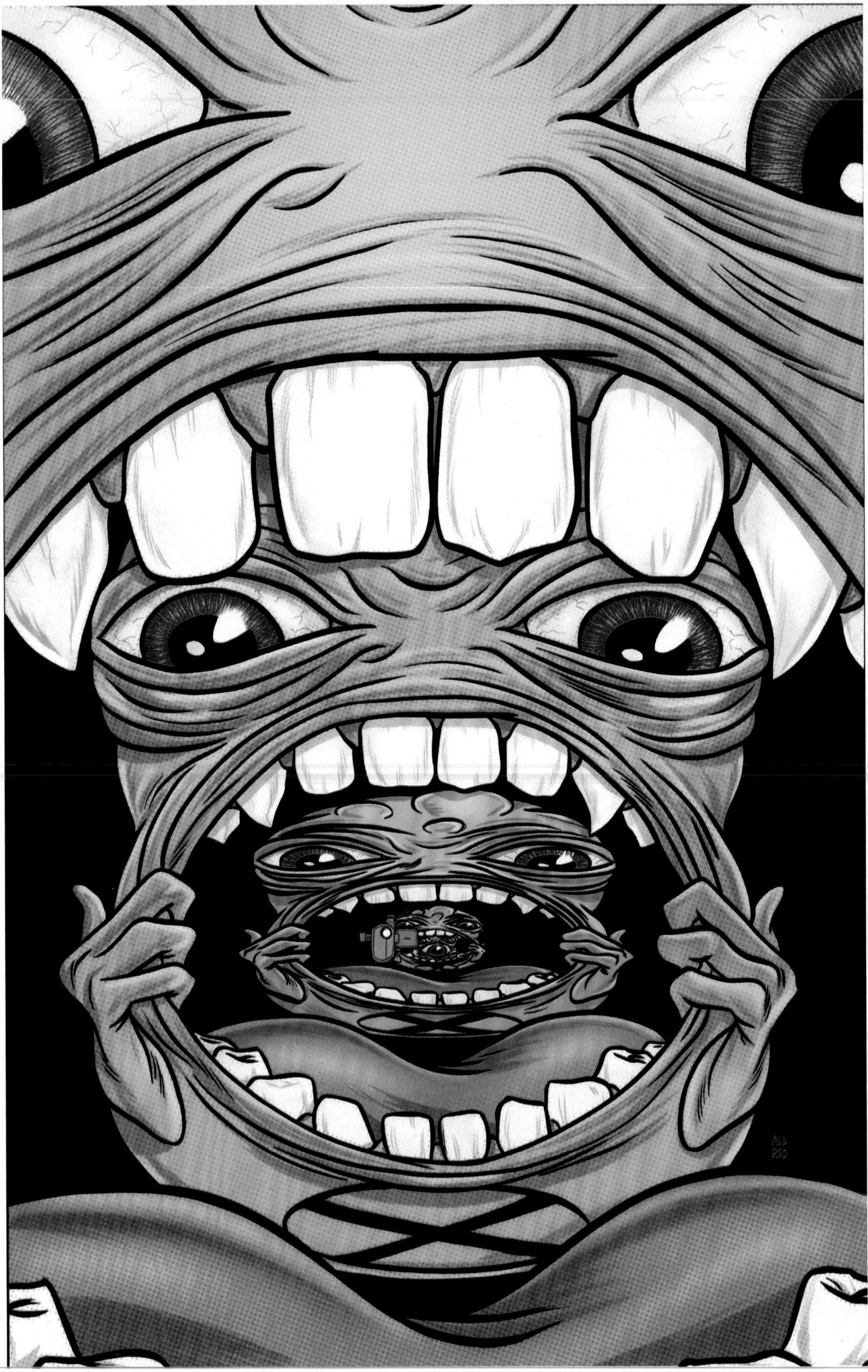
ALL
RED

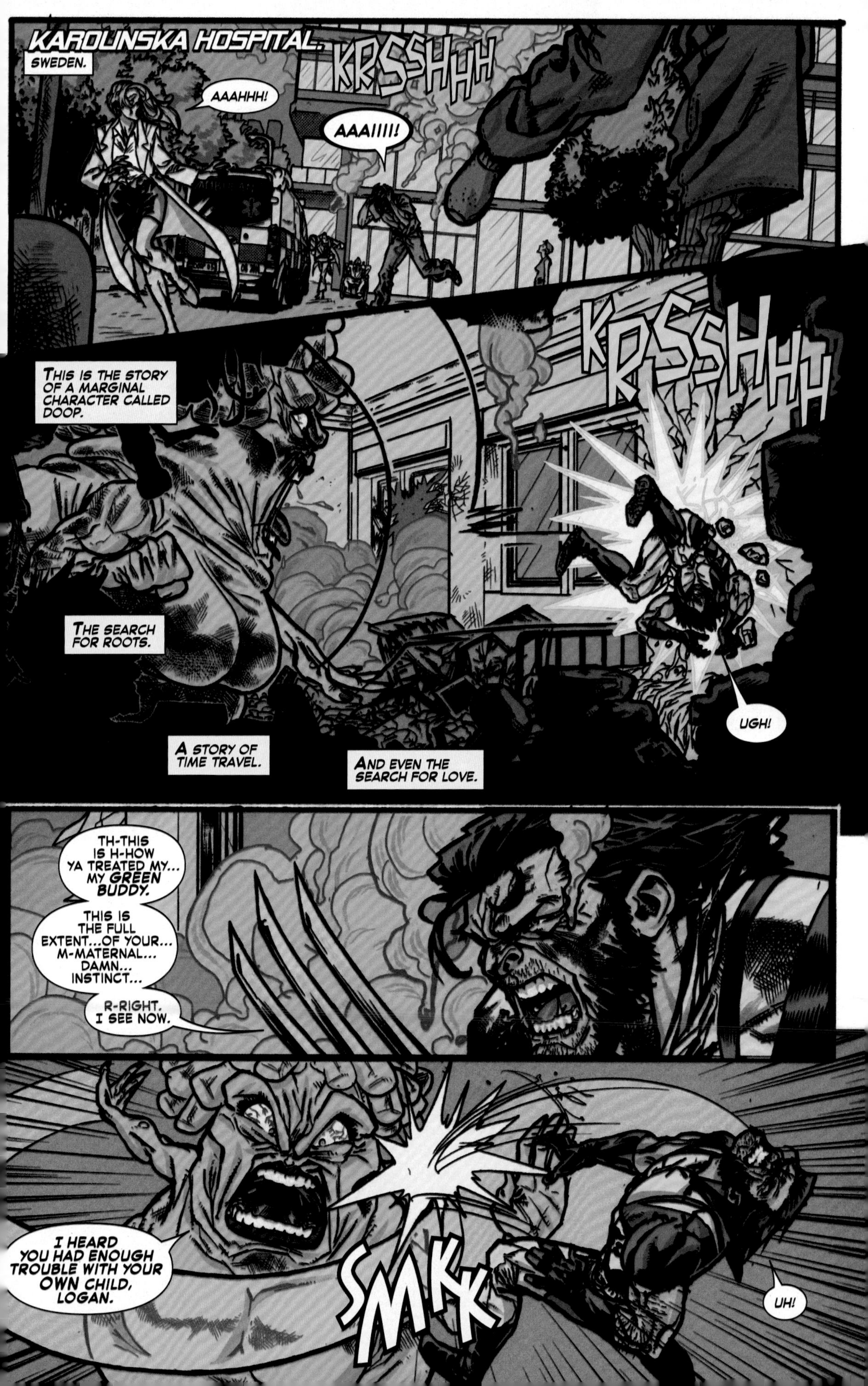
KAROLINSKA HOSPITAL.
SWEDEN.
KRSSHHH
AAAHHH!
AAAIIII!
KRSSHHHH
THIS IS THE STORY OF A MARGINAL CHARACTER CALLED DOOP.
THE SEARCH FOR ROOTS.
A STORY OF TIME TRAVEL.
AND EVEN THE SEARCH FOR LOVE.
UGH!
TH-THIS IS H-HOW YA TREATED MY... MY GREEN BUDDY.
THIS IS THE FULL EXTENT...OF YOUR... M-MATERNAL... DAMN... INSTINCT...
R-RIGHT. I SEE NOW.
I HEARD YOU HAD ENOUGH TROUBLE WITH YOUR OWN CHILD, LOGAN.
SMKK
UH!

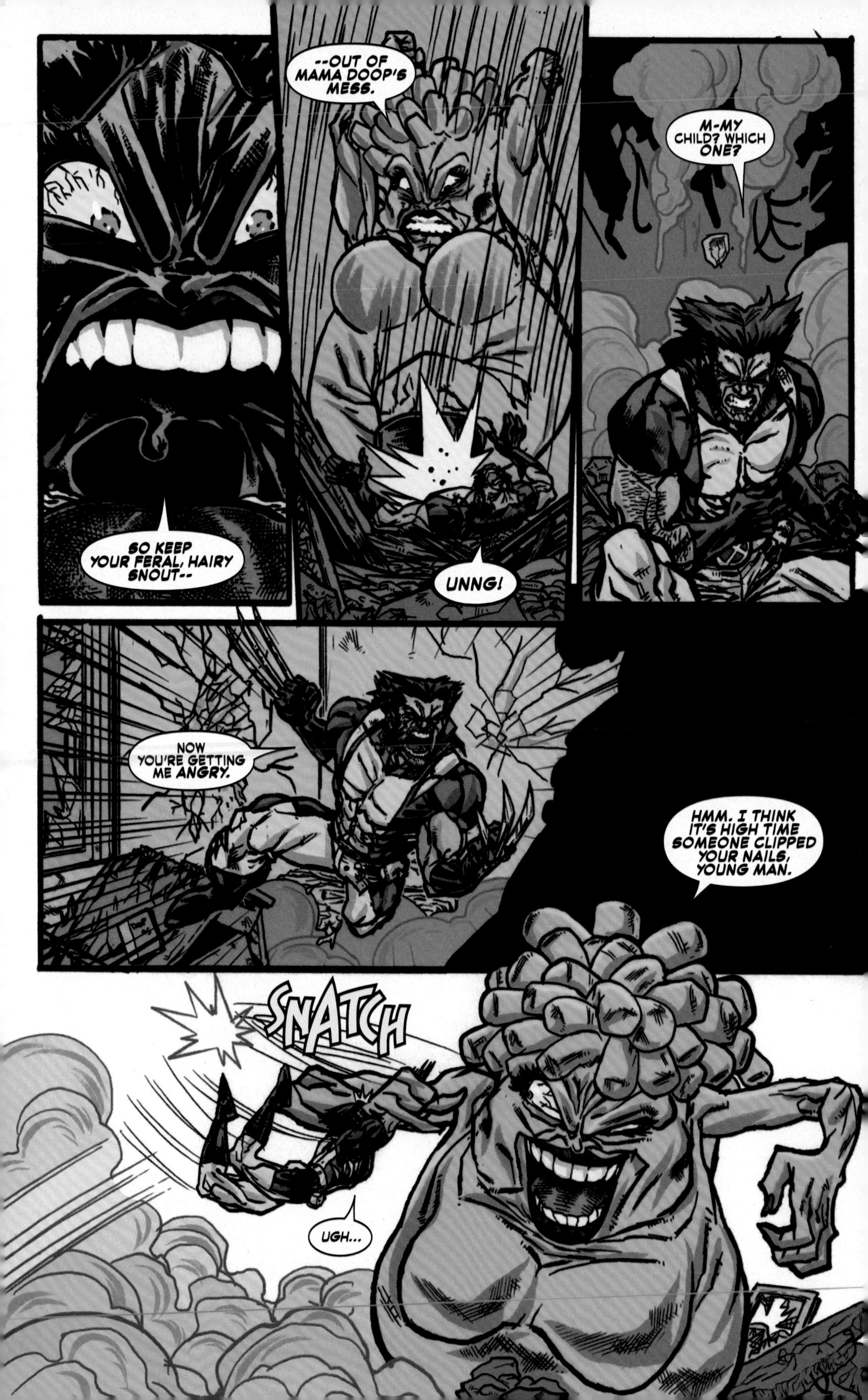
SO KEEP YOUR FERAL, HAIRY SNOUT--
--OUT OF MAMA DOOP'S MESS.
UNNG!
M-MY CHILD? WHICH ONE?
NOW YOU'RE GETTING ME ANGRY.
HMM. I THINK IT'S HIGH TIME SOMEONE CLIPPED YOUR NAILS, YOUNG MAN.
SNATCH
UGH...

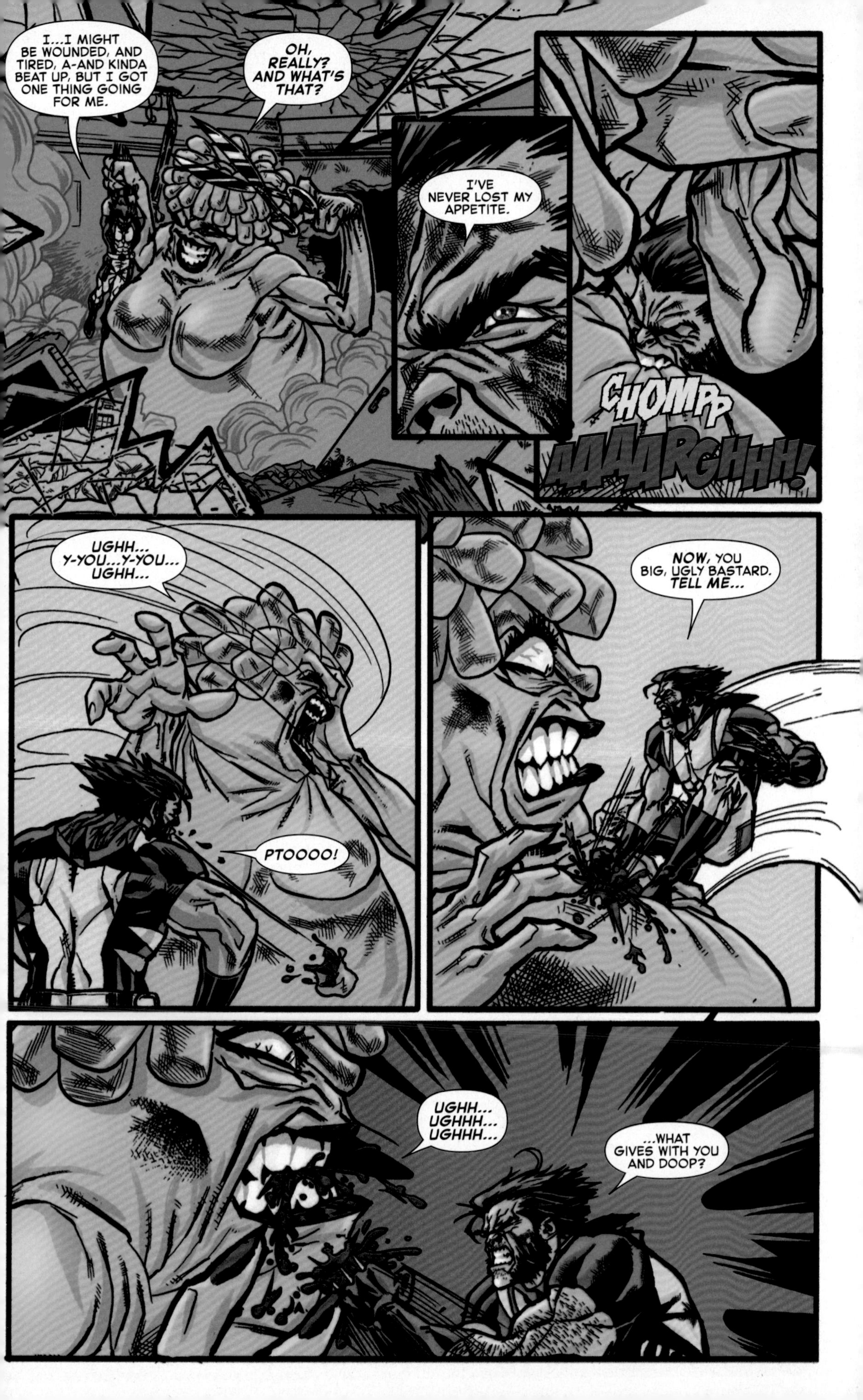
I...I MIGHT BE WOUNDED, AND TIRED, A-AND KINDA BEAT UP, BUT I GOT ONE THING GOING FOR ME.
OH, REALLY? AND WHAT'S THAT?
I'VE NEVER LOST MY APPETITE.
CHOMPP
AAAARGHHH!
UGHH... Y-YOU...Y-YOU... UGHH...
PTOOOO!
NOW, YOU BIG, UGLY BASTARD. TELL ME...
UGHH... UGHHH... UGHHH...
...WHAT GIVES WITH YOU AND DOOP?

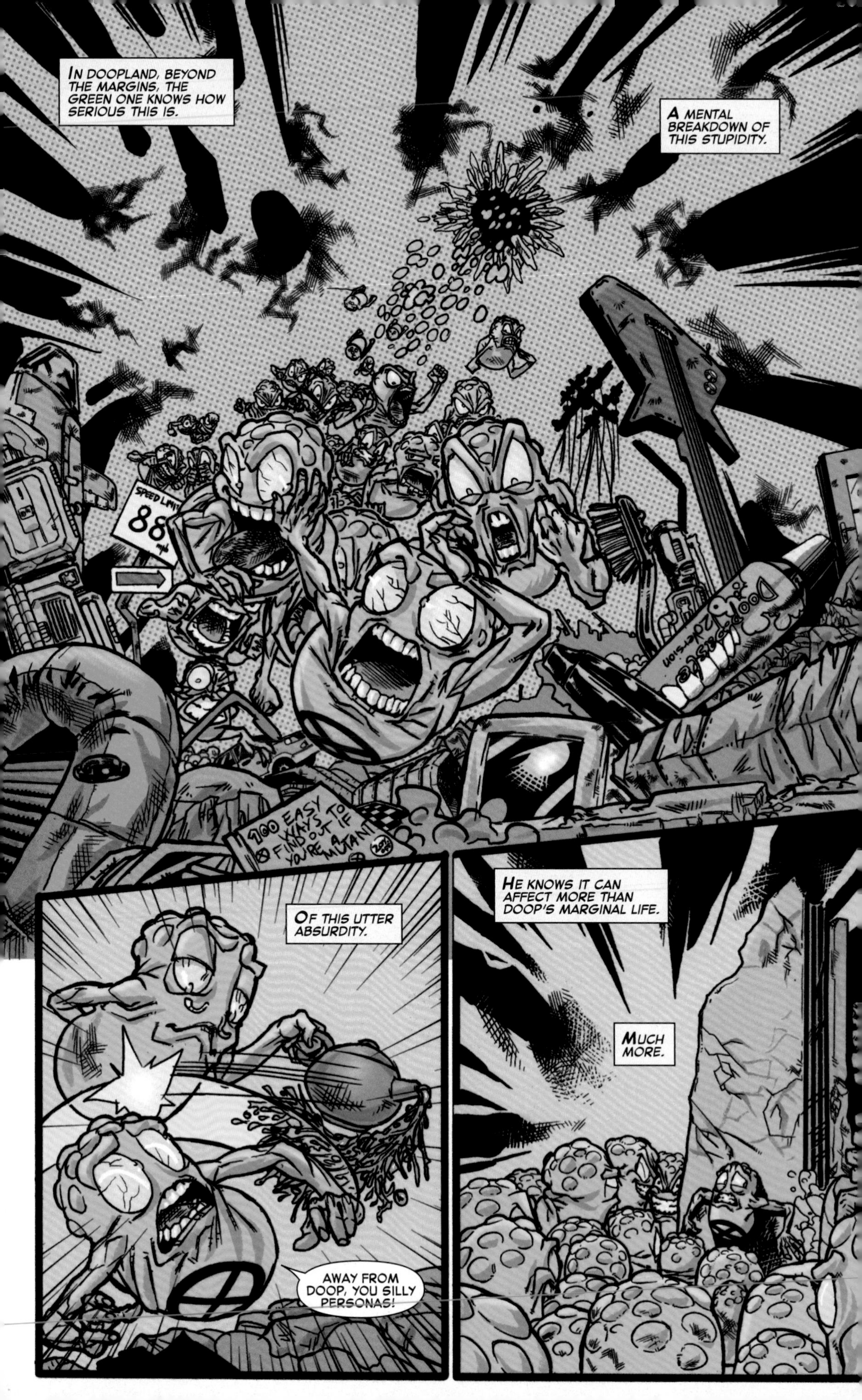
IN DOOPLAND, BEYOND THE MARGINS, THE GREEN ONE KNOWS HOW SERIOUS THIS IS.
A MENTAL BREAKDOWN OF THIS STUPIDITY.
SPEED LIMIT
88
100 EASY WAYS TO FIND OUT IF YOU'RE A MUTANT
OF THIS UTTER ABSURDITY.
AWAY FROM DOOP, YOU SILLY PERSONAS!
HE KNOWS IT CAN AFFECT MORE THAN DOOP'S MARGINAL LIFE.
MUCH MORE.

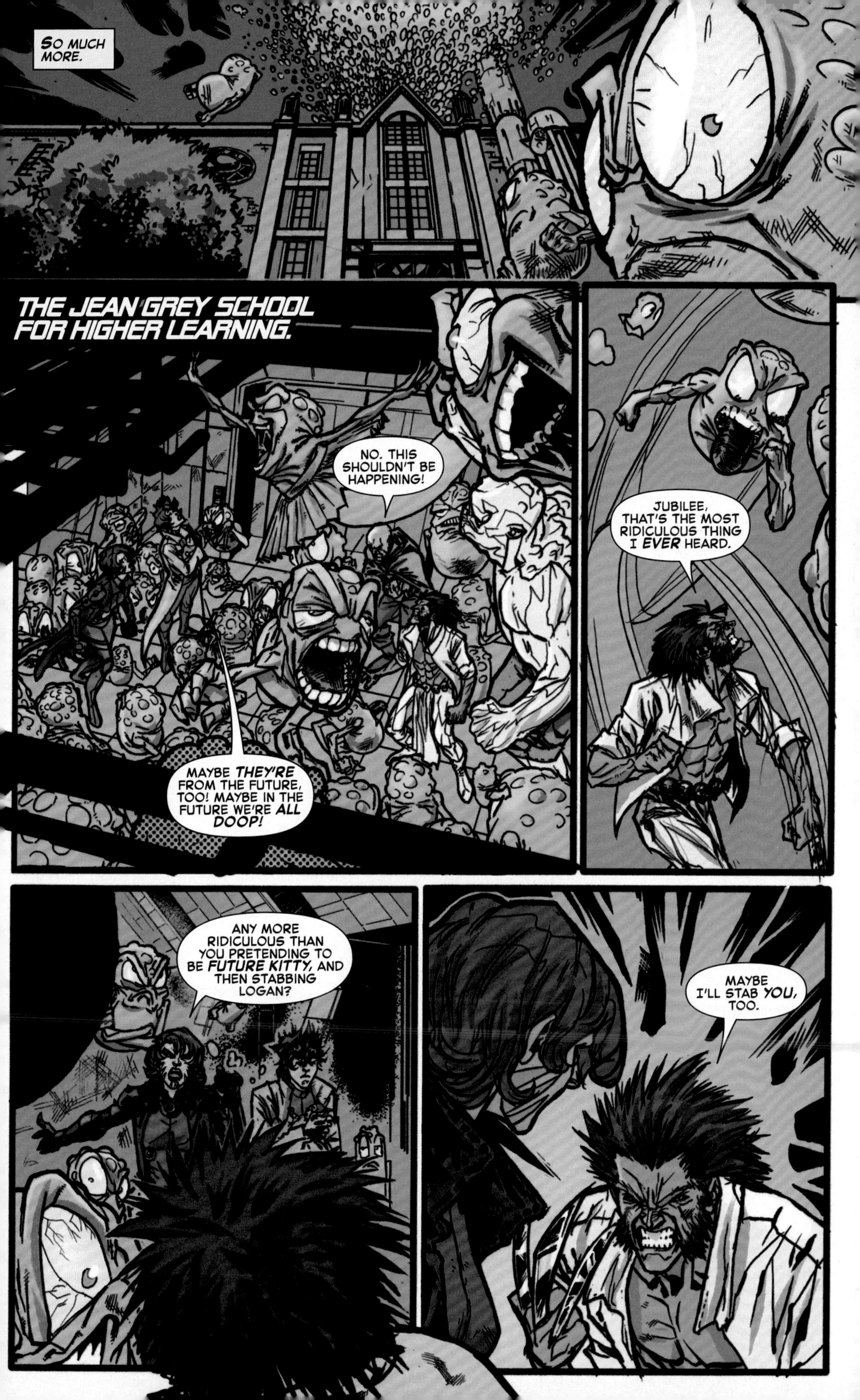
SO MUCH MORE.
THE JEAN GREY SCHOOL FOR HIGHER LEARNING.
NO. THIS SHOULDN'T BE HAPPENING!
MAYBE THEY'RE FROM THE FUTURE, TOO! MAYBE IN THE FUTURE WE'RE ALL DOOP!
JUBILEE, THAT'S THE MOST RIDICULOUS THING I EVER HEARD.
ANY MORE RIDICULOUS THAN YOU PRETENDING TO BE FUTURE KITTY, AND THEN STABBING LOGAN?
MAYBE I'LL STAB YOU, TOO.

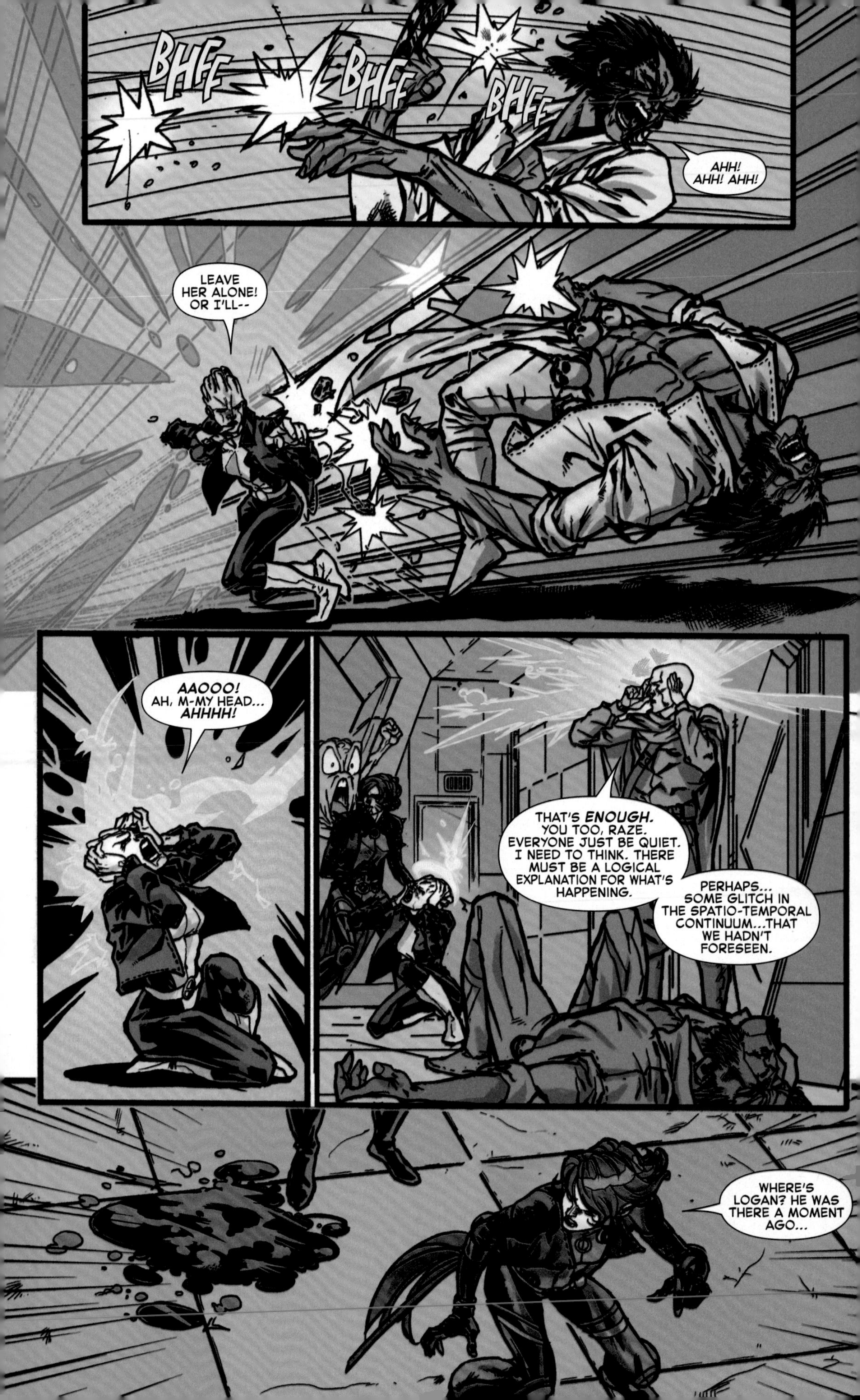
BHFF
BHFF
BHFF
AHH! AHH! AHH!
LEAVE HER ALONE! OR I'LL--
AAOOO! AH, M-MY HEAD... AHHHH!
THAT'S ENOUGH. YOU TOO, RAZE. EVERYONE JUST BE QUIET. I NEED TO THINK. THERE MUST BE A LOGICAL EXPLANATION FOR WHAT'S HAPPENING.
PERHAPS... SOME GLITCH IN THE SPATIO-TEMPORAL CONTINUUM...THAT WE HADN'T FORESEEN.
WHERE'S LOGAN? HE WAS THERE A MOMENT AGO...

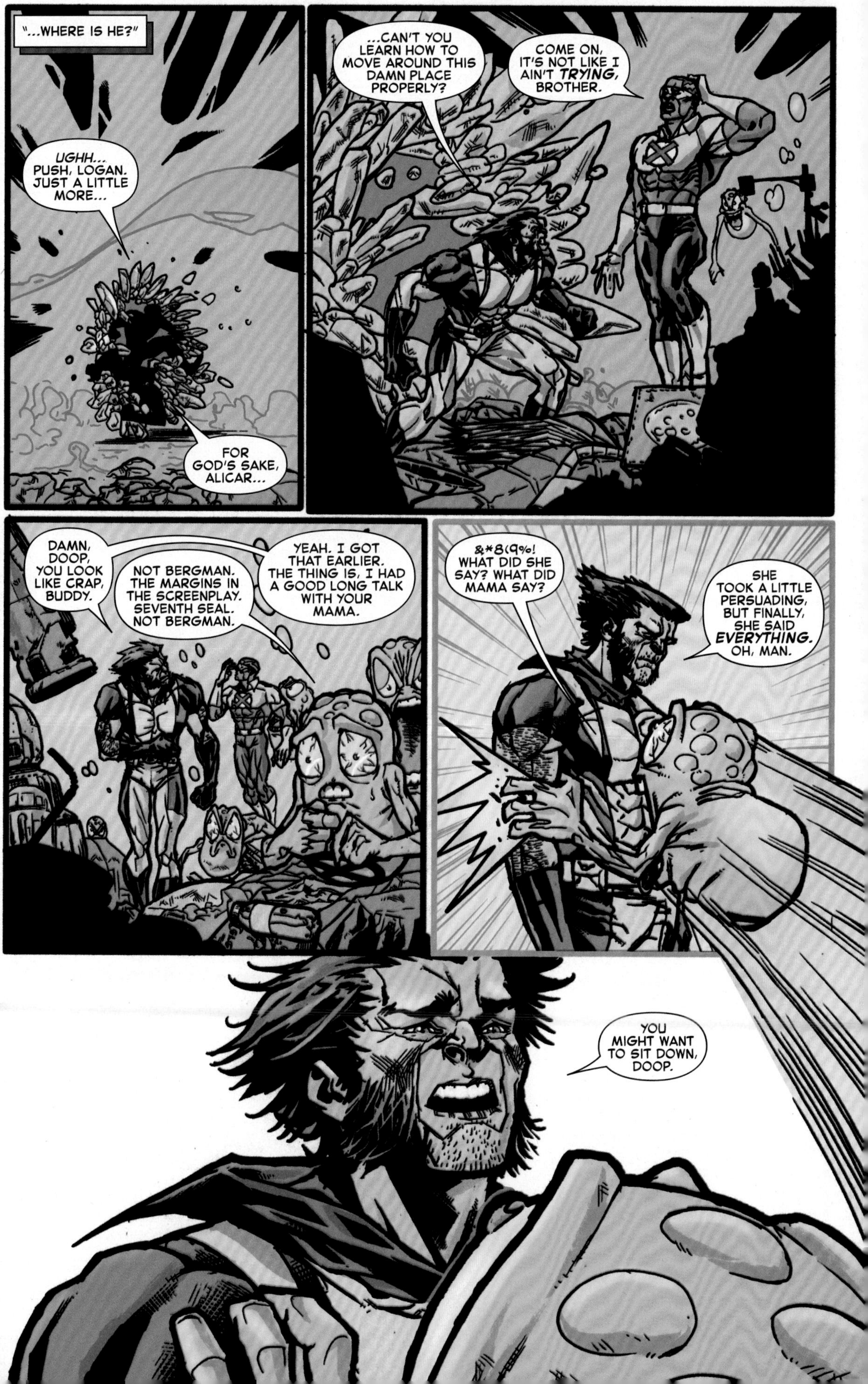
"...WHERE IS HE?"
UGHH... PUSH, LOGAN. JUST A LITTLE MORE...
FOR GOD'S SAKE, ALICAR...
...CAN'T YOU LEARN HOW TO MOVE AROUND THIS DAMN PLACE PROPERLY?
COME ON, IT'S NOT LIKE I AIN'T TRYING, BROTHER.
DAMN, DOOP, YOU LOOK LIKE CRAP, BUDDY.
NOT BERGMAN. THE MARGINS IN THE SCREENPLAY. SEVENTH SEAL. NOT BERGMAN.
YEAH. I GOT THAT EARLIER. THE THING IS, I HAD A GOOD LONG TALK WITH YOUR MAMA.
&*8(9%! WHAT DID SHE SAY? WHAT DID MAMA SAY?
SHE TOOK A LITTLE PERSUADING, BUT FINALLY, SHE SAID EVERYTHING. OH, MAN.
YOU MIGHT WANT TO SIT DOWN, DOOP.

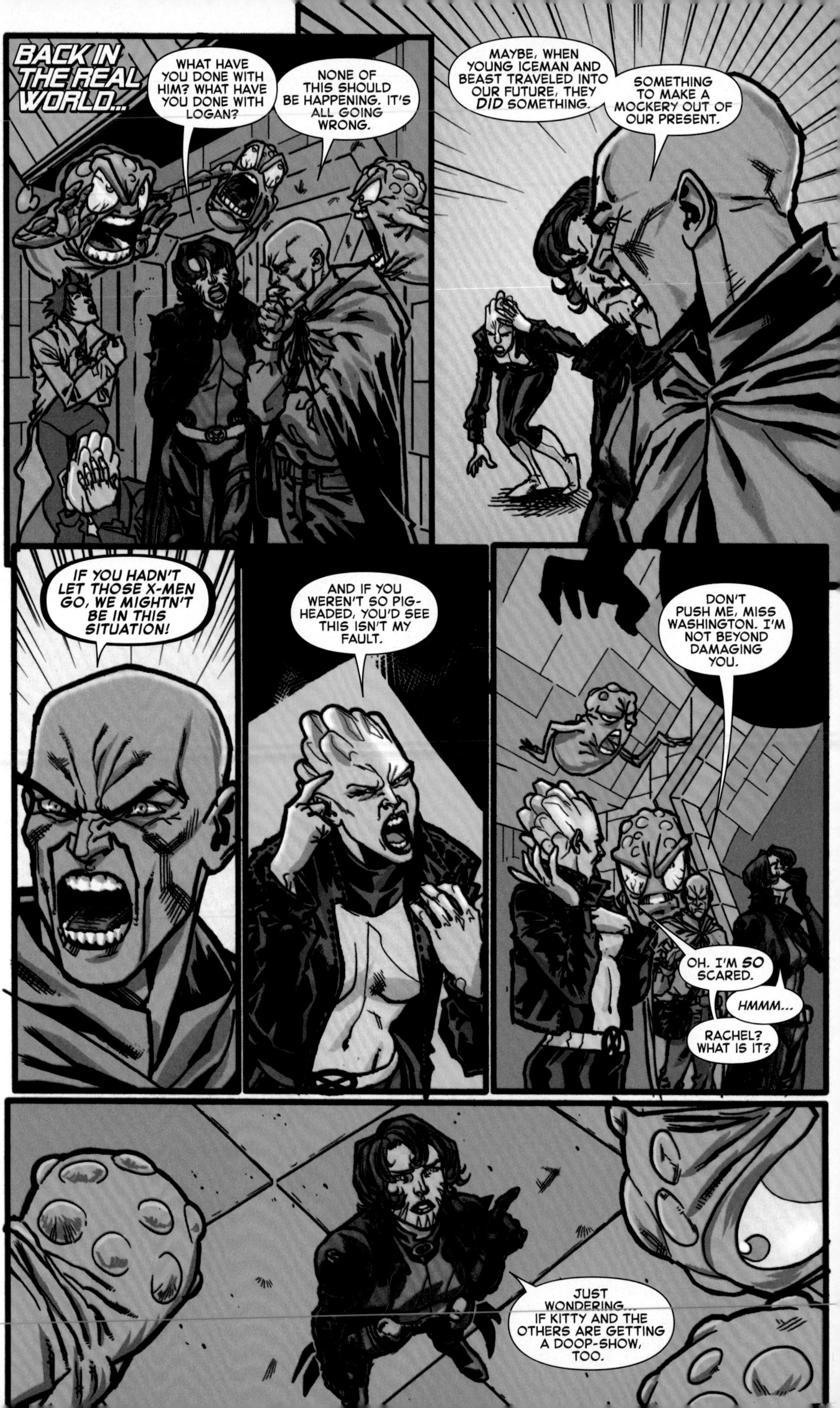

BACK IN THE REAL WORLD...
WHAT HAVE YOU DONE WITH HIM? WHAT HAVE YOU DONE WITH LOGAN?
NONE OF THIS SHOULD BE HAPPENING. IT'S ALL GOING WRONG.
MAYBE, WHEN YOUNG ICEMAN AND BEAST TRAVELED INTO OUR FUTURE, THEY *DID* SOMETHING.
SOMETHING TO MAKE A MOCKERY OUT OF OUR PRESENT.
IF YOU HADN'T LET THOSE X-MEN GO, WE MIGHTN'T BE IN THIS SITUATION!
AND IF YOU WEREN'T SO PIG-HEADED, YOU'D SEE THIS ISN'T MY FAULT.
DON'T PUSH ME, MISS WASHINGTON. I'M NOT BEYOND DAMAGING YOU.
OH. I'M *SO* SCARED.
HMMM...
RACHEL? WHAT IS IT?
JUST WONDERING... IF KITTY AND THE OTHERS ARE GETTING A DOOP-SHOW, TOO.

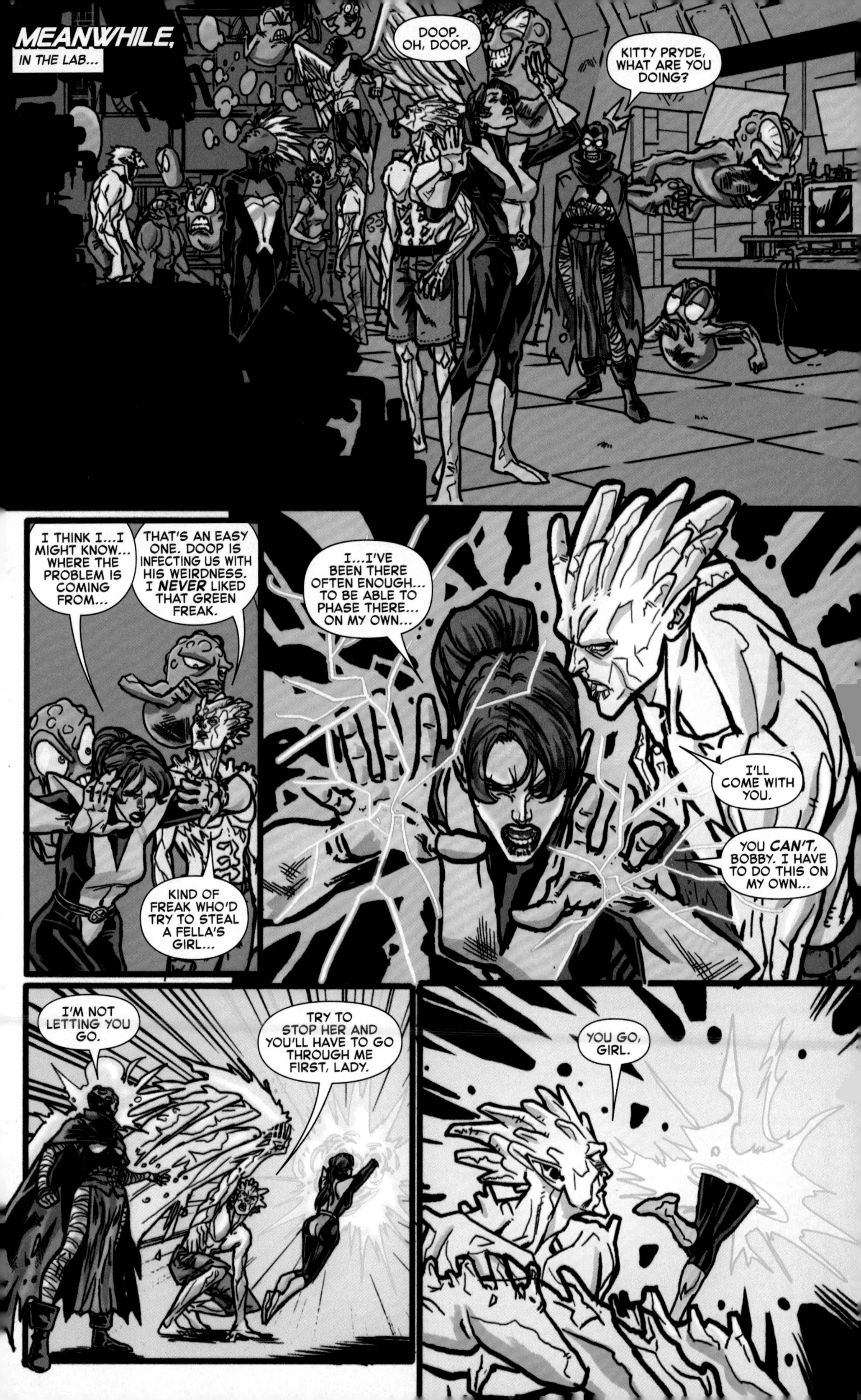
MEANWHILE, IN THE LAB...
DOOP. OH, DOOP.
KITTY PRYDE, WHAT ARE YOU DOING?
I THINK I...I MIGHT KNOW... WHERE THE PROBLEM IS COMING FROM...
THAT'S AN EASY ONE. DOOP IS INFECTING US WITH HIS WEIRDNESS. I NEVER LIKED THAT GREEN FREAK.
KIND OF FREAK WHO'D TRY TO STEAL A FELLA'S GIRL...
I...I'VE BEEN THERE OFTEN ENOUGH... TO BE ABLE TO PHASE THERE... ON MY OWN...
I'LL COME WITH YOU.
YOU CAN'T, BOBBY. I HAVE TO DO THIS ON MY OWN...
I'M NOT LETTING YOU GO.
TRY TO STOP HER AND YOU'LL HAVE TO GO THROUGH ME FIRST, LADY.
YOU GO, GIRL.

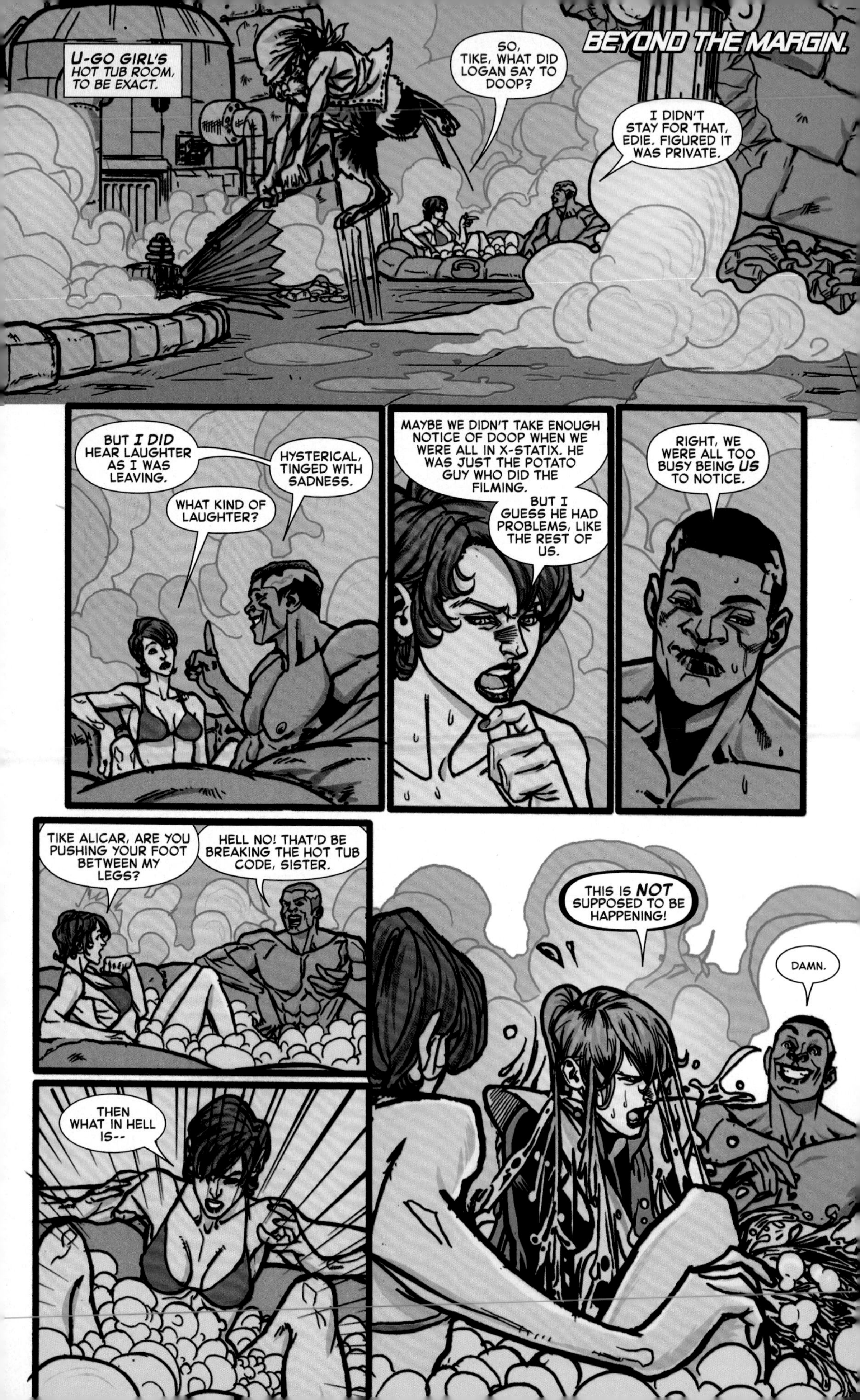
BEYOND THE MARGIN.
U-GO GIRL'S HOT TUB ROOM, TO BE EXACT.
SO, TIKE, WHAT DID LOGAN SAY TO DOOP?
I DIDN'T STAY FOR THAT, EDIE. FIGURED IT WAS PRIVATE.
BUT I DID HEAR LAUGHTER AS I WAS LEAVING.
WHAT KIND OF LAUGHTER?
HYSTERICAL, TINGED WITH SADNESS.
MAYBE WE DIDN'T TAKE ENOUGH NOTICE OF DOOP WHEN WE WERE ALL IN X-STATIX. HE WAS JUST THE POTATO GUY WHO DID THE FILMING.
BUT I GUESS HE HAD PROBLEMS, LIKE THE REST OF US.
RIGHT, WE WERE ALL TOO BUSY BEING US TO NOTICE.
TIKE ALICAR, ARE YOU PUSHING YOUR FOOT BETWEEN MY LEGS?
HELL NO! THAT'D BE BREAKING THE HOT TUB CODE, SISTER.
THEN WHAT IN HELL IS--
THIS IS NOT SUPPOSED TO BE HAPPENING!
DAMN.

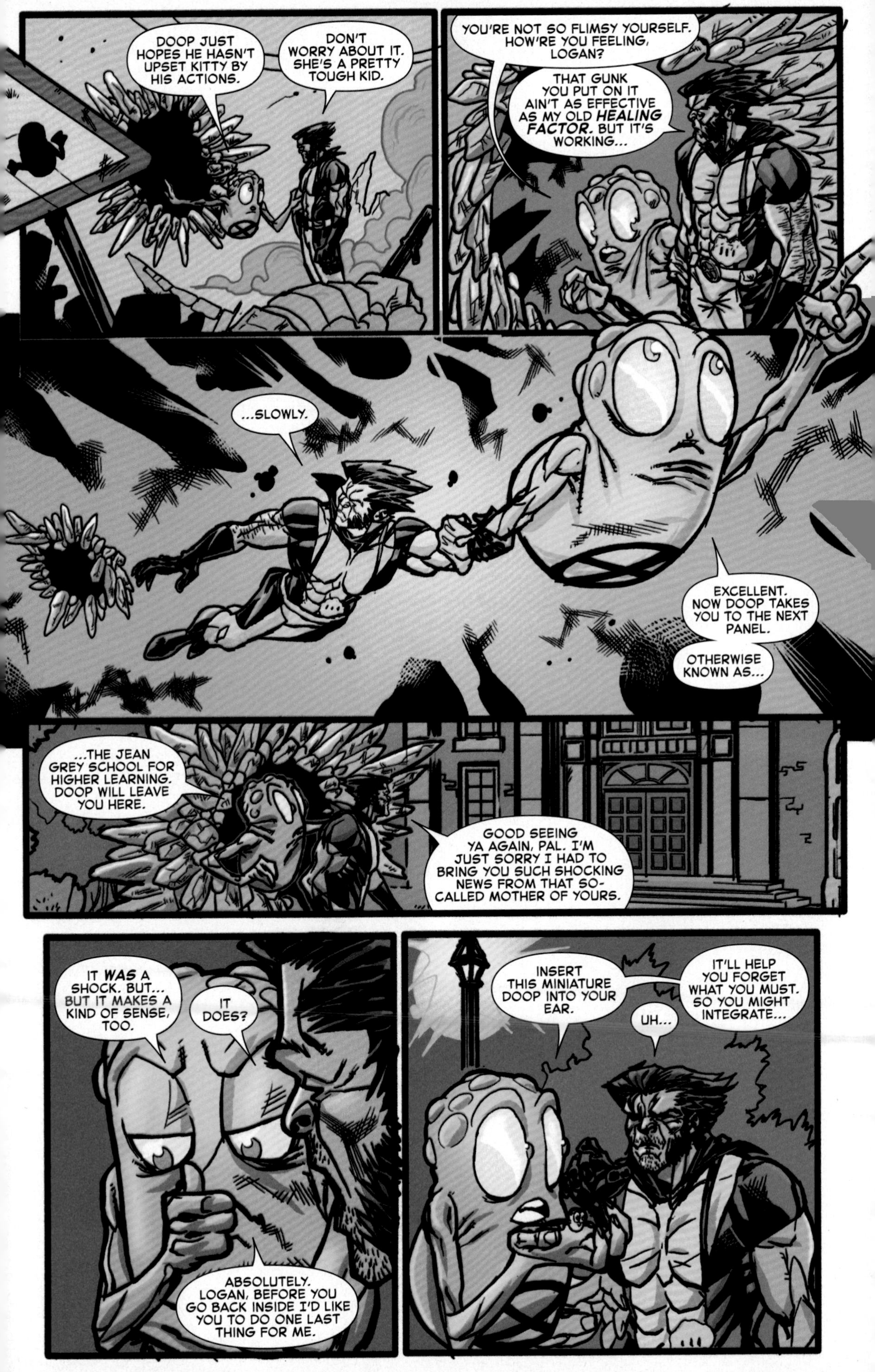
DOOP JUST HOPES HE HASN'T UPSET KITTY BY HIS ACTIONS.
DON'T WORRY ABOUT IT. SHE'S A PRETTY TOUGH KID.
YOU'RE NOT SO FLIMSY YOURSELF. HOW'RE YOU FEELING, LOGAN?
THAT GUNK YOU PUT ON IT AIN'T AS EFFECTIVE AS MY OLD HEALING FACTOR. BUT IT'S WORKING...
...SLOWLY.
EXCELLENT. NOW DOOP TAKES YOU TO THE NEXT PANEL.
OTHERWISE KNOWN AS...
...THE JEAN GREY SCHOOL FOR HIGHER LEARNING. DOOP WILL LEAVE YOU HERE.
GOOD SEEING YA AGAIN, PAL. I'M JUST SORRY I HAD TO BRING YOU SUCH SHOCKING NEWS FROM THAT SO-CALLED MOTHER OF YOURS.
IT WAS A SHOCK. BUT... BUT IT MAKES A KIND OF SENSE, TOO.
IT DOES?
ABSOLUTELY. LOGAN, BEFORE YOU GO BACK INSIDE I'D LIKE YOU TO DO ONE LAST THING FOR ME.
INSERT THIS MINIATURE DOOP INTO YOUR EAR.
IT'LL HELP YOU FORGET WHAT YOU MUST. SO YOU MIGHT INTEGRATE...
UH...

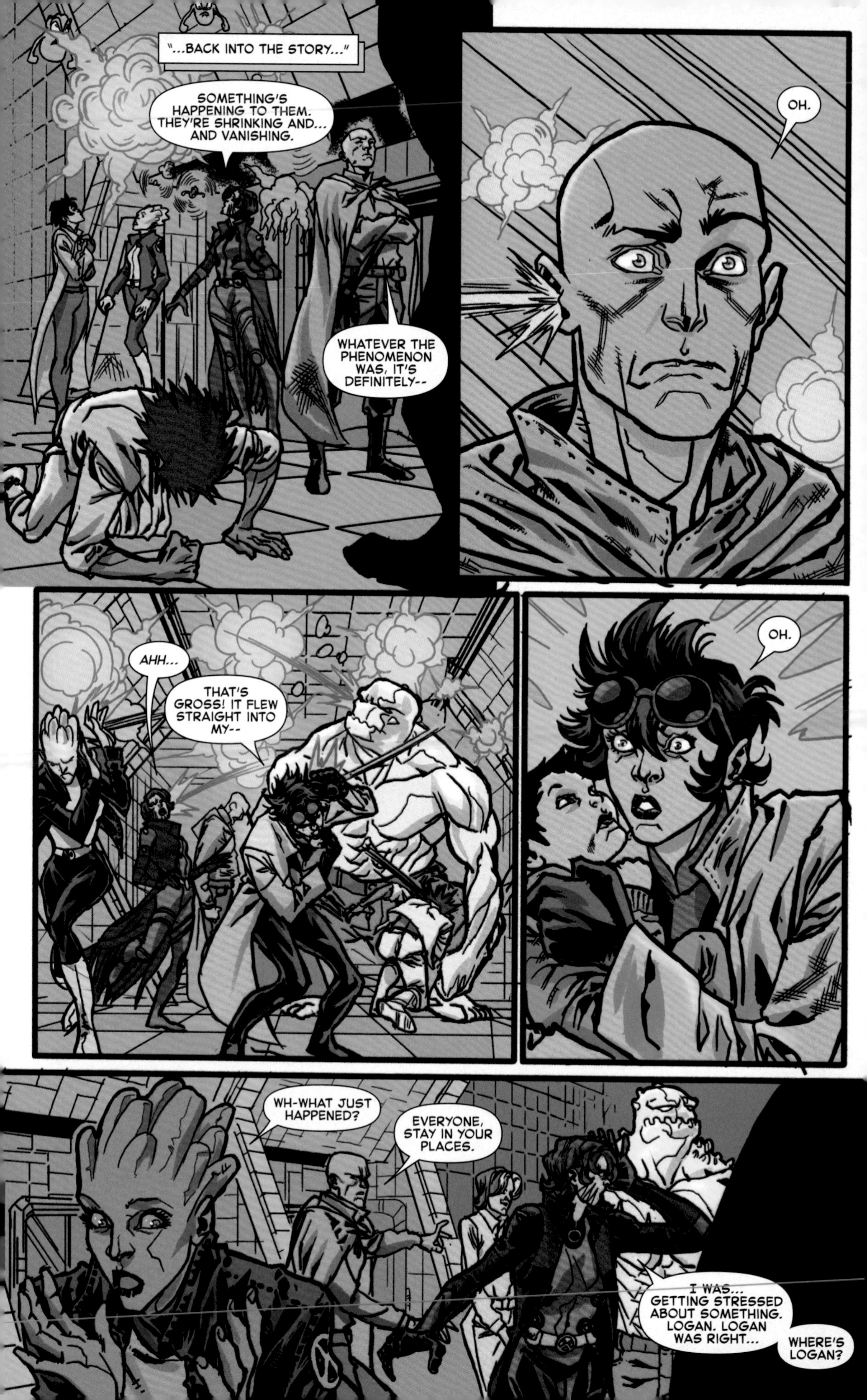
"...BACK INTO THE STORY..."
SOMETHING'S HAPPENING TO THEM. THEY'RE SHRINKING AND... AND VANISHING.
WHATEVER THE PHENOMENON WAS, IT'S DEFINITELY--
OH.
AHH...
THAT'S GROSS! IT FLEW STRAIGHT INTO MY--
OH.
WH-WHAT JUST HAPPENED?
EVERYONE, STAY IN YOUR PLACES.
I WAS... GETTING STRESSED ABOUT SOMETHING. LOGAN. LOGAN WAS RIGHT...
WHERE'S LOGAN?

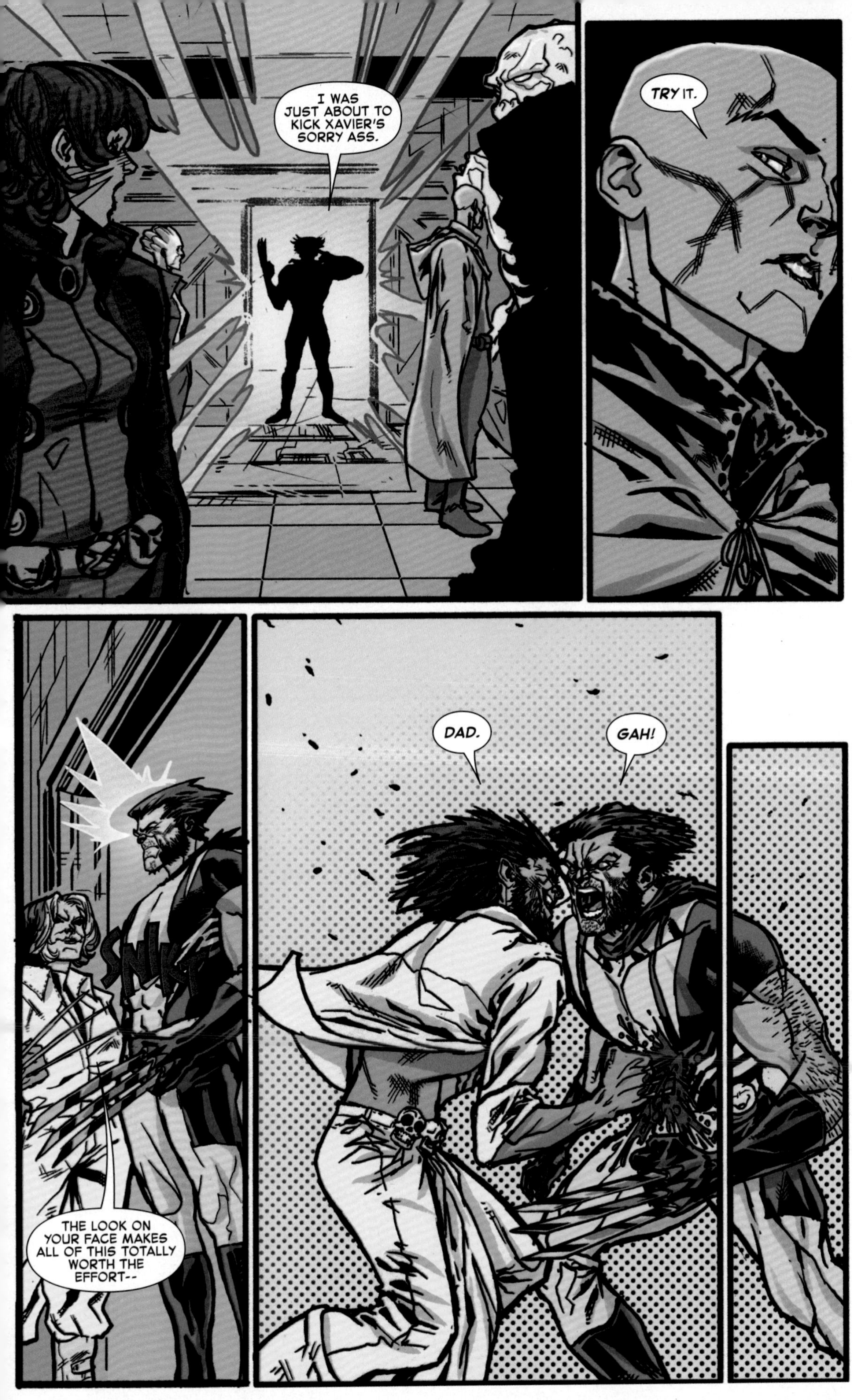
I WAS JUST ABOUT TO KICK XAVIER'S SORRY ASS.
TRY IT.
SNIKT
THE LOOK ON YOUR FACE MAKES ALL OF THIS TOTALLY WORTH THE EFFORT--
DAD.
GAH!

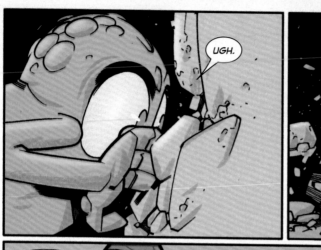

UGH.

UHNN...

YO, DOOP. LOOK WHO I FOUND IN THE HOT TUB.

DOOP!

KITTY, DIDN'T DOOP TELL YOU THAT MOVING THROUGH THE MARGINS TAKES PRACTICE?

DOOP! WHAT'S WITH ALL THE CRAZY DOOPS?

DOOP HAD A MELTING DOWN. A BAD ONE. BUT THEN LOGAN HELPED ME RECOVER.

LOGAN? HOW?

HE FOUND OUT SOMETHING THAT PUT DOOP'S MIND AT REST. ABOUT MAMA DOOP...

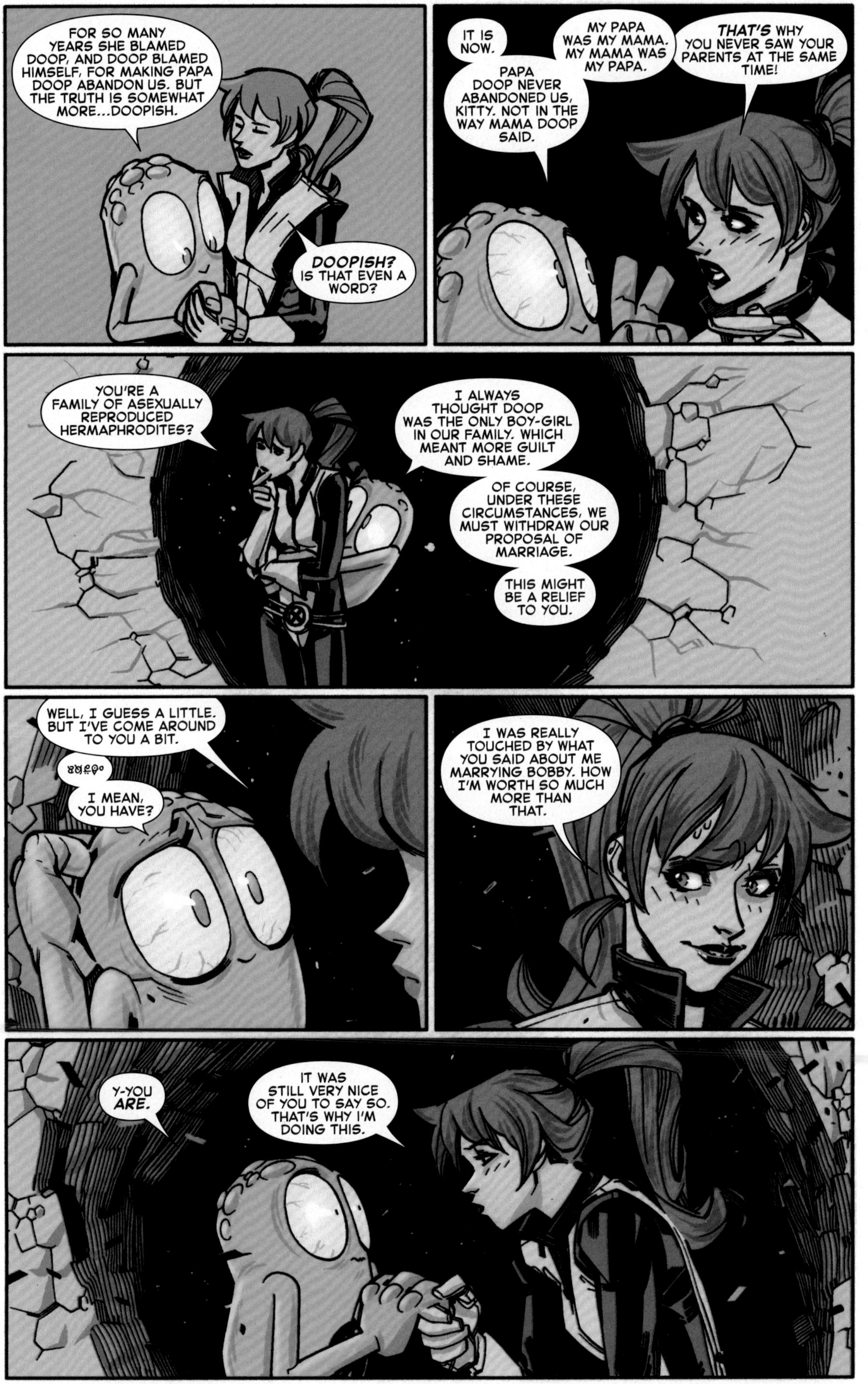
FOR SO MANY YEARS SHE BLAMED DOOP, AND DOOP BLAMED HIMSELF, FOR MAKING PAPA DOOP ABANDON US. BUT THE TRUTH IS SOMEWHAT MORE...DOOPISH.
DOOPISH? IS THAT EVEN A WORD?
IT IS NOW.
MY PAPA WAS MY MAMA. MY MAMA WAS MY PAPA.
PAPA DOOP NEVER ABANDONED US, KITTY. NOT IN THE WAY MAMA DOOP SAID.
THAT'S WHY YOU NEVER SAW YOUR PARENTS AT THE SAME TIME!
YOU'RE A FAMILY OF ASEXUALLY REPRODUCED HERMAPHRODITES?
I ALWAYS THOUGHT DOOP WAS THE ONLY BOY-GIRL IN OUR FAMILY. WHICH MEANT MORE GUILT AND SHAME.
OF COURSE, UNDER THESE CIRCUMSTANCES, WE MUST WITHDRAW OUR PROPOSAL OF MARRIAGE.
THIS MIGHT BE A RELIEF TO YOU.
WELL, I GUESS A LITTLE. BUT I'VE COME AROUND TO YOU A BIT.
I MEAN, YOU HAVE?
I WAS REALLY TOUCHED BY WHAT YOU SAID ABOUT ME MARRYING BOBBY. HOW I'M WORTH SO MUCH MORE THAN THAT.
Y-YOU *ARE.*
IT WAS STILL VERY NICE OF YOU TO SAY SO. THAT'S WHY I'M DOING THIS.

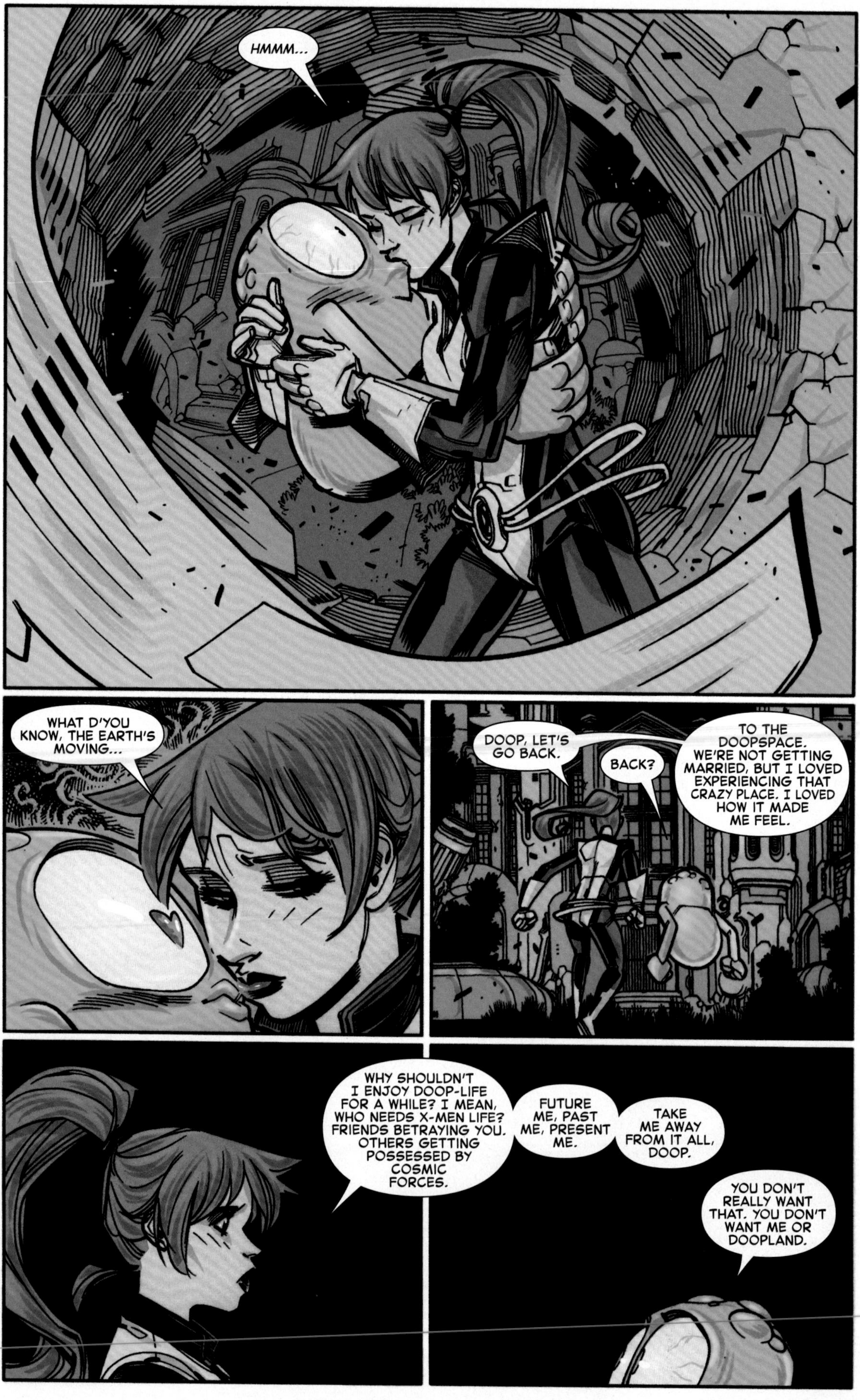
HMMM...
WHAT D'YOU KNOW, THE EARTH'S MOVING...
DOOP, LET'S GO BACK.
BACK?
TO THE DOOPSPACE. WE'RE NOT GETTING MARRIED, BUT I LOVED EXPERIENCING THAT CRAZY PLACE. I LOVED HOW IT MADE ME FEEL.
WHY SHOULDN'T I ENJOY DOOP-LIFE FOR A WHILE? I MEAN, WHO NEEDS X-MEN LIFE? FRIENDS BETRAYING YOU. OTHERS GETTING POSSESSED BY COSMIC FORCES.
FUTURE ME, PAST ME, PRESENT ME.
TAKE ME AWAY FROM IT ALL, DOOP.
YOU DON'T REALLY WANT THAT. YOU DON'T WANT ME OR DOOPLAND.

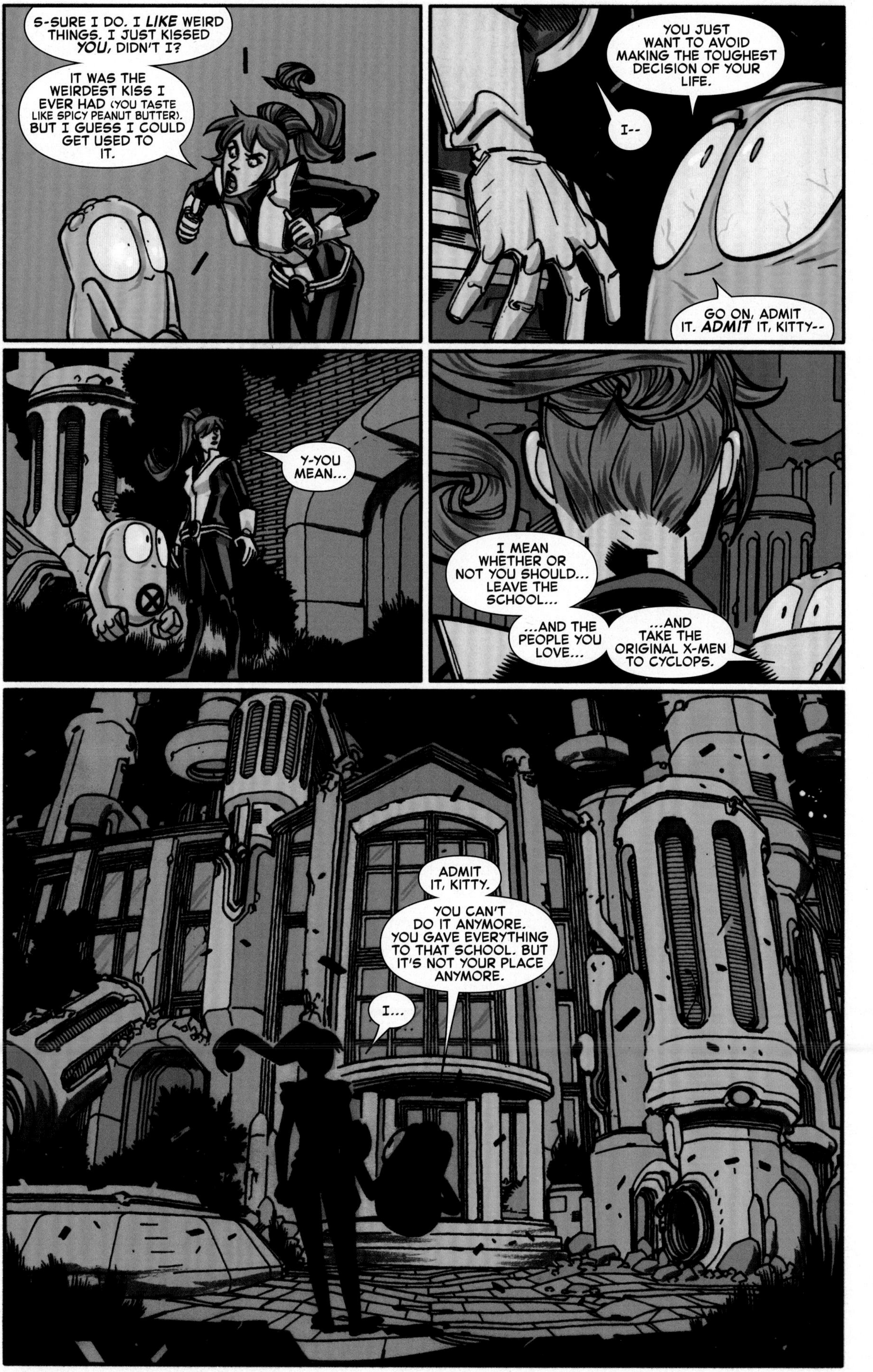
S-SURE I DO. I LIKE WEIRD THINGS. I JUST KISSED YOU, DIDN'T I?
IT WAS THE WEIRDEST KISS I EVER HAD (YOU TASTE LIKE SPICY PEANUT BUTTER). BUT I GUESS I COULD GET USED TO IT.
YOU JUST WANT TO AVOID MAKING THE TOUGHEST DECISION OF YOUR LIFE.
I--
GO ON, ADMIT IT. ADMIT IT, KITTY--
Y-YOU MEAN...
I MEAN WHETHER OR NOT YOU SHOULD... LEAVE THE SCHOOL...
...AND THE PEOPLE YOU LOVE...
...AND TAKE THE ORIGINAL X-MEN TO CYCLOPS.
ADMIT IT, KITTY.
YOU CAN'T DO IT ANYMORE. YOU GAVE EVERYTHING TO THAT SCHOOL. BUT IT'S NOT YOUR PLACE ANYMORE.
I...

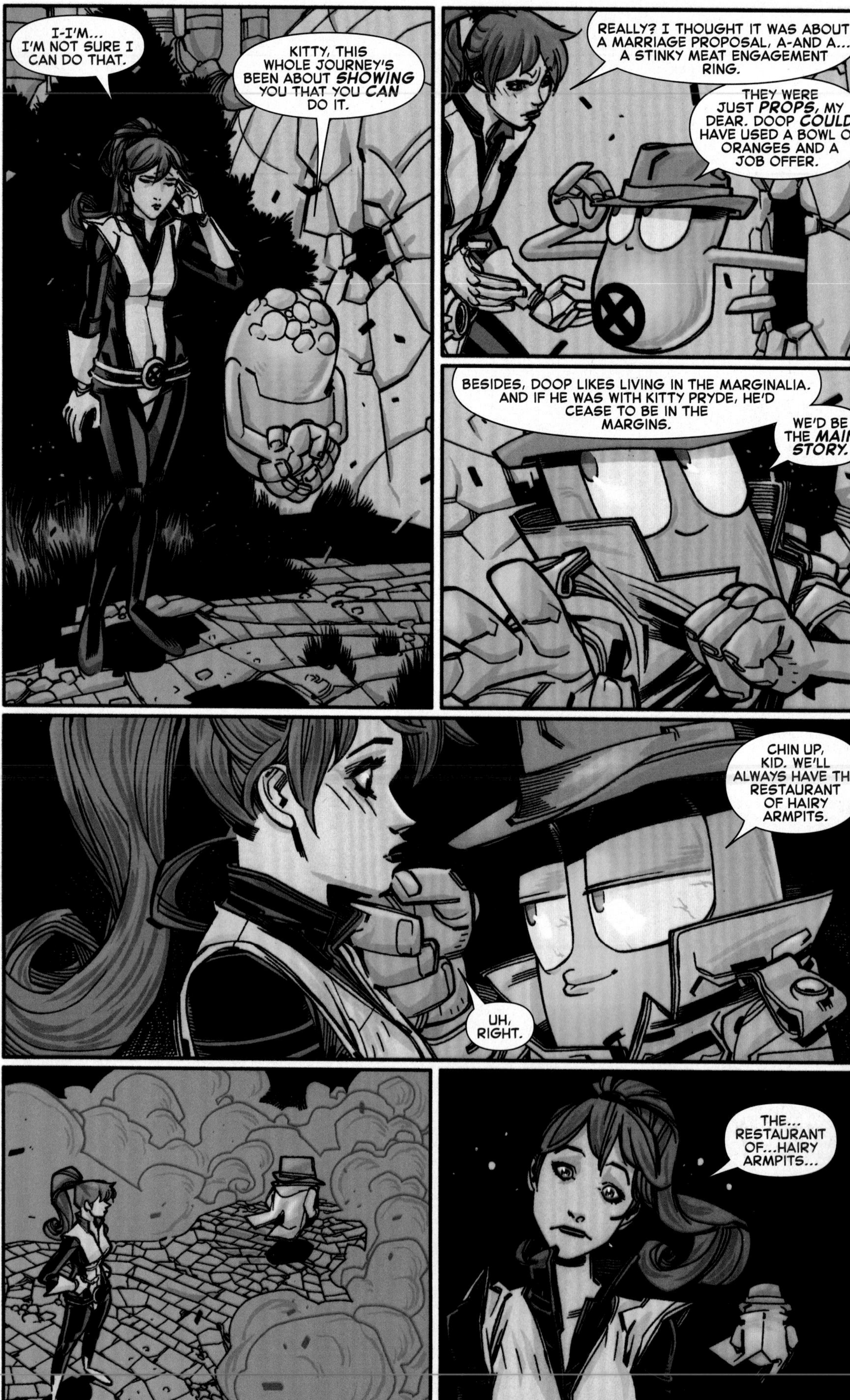
I-I'M... I'M NOT SURE I CAN DO THAT.
KITTY, THIS WHOLE JOURNEY'S BEEN ABOUT SHOWING YOU THAT YOU CAN DO IT.
REALLY? I THOUGHT IT WAS ABOUT A MARRIAGE PROPOSAL, A-AND A... A STINKY MEAT ENGAGEMENT RING.
THEY WERE JUST PROPS, MY DEAR. DOOP COULD HAVE USED A BOWL OF ORANGES AND A JOB OFFER.
BESIDES, DOOP LIKES LIVING IN THE MARGINALIA. AND IF HE WAS WITH KITTY PRYDE, HE'D CEASE TO BE IN THE MARGINS.
WE'D BE THE MAIN STORY.
CHIN UP, KID. WE'LL ALWAYS HAVE THE RESTAURANT OF HAIRY ARMPITS.
UH, RIGHT.
THE... RESTAURANT OF...HAIRY ARMPITS...

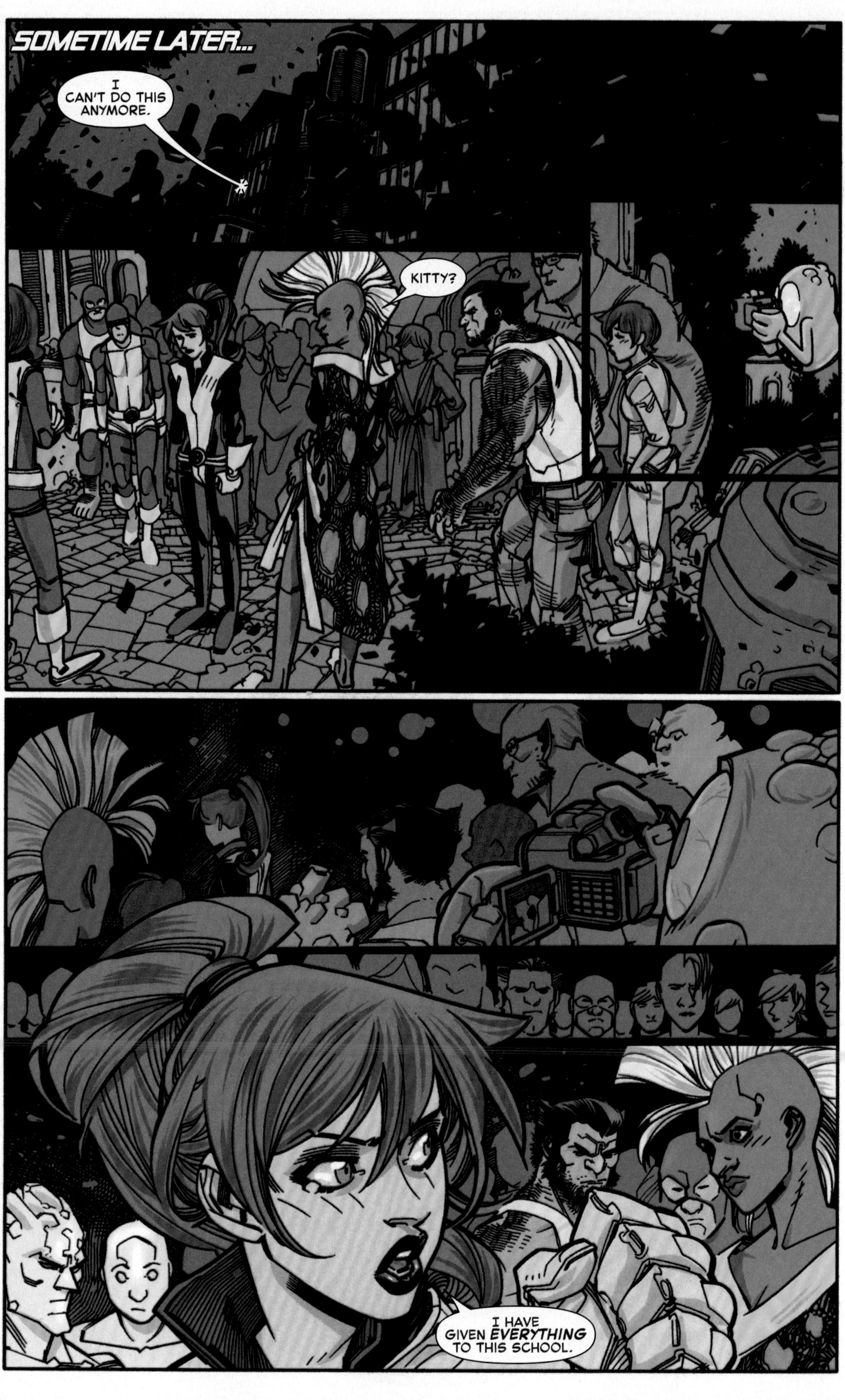
SOMETIME LATER...
I CAN'T DO THIS ANYMORE.
KITTY?
I HAVE GIVEN EVERYTHING TO THIS SCHOOL.

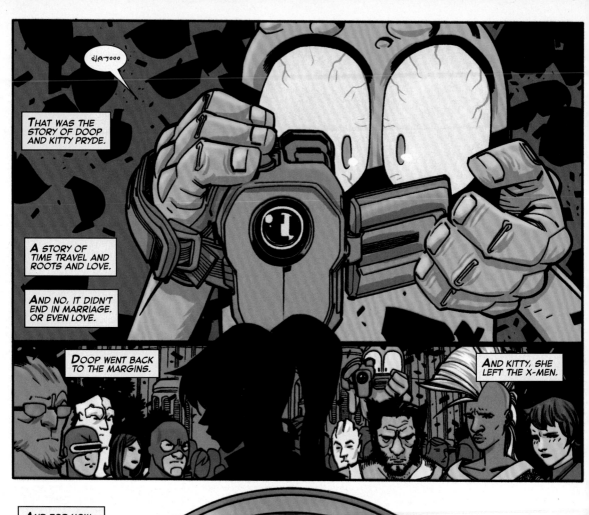

THAT WAS THE STORY OF DOOP AND KITTY PRYDE.

A STORY OF TIME TRAVEL AND ROOTS AND LOVE.

AND NO, IT DIDN'T END IN MARRIAGE. OR EVEN LOVE.

DOOP WENT BACK TO THE MARGINS.

AND KITTY, SHE LEFT THE X-MEN.

AND FOR NOW...

...THAT SUITS THEM BOTH JUST FINE.

STOP

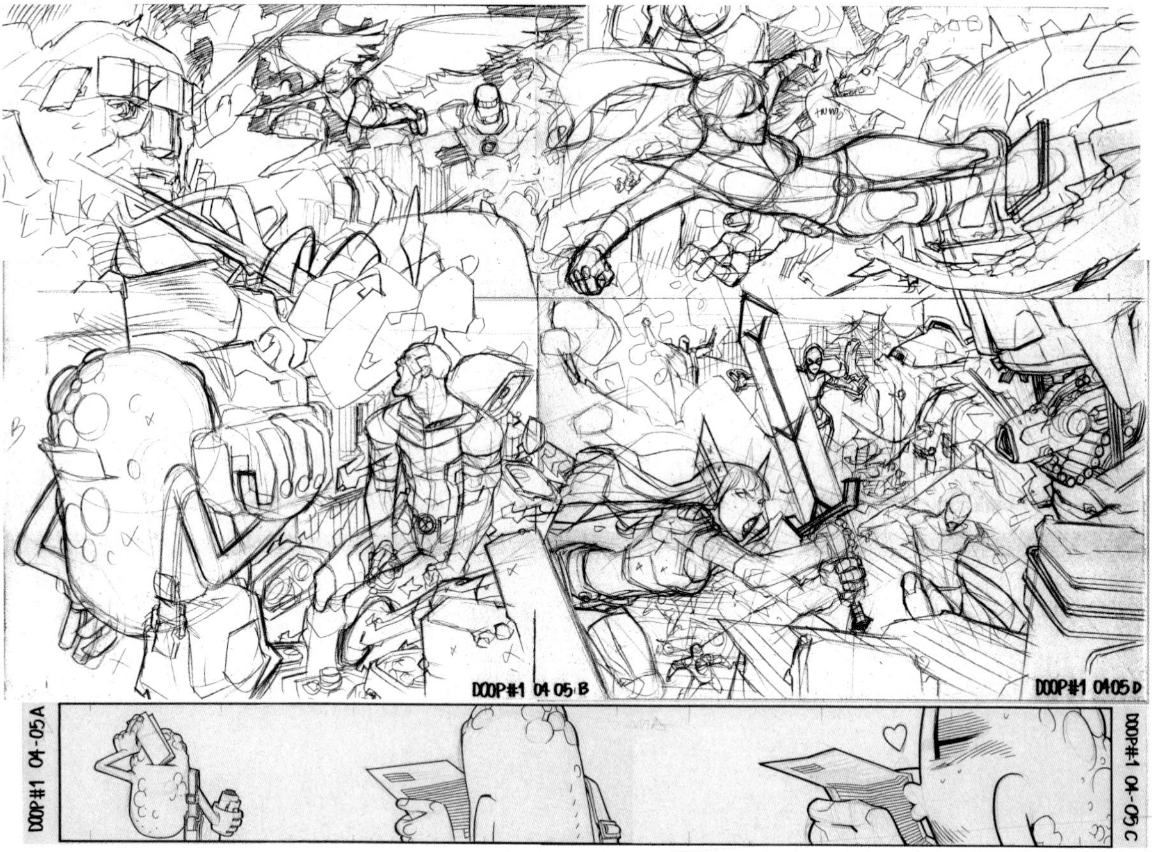
DOOP#1 04-05 B
DOOP#1 0405 D
DOOP#1 04-05A
DOOP#1 04-05 C

ALL NEW DOOP #1 PAGES 4-5 PENCILS BY DAVID LAFUENTE

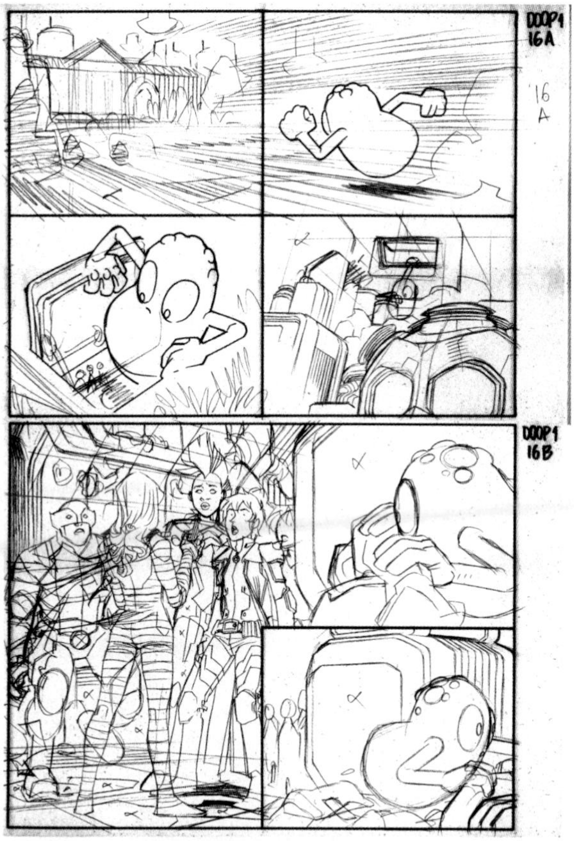
DOOP1 16A
16 A
DOOP1 16B

ALL NEW DOOP #1 PAGE 16
PENCILS BY DAVID LAFUENTE

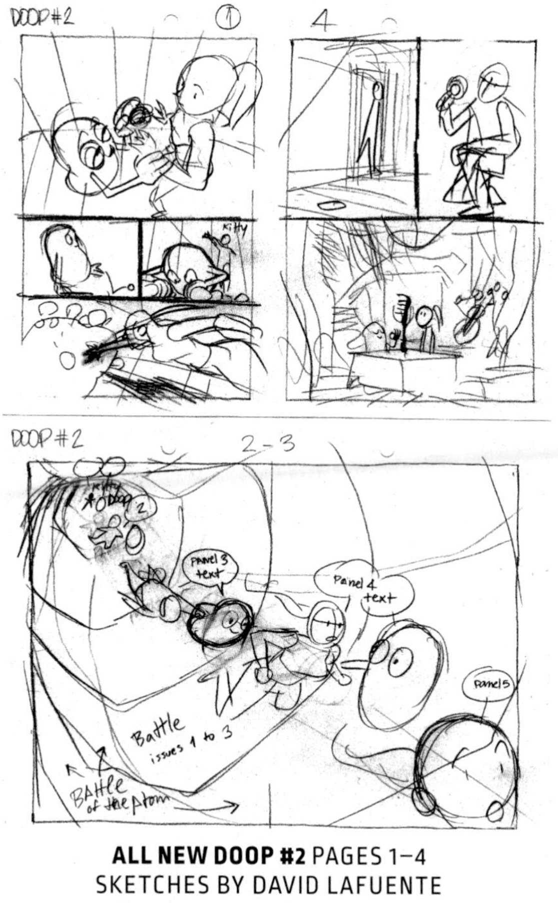
DOOP#2
1
4
Kitty
DOOP#2
2-3
Panel 3 text
Panel 4 text
Panel 5
Battle issues 1 to 3
Battle of the Atom

ALL NEW DOOP #2 PAGES 1–4
SKETCHES BY DAVID LAFUENTE

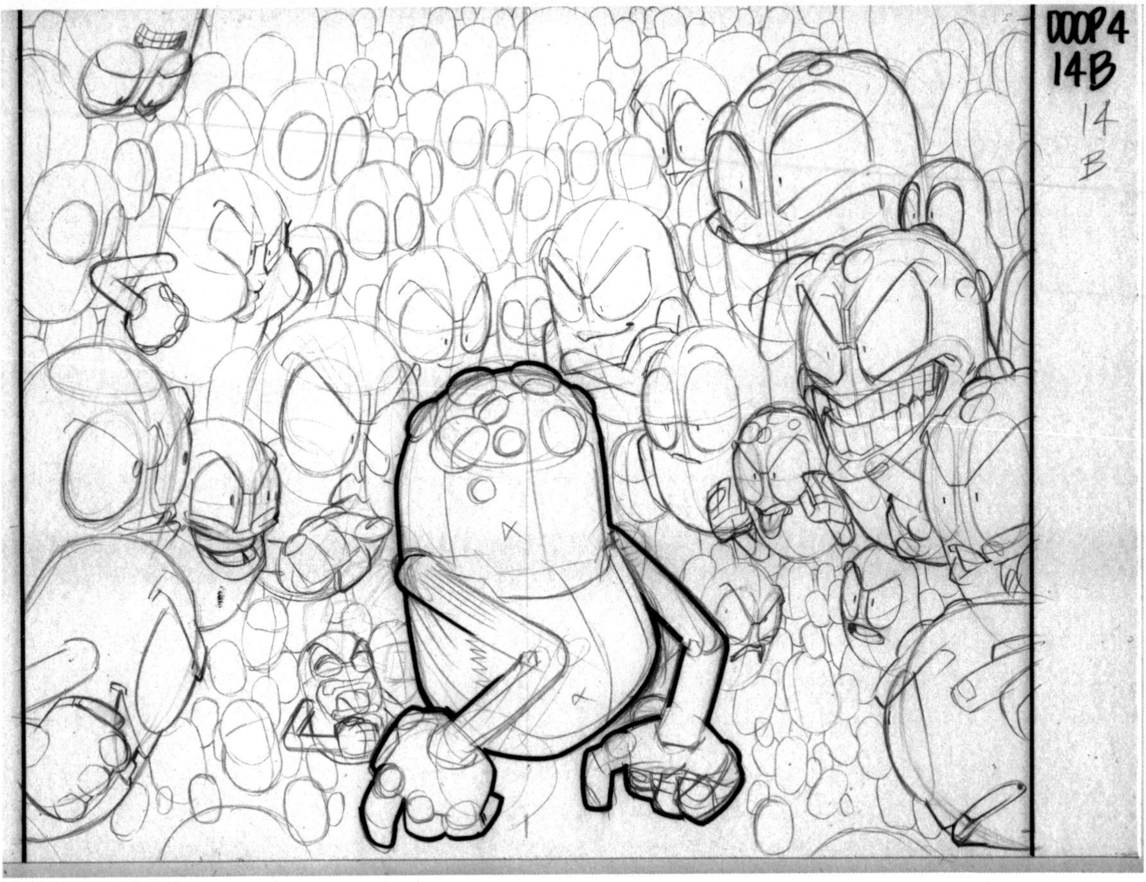
DOOP 4
14B
14
B

ALL NEW DOOP #4 PAGE 14 PENCILS BY DAVID LAFUENTE

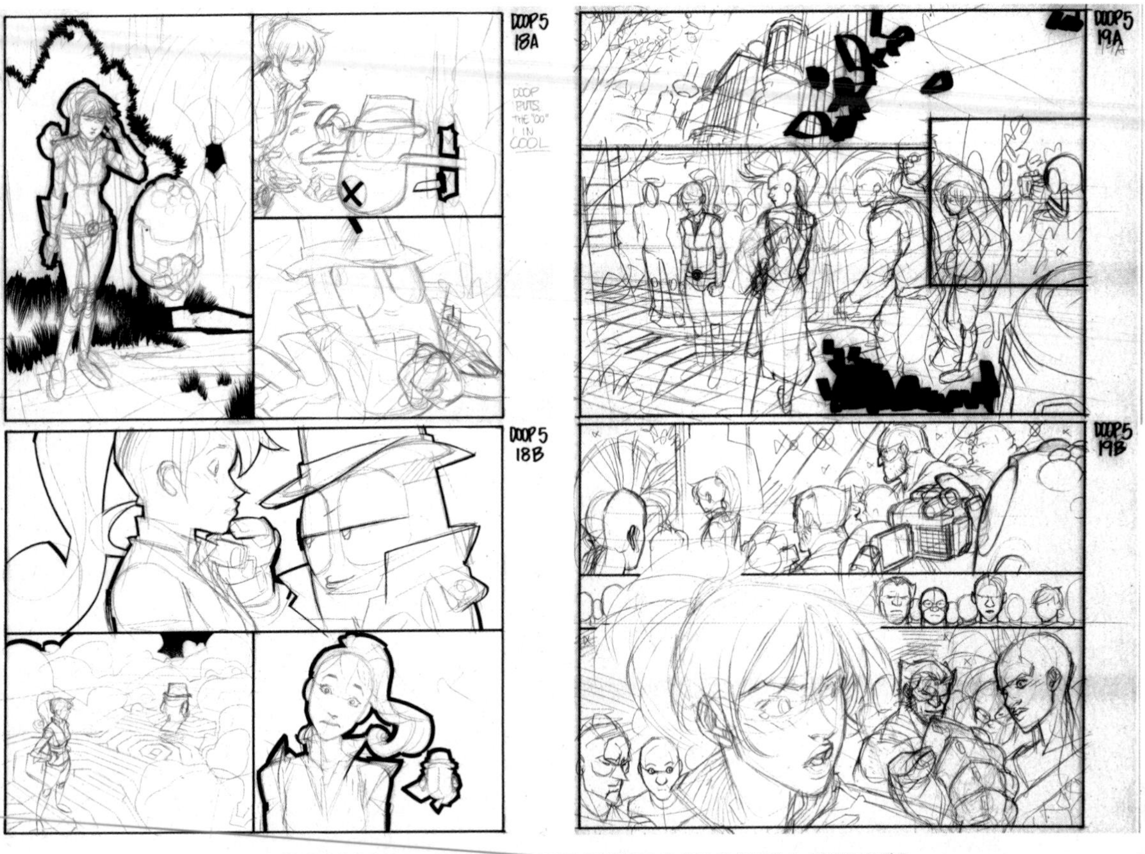
DOOP 5
18A
DOOP PUTS "THE "OO" IN COOL
DOOP 5
18B
DOOP 5
19A
DOOP 5
19B

ALL NEW DOOP #5 PAGES 18–19 PENCILS BY DAVID LAFUENTE